```
I0117301
```

THE SCHOOL OF HOLISTIC PSYCHOLOGY

A MANUAL FOR THE HARMONIZATION AND ENLIGHTENMENT OF YOUR PERSONALITY

Book #1
2011

By Alexander Pint

Translated by Emin Kuliev, MD

www.pint.ru

https://caterpillartobuterfly.wordpress.com

© Alexander Pint 2018

All rights reserved. Neither this book nor any part may be reproduced or transmitted in any form or by any means, electronic or mechanical, including photocopying, microfilming, and recording or by any information storage and retrieval system without permission in writing from the publisher.

Visit www.SkyrocketPress.com

Cover art by Freydoon Rassouli
Cover Designed by Emma Michaels
Interior Design by Laurisa White Reyes

ISBN: 978-1-944722-08-1

RESPECTED READERS!

We are offering you verbatim transcription of the webinars conducted by our School during 2010 and 2011. These materials carry great practical value for your Holistic understanding of yourself and problems you encounter in life.

By studying these materials, you will be able to see what happens to you from the point of view of Holistic psychology, which offers you an opportunity to see not just the symptoms and the consequences of your basic problems, but their essence and mechanisms of appearance. All these problems arise because your personality is a dual structure; it consists of opposite tendencies. We call these opposite tendencies of our personality personal dualities.

Some of these opposite tendencies of your personality you consider to be "positive" or "good." You deem other tendencies "negative" or "bad." Rejecting bad tendencies in yourself, you maintain your inner separation. As s a result, you prolongate the state of internal and external war you wage with yourself. Such a perception causes disharmony and disbalance in your personality, gives birth to problems, pain, suffering, accidents, and diseases. The materials you are about to read review the mechanisms of functioning of basic personal dualities that create main lessons of your earthly life.

In other words, this is the practical manual of en-light-enment, which will "introduce light" into every shadow part of your personality. Using these materials, you will be able to solve your life lessons and problems in full awareness of what you are doing. You will clearly see the mechanisms of conflict appearance and true reasons that stand behind them.

Harmonization of the disbalance of your personal dualities will allow you to solve your most challenging problems, even those that are considered to be unsolvable here. **This work will allow you to become fully aware of your personal program and to get to the next level of consciousness.** You will transform from the personage of a show who mechanically experiences his life into a programmer of your life.

– Alexander Pint

My grandmother didn't teach me, "To be or not to be."
My grandmother taught me, "To be—Not to be."
—Rumi

TABLE OF CONTENTS

CHAPTER 1

HOW TO STOP THE FIGHT OF YOUR PERSONAL OPPOSITIONS AND TO BECOME WHOLE IN THE DUALITY "TO GIVE—TO RECEIVE"

— We are about to start our first webinar today. What kind of a webinar is it? I see it as the first step to enter a lobby of the School of Holistic psychology. This is not the hall of Holistic psychology yet. This is just a lobby, where many important questions must be solved before you can enter a hall of the School of Holistic psychology.

Why did I create the School? I did it because time of wholeness has come. What does it mean? It means, we have entered "The Quantum Leap of 2012." Perhaps, some of you have heard about it. What is the Quantum Leap? Quite a lot is being said about it nowadays. I will share my vision of Quantum Leap with you. Quantum Leap is a cosmic process which starts on Earth. Currently, the Earth is in the zone of attention of many entities, planets, stars, and galaxies. The experiment that is being conducted here has never been conducted before. It doesn't mean we have not experienced leaps before. There were plenty of them, but the one that

1

occurs now is very unusual. Cosmos is a big organization, which conducts its own experiments and searches for different methods to realize its agenda. Quantum Leap is one of these experiments. I will touch upon some basic moment that we, humans, need to be aware of to go through this experiment.

What is the essence of this leap? To simplify, **we are being asked to elevate the level of our consciousness and to transfer to the next level of consciousness.** Consciousness is a substance that has a certain structure. Presently, the substance of consciousness of people populating the Earth is structured based on the **axiom of survival**. For many centuries, our consciousness was intricately interconnected with the idea of survival. This structure starts to change. Energies of different qualities are coming from Cosmos. These energies carry new ideas. One of the main ideas we are going to explore is the idea of Wholeness. The mode of survival in which we spent hundredth of lifetimes and continue to be in now is based on **the idea of separation**. We have been acquiring the experience of separation in the form of conflicts, competitions, wars, and suffering for a long time. You are familiar with this experience of separation as well as I am.

Earth is starting to move to the next level of consciousness now—consciousness of Wholeness. The main task of a human being during the Quantum Leap is to become whole. Talking about Wholeness, we should not forget about its opposite side—separation. We see and encounter separation all the time. We live in it. We survive in it. How was it fixed in us? Where are the roots of this separation?

The roots of this separation lie in the inner world of a human being, in his personality. Let's look at what a human being is now. How can we define him? I will share my vision with you. A human being consists of the physical body. Each one of us receives it at birth. As soon as the physical body is born, personality starts to form in it. This process takes years. It is the personality we acquire that is responsible for our inner separation. It is the reason behind every negative event we experience in life. These negative events represent the lessons or assignments we have come here to solve.

This is a revolutionary point of view. Usually, a human being thinks, "I want this, and I want that. I am setting this and that goal for myself," and he tries to reach these goals. These goals come out of the desires of his personality, i.e. a man tries to satisfy the desires of his personality without any understanding of what his personality represents. I want to accentuate your attention on this fact. People try to satisfy desires of their personalities without any understanding of what their personality is and why was it given to them.

Why don't they ask this question? They don't ask this question because they consider themselves *to be* personalities. They say, "I am a personality." This personality navigates their bodies the same way a driver navigates a car. Personality pretends to be the driver and the owner, and the possibility of presence of another owner does not even occur to people. But the true owner is in us. So, who is the true owner of our car, a car that includes both the physical body and the personality? It is the Supreme Aspect.

I am not going to discuss the nature of our Supreme Aspects now. We will do that later. Presently, I want to reiterate that aside from the personality, i.e. the false owner, we have the true owner, the true driver—our Supreme Aspect. The idea of seeing personality as something separated from the rest of me arose in me when I started to see the Supreme Aspect as one of the most important parts of my structure. I am not just Pint's personality. I am not just Pint's body. I am Pint's

Supreme Aspect, too. It is my Supreme Aspect that conducts my investigation. I have been investigating my personality for forty years. I have sorted out how it was constructed and how it resists to be penetrated by the voice, energy, and intention of the Supreme Aspect.

Let us review now how the personality of a human being is made, as it is the makeup of our personality that provides us with experience of separation. **We come to Earth to receive a certain experience.** Different dimensions of the universe serve as playgrounds for us. We receive different kinds of experiences there. We are on Earth now, and we will investigate the specifics of this stage, the stage where we play certain roles, and because of playing these roles receive the experience our Supreme Aspects need.

So, how is the personality of a human being made? Personality of a human being is determined by certain qualities. If I were to ask you to describe your personality, you would list several qualities. For example, smart or stupid, active or passive, feminine or masculine, etc. You may list many more of such qualities. But when we look at them from the point of view of Holistic consciousness, we see that all of them are dual. For example, we see that the opposite poles of duality "smart—stupid" represent two sides of one scale. Let's look at duality, "obedient—disobedient." Qualities "obedient" and "disobedient" represent two separate parts of our personality or one scale. This is very important to understand. Let's say you are obedient. This is one part of your personality. Another part of your personality is disobedience. But that is not how people see themselves. They do not see negative and positive qualities of one scale of duality as one. No, they see them as two separate qualities or two opposite sides. As a result, these opposite sides are at constant war with each other. We call one side of duality good, right, and necessary. We call another, opposite side bad, wrong, and unnecessary.

What were your parents teaching you in the process of your upbringing? Acquisition of which qualities did they emphasize? They used to say, "Be better! Do this! Do it this way!" They praised you for doing things the right way. If you didn't do something the way they wanted you to do it, they reprimanded you. This is how separation of the opposite sides, with the following conflict relationship between them is introduced into a growing personality of every child. To become better, you had to fight the side your parents called bad. As a result, you don't want to acknowledge the presence of "bad" in you. What happens in this case? You project whatever you don't accept in yourself onto the external world and people that inhabit this world. You start to fight these people. In reality, you fight yourself.

We have briefly reviewed the makeup of our personality, which was necessary to understand the essence of separation. Where does separation come from? Why are we in it? Where does it lead to? Those are very important questions to pose as our entire experience here, in this reality, is experience of separation. Let's review the mechanisms using which we acquire the experience of separation.

We can compare a human being to a computer. As you know, every computer is built on the dual principle: yes—no, one—zero. This simple principle gives birth to different programs. Our mind is built on the same dual principle. Those of you who studied neurophysiology know that brain is composed of two hemispheres divided by a partition—corpus colosum. You may also know that we have consciousness and subconsciousness. For example, if you happen to be in the body of a man, you are conscious of the fact that you are a man. But are you conscious of the fact that you are also a woman? One side of duality is present on the conscious level— you say, "I am a man." Another side submerges into subconsciousness. You don't see that side and you deny it, "I am not a woman." **Our being conscious of only one side of our personality gives birth to duality, i.e. half-sidedness or one-sidedness of our perception.**

The experience of separation can be acquired only if your perception is separated or one-sided. Do we see that? Do we see ourselves holistically? Do we see other people holistically? Do we see the world holistically? No, we do not. We do not see ourselves or the world holistically, because of the way our perception is set up now. The knowledge about the makeup of our perception that I discuss with you comes from my Supreme Aspect, which resides in the world of Wholeness and has an ability to see holistically. It allows me to see the structure of my personality and every other personality clearly.

The root of separation is in our divided mind that gives birth to dual or half-sided perception. This one-sided perception leads to inner conflict; we fight ourselves. People say, "If we want to be better, we have to fight our bad side." But, these better and worst, irrespective of what they are, are two sides of one whole in you, in your personality. In that case, what are we doing when we fight for the best in ourselves, in our wives, in our husbands, in our kids, in our families, and in the society, we live in? Not being aware of it, we fight ourselves. This is what hell is all about. What is hell? Hell is the fight that occurs inside us. There are no winners in this fight and there cannot be any. There are only losers there, and we are those losers. This is very important to understand. This is a paradigm—a perception shared by society that contains the basic assumptions, ways of thinking, and patterns of how

6

things work in the world—we are living in. It's precisely on this paradigm, on the paradigm of one's fight with oneself that the entire system of survival in every aspect of it—religious, political, economic, cultural, and moral—is built. Recall geometry where everything starts with an axiom. One of the axioms states that two parallel lines never intercept. Later, you are offered multiple theorems and assignments to prove this axiom. Change the axiom, and all these theorems will fall as a house of cards. Why? They will fall because the axiom is the foundation that supports them. When you remove the axiom, every theorem that arise out of it stops to work. The School of Holistic Psychology offers you a new axiom, an axiom which suites a new time. The axiom of old time is an axiom of survival. The axiom I discuss with you is the axiom of Partnership and Wholeness. You may not understand everything now, but as you work and move toward wholeness, you will understand more and more.

Let us return to the topic of inner separation of our personality, which maintains and continues the inner conflict that rages inside us. What is going on in the world now? We see endless conflicts and wars. The same scenario plays itself out in the life of common people around us. Behind all these conflicts is inner separation. The external world reflects this inner separation as a mirror. We can neither heal this separation nor solve these problems by changing the external world. That's what most people, who happened to live in the axiom of survival, try to do. One should work with a cause, not with its reflection. The external world is just a reflection of our inner separation, a separation that gives birth to the war inside us.

The first and the most important step on your way to Wholeness is the *intention* to stop the conflict that is

raging inside you. To come to this intention, you should live through many lives and experience every peculiarity of inner conflict and separation. You can only acquire this experience if you don't understand that you are fighting yourself. It *appears* to you that you fight the external world. It *appears* to you that you want to carve a place for yourself under the sun. It *appears* to you that you want to triumph over someone and to become successful. You are fighting yourself. I don't negate this experience; I am grateful for it. This experience has brought us to discuss the topic we discuss now. **I want you to notice that there is no denial and no condemnation in my words.** I do not disapprove, and I do not condemn anything that happens around us, because I see that at the end every experience directs us toward the impulse to stop the war and helps us acquire wholeness. That's where the entire humanity is heading to.

The process of Quantum Leap will proceed in a stepwise fashion. The first step is to gather your personality together. Then, we will unite on the social scale. Later, we will address unity in other dimensions.

But, how do we make the first step? How do we start on this path? There are many seekers around. People walk in the dark, bumping into each other and stepping onto each other's toes. Most of them are not aware of where they are going and why. This transfer from searching for the path to getting on the path is a very important step. I call the path I follow the path toward Wholeness. Are you ready to stop searching for the path and to start walking the path? You are not even searching where you have lost. People commonly search in places that are better illuminated, noisier, and more popular. They search in places that are better known and bring more money, i.e. where certain survival tips are offered. They are searching not where they need to search.

So, how can one get on the path to Wholeness? I can tell you how I did it. It was not a simple process. As all of you, I have spent many lifetimes here. As all of you, I fought during these lifetimes. In this lifetime, I came to decide to stop this war. I was tired of it and I felt hopeless. On the emotional level, I felt as a prisoner on the death road. That's how I experienced it. At some point, a tremendous inner passion brought me to understand what was happening to me. This passion allowed me to stop this inner war. That's how I experienced it. You will have to experience it on your own. This is the revolution that you will have to go through in your inner world. I am discussing the pointers on the way I went through and continue to follow, but you will have to do it on your own. You will start on this path when you finally get to understand that you are fighting yourself. **When you fight and try to prove something to your kids, wives, husbands, parents, or coworkers, you try to prove it to yourself and you fight yourself.** You want to convince them that you are right. When you do that, you fight yourself. I cannot say there is no pleasure in it. There is plenty of pleasure in it. If you are still interested in this pleasure—you want to continue the fight. You want to convince people. You want to win. You will win, but in the end, your victory will turn into defeat. If you continue to fight, you are not ready to walk the way of Wholeness. When, constricted by the ropes of dual problems, you start to feel very bad, you start to search for the exit the way a drowning man searches for a breath of air. You will be able to start on the way to Wholeness when the level of your passion to stop the war will approach the level of the passion of the drowning man. Only then you will be able to walk the way of awareness. But the first and the most important step you will have to make is to experience the need to love yourself and to become your own partner.

Many people suffer thinking no one loves them. They search for love in the outside world. They want other people to love them. In reality, they don't love themselves. The external world just mirrors them the state of their affairs.

So, the first step you will have to make is to start seeing that you are fighting yourself. This step will give birth to *the intention* to stop the fight. When you make this step, you will need Holistic Psychology as the drowning man needs air, because it describes this path clearly and in minute details. It points out every trap on the way.

You can only understand yourself holistically when you start to observe your personality and become aware of yourself. As I have mentioned already, the personality of a human being represents a set of assignments, like a set of textbook assignments a high school student must solve to graduate. Our personality is such a textbook. It has many assignments. Our work is to solve the assignments written in our personalities and to understand ourselves holistically. This path consists of many steps.

Many people are still on the kindergarten level of consciousness. This is not a condemnation, but a characteristic of the age of the souls present on Earth. Many souls are at the level where they believe in miracles. They believe they will meet a great guru who will tell them that they have been chosen and will soon be enlightened. Many people await that. This is not the way it will happen.

You will have to take many steps to become whole. To complete a high school physics course a student needs to solve every assignment related to the course and to pass the final exam. Only then, he can be transferred to another grade. We are dealing with a similar but much more complicated situation here.

You will face many temptations on this path. I will tell you about some of them. A man called me yesterday asking for a consultation. He was screaming, "I am dying! I must see you now!" An hour later he called again to inform me that his car has broken down and he cannot make it. What happened? This is a temptation. This is the way personality fights for survival.

What is survival? When people think of survival, they usually think of the need to pay for food and shelter. I will broaden this notion. **From the standpoint of Holistic Psychology, to survive is to preserve a certain structure in the form it exists. Our personality has been created as a separate entity, and for it to survive it must preserve itself the way it is, in the form that can continue to fight.**

What does your personality feel when you read my books or listen to what I say? It starts to feel threatened for its survival, because I speak of another axiom, of the axiom of life. When your personality hears me, it gets scared. What is it afraid of? It is afraid of changes. It is afraid of not being able to function as a survival mechanism anymore. It is afraid of turning into something else. Every one of you will have to pass through this step. Many of you will stop here. They will not be able to go further. **This is a temptation by survival.**

Moving on the path of Wholeness, you will have to make choices. The world of survival will repeatedly tempt you by offering you money, status, advancement on a career ladder, etc. What will you choose? Will you choose survival or Wholeness?

Why do I keep moving in this direction for many years? I do that because I have made a choice and I continue to make it daily. It is not an easy choice to make. I am sharing my experience with you, because that's what you will have to experience, too.

To perceive yourself holistically, you will have to become aware of your personal program. I call personality a personal program. This is a real program. It works similarly to the Windows program in a computer. This program was downloaded with certain information, and it will only regurgitate what was downloaded into it. So, what exactly was downloaded into your personal program? The personal program of every human being is unique. All snowflakes appear to be the same, but when you look at them under the magnifying glass, each one of them is different. Similarly, the personality of every human being is unique. You will not find information about your personal program in any book. You will have to investigate your personal program yourself. I call our way the way of self-investigation. Investigation of your personal program will provide you with an opportunity to become whole. Thorough investigation and knowledge of your program will allow you to change it. That change will turn you into a human being of the next level of consciousness.

It is very important for us to know who inculcated our program. The origins of our program are rooted in our parents and their conflicts. If you are not living with them or they have passed away, they are still with you. Our main work is to investigate the program inculcated into us by our parents.

We need to review another important question that deals with enlightenment. Many people that call themselves spiritual seekers search for enlightenment. The material people want to acquire material wealth, status, and power. The spiritual people want enlightenment. What is enlightenment? Perhaps you have read about cases of enlightenment. They have been described in the spiritual literature. A man is suffering and searching for something for many years. Suddenly, he experiences a rupture and transfers to a different level of consciousness. However, he cannot describe how he transferred there. That's the way it used to happen. These cases have been described. These people have existed, and they exist. What I and the School of Holistic Psychology address as holistic consciousness is something else. I cannot tell you anything about the discrete moments of my enlightenment. I can share the process with you. I can take you on the way with me. It's a difficult, steep road that ascends higher and higher. I move toward wholeness one step at a time.

What kind of steps do I take? Let's look at them from the point of view of the structure of our personality. As I have mentioned already, our personality represents a set of interconnected dualities.

What is enlightenment? Enlightenment is introduction of light into our personal structure. En-light-enment. Presently, our personal structure is in the dark, i.e. in separation. It's in this darkness that your fight with yourself occurs. Would you fight yourself if you were to clearly see and understand that you are fighting yourself? That would be absurd. You would not do that. So, why do you do that? You do that because you are in the dark; you don't see what happens here. You need to investigate your inner house, i.e. your personal structure. You need to bring light into its every corner. Imagine your world as a big house that has many rooms. You have not set your foot in many of them. You are living on the northern side of it. You don't visit the south side. Some rooms of your house are full of light, others are dark. You don't even know you have the dark side. You think you only move on one side, the north side. You don't see the other side. You don't think it is yours. But it is yours. The entire house is yours.

How can we bring light into our house? To do that we will need to explore and investigate dualities. By seeing the mechanisms of conflict between the opposite sides of duality, you will introduce light into these rooms. We can say that the number of rooms you have is equivalent to the number of inner dualities of your personal program. When you investigate one of your dualities, when you illuminate it with the light of awareness, and clearly see the mechanism it operates on, the conflict resolves. The path to en-light-enment or Wholeness is a step by step process. You will have to investigate your every duality. You will have to see how these dualities interconnect. We will thoroughly investigate the mechanisms based on which your dualities work. You will find that every duality we discuss relates to you. You will find that some of these dualities are related to you more than others. You will only be able to feel and understand that if you continue to participate in this Process and to attend the School seminars and webinars.

The way I present the material during these webinars is new. The information you find on our site today reflects fragments of my investigation. My investigation has been completed. I can present my results to you in the proper form now. I have received the keys that can open every duality. This revolutionary discovery will allow us to transfer from separated consciousness to Holistic consciousness in a step by step fashion and in full awareness of how it is to be done.

We will explore the duality **"To give—to receive"** today. Let's start with the experiment that was introduced into this webinar from the start when I announced that you can decide how much to pay for it. Financial questions are the most important questions in the world we live in, the world governed by the axiom of survival.

Money provides us with an opportunity to survive. That's why people pray to money. Money has turned into a god. I am not saying money is something bad. I am not saying money is something good. For me, money is a chip in the game. It's just a chip. Let's look at this chip. How did you move it today? Where did you move it? What did you feel moving it? What did you think when you paid for today's webinar?

My announcement has stipulated the rule: "You can receive as much as the amount of energy you have invested." I have asked you *to feel* your reaction to this statement. As the structure of our personality is dual, it might have caused you to experience both positive and negative thoughts and feelings. Thus, if you are conscious of the fact that you have experienced only negative states, you need to know that you have also experienced the positive states—you just have not noticed them. If you only experienced positive states, you need to know that you have also experienced negative states—you just have not noticed them. When you see both positive and negative states simultaneously, you will perceive yourself holistically. At that time, you will have a choice.

Quite a lot is being said about choice nowadays. People say, "I choose this, and I choose that." But do they really have a choice, or do they have an illusion that they have a choice? For example, while in a state of one-sided perception, you say: "I am good." Is that a choice? No, this is just a statement of one-sided perception. You have a choice when you can say: "I am good, and I am bad. Presently, I choose to be good." When you say, "I am good" and insist on it, it is not a choice. Those are very important nuances of our work. The opportunity of a choice appears when you start to see two opposite sides of every phenomenon—positive sides and negative sides—at once. These terms, positive and negative, are just technical terms in my vocabulary. When I say positive, I don't mean good, and when I say negative—I don't mean bad. I am talking about a battery equipped with positive and negative poles. When you connect these poles, your battery can perform useful work. When you say that positive is good and negative is bad, you refuse to touch the negative pole. As a result, you cannot receive energy from the battery of your personality.

Let us return to the experiment we started this webinar with and to my assertion that **you can only receive as much as the amount of energy you have invested**. What kind of energy does a human being possess? There are at least three types of energy. There is mental energy—the energy of the mind, thoughts, and images. The energy that appears in your mental sphere because of our experiment is the energy of a question. You participate in the webinar and you come up with a question. I don't think you came here without one. The fact that you came here indicates that you have a question.

The next question, "How powerful is your question?" You can say, "I am interested." What do you mean by that? How powerful is your question? This power or energy is related to the emotional or feeling sphere. How do you feel your question emotionally? How high is its level? I have told you about the power of my question already. Imagine a man. His head is submerged in water. He is desperate for a breath of air. Another man just stands there taking small, shallow breaths. He is not desperate yet. Which one of these men are you?

The third component is physical. It deals with the question of how much money you are ready to invest in your request.

How much time are you willing to spend on it? What other physical effort are you ready to apply? The physical component will show the power of your question. Did you pay for it? How much did you pay for it? Did you want to pay for it? This is a physical realization. Why did you pay ten dollars for it? Why did you pay fifty dollars for it? Why did you pay five hundred dollars for it? The amount of money you spend depends on the power of your question.

Monetary payment is a good physical indicator. What happens in your mental and emotional spheres? I will not know that until I speak to you. But the amount of money you paid for the webinar allows me to see what happens on your physical level clearly. That's why the question of money is so important. The sum of money you paid for this webinar is a result of mental and emotional effort your personality spent on the question it wants to be answered during the webinar. What is the power of your question? The physical component— money you paid for this webinar—shows its strength.

Moreover, when you give something, you free up space for something new to come in. Imagine you have a room. It is filled with old furniture. You have been living in this room for a long time. One day, while walking through a store, you decide to buy a new chair. But your room doesn't have space for it. You need to free up some space to fit this new chair in. The same can be said about new knowledge.

Every personality is full of knowledge. Every one of you is full of information you received from your parents and school teachers, but not one of you knows why you need this information. Every bit of this knowledge deals with survival. I transmit a different type of knowledge, but do you have the space necessary for this knowledge to enter you? You probably know the old parable about the glass that was full of water. If your glass is full, you will not be able to pour anything in it. First, you need to empty it. What we discuss now—giving money for something—is more than money. We are freeing space in your mental-emotional sphere. If you are full to the brim with knowledge about survival and self-importance, this new knowledge will not enter you. How strong is your longing for this new knowledge and how much space are you willing to free in your inner world for it?

Let's now explore these topics by using real-life situations, such as difficulties you have encountered paying for this webinar and other problems that arose while you were investigating duality "To give—to receive."

— You have said that in the process of self-investigation, we will encounter numerous temptations and will have to make a choice toward Wholeness. But how can we even make this choice if the personal program installed in us predetermines everything?

— If we only consisted of the personal program, created for our survival, we would not have any other choice but to explore different modes of survival. We would never be able to get to Wholeness. But as I have mentioned already, we have another, very important part—Supreme Aspect. It has sent us here in the form we are in—in the form of personality and physical body. The Supreme Aspect has its own vision of what is important for us and what is not. For the Supreme Aspect, our Wholeness is of utmost importance. We have just entered a new period of evolution, which will allow us to work on our awareness and wholeness. Only a few people could do this work before. Now, all of us can do it. The direction you choose will depend on you. My task is not to force you toward wholeness. This will not only be meaningless; it will be impossible. This would be like forcing gratitude out of someone. If I were to do that, you would experience opposite

18

reaction—you would hate me. **My task is to show you things the way they are.** How will you perceive these things? That depends on you. Depending on the way you perceive this, you may have a choice. If you perceive this as an opportunity for your Supreme and lower aspects to interact, you will have a choice. If you don't, you will not have a choice—you will continue to navigate this reality in the survival mode.

— *So, I do decide something after all.*

— Is this a question or a statement?

— *It is a question.*

— You will have to answer this question yourself. I will return your question to you, "Do you decide anything or not?"

— *I got it. Thank you. Let me ask you another question. While reading esoteric literature, we frequently encounter the notion of intention. Do you use this notion, too?*

— We do encounter this word—*intention*—quite frequently nowadays. **What is the difference between intention and desire?** Quite frequently people use the word "intention" as a substitute for the word "desire." For me, those are two totally different notions. For me, *the intention* is something that comes from my Supreme Aspect, which happens to reside at the level of Holistic consciousness. The intention that comes from There is not dual. This is very important to understand. Here, on the other hand, in the dual world where our personalities reside, our desires are dual and opposite. When you desire something, only one part of you desires it. The other part of you desires something totally opposite to what this first part of you desires. The discernment between intention and desire requires awareness and an ability to see the difference between the Supreme Aspect which resides at the level of consciousness of unity and the lower aspect which resides at the level of consciousness of separation.

— *What about the Observer? Do these two notions—Observer and Supreme Aspect—mean the same thing in your dictionary?*

— The notion of the Observer is being used by many schools of psychology, but let us make a distinction between the way they use this term and the way I use it. Can you share some of your observations of your personality?

— *I like to be told that I am active and energetic. Recently, I received an evaluation from my boss, where he describes me as a passive and lacking initiative. This caused me to experience an aggressive outburst and suffering. I could not accept it. I identify myself with an active, self-assured man, and when someone tells me that I am not, that I am something opposite, I start to fight him. How can I accept this part?*

— You have brought up a very good example. I want to thank you for it. You have said that you identify yourself with the positive, active, successful, and full of the initiative side. When someone tells you that you are something opposite to it—passive, not successful, and not initiative, you get upset and take an offense. Is that the case?

— *Yes, I get very upset!*

— Of course, you get very upset. You consider yourself to be something, and you are told you are something totally opposite. What does this situation tell us about? It tells us about the fight that goes on inside you. It seems to you that you are active, successful, and full of initiative. This is a one-sided perception. You don't know the inner duality that is present in you, and you don't want to accept your opposite side. Am I correct?

— *Yes.*

— Now, how did your mind come up with the judgment that you are active, successful, and full of initiative? What does it lean on when it creates such a judgment?

— *It leans on the external world, on people who give me these characteristics.*

— Let me put it differently, "How do these people come up with these characteristics?" For you to understand what it means to be an aim driven man, you need to know what it means to live without an aim. For you to understand what it means to be successful, you need to know what it means to be a failure. For you to understand what activity is, you need to know passivity. You can determine your position on a scale. Presently, we are dealing with three scales: "success—failure," "active—passive," "hard-working—slacker." Next, you mark up one side of a scale, and you say, "I am here." But take a closer look, we are dealing with one scale. Positive and negative qualities are just the extreme sides of one scale. However, you set up a mark, and you say, "I am very close to being a success." And you reject the rest of the scale. You reject it inside yourself.

I must maintain our conversation in a certain format. I think the format question—answer is very primitive. I am not interested in it. I conduct constant self-investigation. Every conversation we have will turn into an investigation. Presently, we investigate how you perceive yourself. And what do we see? We see that you are stuck in one-sided perception. You want to be positive and only positive. When you are told that you have negative qualities, you vehemently deny it. In that case, you cannot accept yourself Holistically. This is very important to understand. I am not saying that something is wrong with you. I am just showing you how things are now. Perhaps, you need to continue to accumulate the experience of conflict to reach a higher level of self-esteem or another one-sided quality. Are you ready to see yourself as a whole? I don't know. You can only answer this question yourself. But if you are ready, you will use the information your boss and other people are sharing with you. Their words are directing you to see your opposite side. You will be grateful for the help they offer you to see your own, invisible to you, side. You need to accept your opposite side. Both sides are equally important.

Look, if we feel bad today, we will feel better tomorrow. If we were sick and suddenly started to get better, we say, "I felt bad yesterday. I feel better now." Your tooth was hurting you. You went to see a dentist. Your tooth is not bothering you, and you feel better—you feel as good now as you felt bad before. We feel as good as we felt bad before. For you to feel better, you need to feel bad. This is the principle of life here: the worst you are, the better you will be. But this is a mechanical way of life. A human being receives his positive and negative experiences, his pleasures and sufferings whether he is on vacation or in jail. Moreover, as paradoxical as it may sound, he receives them in equal quantities. Why? It happens because we are dealing with a mechanism. While in jail, a man is told, "You are going to be hanged tomorrow." Tomorrow comes and he is told, "No, we are not going to hang you." He feels great. Checking out of a hotel on a tropical island, a man is told, "You have not settled your bill in full. You owe us three thousand dollars." Ten minutes later, the concierge tells him, "I am sorry. I have made a mistake. Your account has been paid in full." A man is happy. All these disappointments and excitements are mechanical. People do not understand this mechanism. I invite you to see this mechanism and to control it. You can say, "I don't want to control it. This is fate. I cannot control it." This is another approach to life. There are many ways to perceive life. The perception I share with you differs from the perception of "sleeping" people. Are you ready to move to a higher level of perception?

— *You have mentioned gratitude. The way I understand it, gratitude is a result. Is gratitude a result of self-investigation?*

— Yes. Gratitude is not an affirmation. Many techniques are available today. Affirmative positive thinking is one of these techniques. What do people who practice it do? They repeat affirmations as other people recite prayers in church. In church, a man prays, "In the name of the father, the son, and the Holy Spirit." Here he repeats, "Love you, love you, love you." What does it lead to? It activates his opposite side: "I hate you, I hate you, I hate you." But as he decided to manifest only the positive side, he starts to suppress this opposite, negative side. In the end, this leads to a serious disbalance, which manifests itself in personal dramas, accidents, and diseases. Why do I say that work with Wholeness is the most important work here? I say that because this work is connected to the most important things in your life, to your health. When you are in an imbalanced state, i.e. when you see only one side of duality and reject the opposite side, you create a serious disbalance. This disbalance will manifest itself in the form of diseases, accidents, and failures. It will always manifest itself physically. All these dramas we experience in our lives are directly related to inner disbalance that we don't even see. I am teaching you how to see it. The work we do here will harmonize your inner life. Consequently, your external life will also be harmonized.

— *Duality "successful—not successful" has become active in my life recently. I have been out of work for a long time. My husband and my son work. My son gives me money from time to time. When I learned about this webinar, I decided to pay for it using some of his money. You have asked us to observe the thoughts and feelings that will appear in connection with paying for this webinar. I would like to share my observations. The first thought I observed was a happy one, "I will talk to Pint today." I yearned to talk to you since I read your first book. However, another part of me got activated an hour later—the greedy part. It said, "Why do you want to spend that much? You can send him half of the amount you want to send." Eventually, I sent as much as I intended to send.*

Four years ago, I was fired from a job. A year later I opened a business, but it didn't succeed. The more inner tension I created forcing myself to act, the more resistance I experienced. Finally, I got so tired of hitting my head against the wall and fighting myself that I screamed, "Why is this happening to me?" This is not the first time I experienced this situation. My husband makes money; I spend. I only spend. I only receive. What do I give back? I love to work. I worked since I was seventeen. While in college, I worked full time. I was independent once. Why can't I earn any money now?

— I will ask you to formulate your question better. You have described your situation well, but it can be seen from many angles. Please, be more specific.

— *Why can't I earn any money? Why can't I satisfy my needs on my own?*

— Okay. You need the money to satisfy your needs. What are those needs?

— *I am talking about desires of my personality. I want to buy expensive things. I want to go on exotic vacations.*

— The aims you have listed are connected to survival and higher quality of survival. I want you to see that, and I want you *to discern* something here. There is survival and there is what I call Wholeness or Life. Do you want to understand yourself? Do you want to get to know yourself? Do you have a question that is not related to survival? We have not gathered here to improve our survival techniques. We are here to investigate the mechanisms of survival. This is an important distinction. You have said that you wanted to be on my webinar. You probably had an idea about what we do here. I am not here to improve the quality of your survival. Many people do that, and you can visit their seminars. However, you have decided to come here. That means your question deals with something that is more than survival. What else do you want to know?

— *I want to understand myself. What am I living for? Why am I here?*

— Those questions belong to a different category. An exotic vacation or a luxury car belonging to one category of aims. You have just brought up a totally different category: "Why am I here? What is the meaning of my life? What is my assignment?" This is an entirely different category of questions. A human being concerned with where to go for a vacation, how to buy an expensive car, or how to acquire a higher status does not ask these questions. The quantum leap will stress people out. Many people will start to ask questions not out of their personalities, which operate in survival mode, but out of their Supreme Aspects.

Let's look at the strength of your inquiry to understand yourself and compare it to the inquiry of your personality to survive. Let's put the questions and inquiries of your personality on one side of a scale and questions and inquiries of your Supreme Aspect geared to understand yourself on another side of a scale. Which side will outweigh another?

— *The side that wants to understand itself will outweigh another side, of course.*

— Really? How much money do you spend on survival and how much money do you spend to understand yourself?

— *I don't work now. I don't earn any money.*

— You don't earn any money, but you have money. If you didn't have any money, we would not talk now. You would not be here. You do get these monies one way or another. You don't earn them yourself, but you do get them from someone.

— *I get money from my husband and my son.*

— **There are two modes of survival here: feminine and masculine. To survive using feminine mode of survival is to find a man who will provide you with the money you need and to survive behind his back. A woman will orient herself toward this man. She will fight other women and have him bring his money to her. Moreover, she will insist he brings her more and more money. The effort she will invest in this activity is not any weaker than the effort a man spends to earn this money.**

Then, the question is what do you spend this money on? I am asking you the same question I asked before. You have told us, you don't have money because you don't earn any, but as we know now, you do have the money you need. We have learned that your man gives you money. Our next question is what does he allow you to spend this money on and how vigilant is he about checking where his money go to? He says, "I will give you money to buy a nice dress, but I will not give you money to attend to your spiritual needs. I will not pay for Pint's seminars." Is that the case?

— *If I were to choose between buying a dress and coming to a seminar, I would choose to come here.*

— I will ask you to make an assessment. How much money do you spend to understand yourself, and how much money do you spend on survival, including housing, food, and clothes. Give me a rough estimate.

— *I spend ten percent of my money to understand myself.*

— That tells you how important it is for you to understand yourself. What I say is not a condemnation. I am not here to condemn anyone. **My task is to describe what is the way it is.** However, your personality may react to this information differently. The strength of your inquiry to survive overwhelms the strength of your inquiry to understand yourself. When I shared my personal story with you, I have mentioned that I faced many choices in my life, and I continue to face them. They appear all the time. I must constantly make a choice: survival vs. life. I keep choosing Wholeness. I choose to understand myself, but I see both sides. I say, "This is what important for me now." I am not saying that one of these sides is bad and another is good. No. But I choose what I choose. You must direct at least fifty-one percent of your energy toward understanding yourself. This is the minimum required here. And the more energy you direct in that direction, the more you will understand yourself. Otherwise, you spend all your money, i.e. energy on survival. Quite frequently, all your effort to understand yourself get lost because silently you choose survival. This is a very important question. Thank you for asking it.

You have asked me, "What should I do to earn money for my necessities?" This question is about changing the mode of your survival. If you are in the feminine mode of survival, you survive on the account of your man; it requires no less effort from you than earning money on your own using the masculine mode of survival.

Why do we observe feminization nowadays? Previously, a wife was a part of her husband. In some cultures, when a man died, his wife was buried with him alive. Things have changed since. We can hear women express a lot of dissatisfaction with men, "Men cheat and drink. They don't take care of their children." Some women choose to work and to make money on their own in order not to depend on men. Many women, while being in the female bodies, choose the masculine mode of survival. This is a widespread phenomenon nowadays. How does it happen? It happens through suppression of the inner feminine part and reinforcement of the inner masculine part. If your inquiry is to experience that, you will have to intentionally switch to your masculine side. Do you know your masculine side? Have you developed it? How strong is it? Those are the questions you will need to ask yourself. I have answered your question. If you really want to control your finances and to determine what to spend your money on, instead of turning to your husband for help, you need to move to the masculine mode of survival. This transformation, however, will bring up many changes in to your life. You will face a marital discord. You may face separation or divorce. That will allow you to live independently. You must pay for everything here. If you are waiting for me to say, "Do this and do that and you will have the money you need," you are mistaken. I will not do that. I can show you the consequences of you moving in this direction. This is neither bad nor good. This is just an experience. That's how I look at it. But do you need this experience? Will you choose this experience? Why would you choose it? Those are the questions you will face. You can choose to experience that to achieve Wholeness. You may choose to experience that to acquire the experience of the opposite mode of survival. That's my answer to your question.

— *Thank you.*

— Thank you for bringing this important question to the table.

— *I would like to share the states this webinar and paying for it activated in me. I have experienced very unusual, scary states. I didn't have any troubles deciding how much money to pay for the webinar. A day prior to the webinar I spoke to my dad. He mirrored my inner part to me, the part that I didn't want to see. He said any spiritual evolution one needs to pay for is nonsense and illusion. This is something I am afraid of. I've had the experience when I thought I was evolving spiritually, while for two years I just lived in the illusion, which just intensified the pride of my spiritual side. I felt hopeless and helpless. I was stuck. Dad thinks that a man can only progress on the pass of spiritual evolution by working solo; no one can help him do this work. I don't know what brought me to this webinar? Was it the desire of my personality or the request of my soul to evolve spiritually?*

— This is a very good question and it brings us to **duality "material—spiritual."** As you will see, we almost never work with one duality alone. Our structure is complex and many-sided. We will explore every duality you bring. Later, we will summarize everything and figure out how all these dualities are connected to the theme of the webinar. The duality "material—spiritual" is very important. Let's explore it. Let's look at people who live through the material aspect of this duality. They are interested in status, money, and power. They are interested in houses, square footage of these houses, cars, and models of their cars. These things are subject of their conversations.

Other people call themselves spiritual. They are concerned with whether they are enlightened or not. They are concerned with the Truth they carry, the power of their Truth, and how much better their Truth is in comparison to the truth of other spiritual and esoteric groups. Those things are subject of their conversations. So, what do we see? We see that the basic quality that material and spiritual people share is pride. The only difference is that their pride is supported by different means. Do you need to acquire the material or the spiritual experience? You need to acquire both. We are sent to this reality by our Soul to acquire experience. That's our main assignment. The experience we acquire here is connected to the energy we accumulate. In the end, we send this energy to our Soul. Our soul needs this energy. For us to become whole, we must have experience of living through opposite sides of multiple dualities. You will not be able to bypass this experience, as this is your main assignment here. Let's look at what your dad was saying to you. Which side of this duality is he living through: material or spiritual?

— *He can barely earn enough money to support himself. The questions of survival are of paramount importance for him. He keeps repeating, "I make enough money to have bread on my table and roof over my head. I will never pay for spiritual stuff."*

— Your father is a typical example. A human being who doesn't have money rejects it. I say it without condemnation. I simply review the facts. If he was living through the material side of this duality, he would be very upset to be told, "You say you are material, but you don't have any money. How come?" But as we can see, he says, "I don't have money, because I am spiritual. People who belong to the spiritual sphere don't need money." Moreover, he asserts that a man who moves toward the spiritual sphere should reject the money. He says, "A spiritual teacher who accepts money is not a real teacher; he will fool you." He separates the material side from the spiritual side. Many people do that, and this is not bad. This is a necessary stage people must pass to separate dual sides and to experience one of them. When you enter the material side, you start to reject the spiritual side. When you move to the spiritual side, you start to reject the material side. Your inner conflict exacerbates. Receiving the experience of only one side presupposes a strong rejection of the opposite side. It is based on this rejection that you start to reinforce and accumulate the experience of the side that you chose to experience. Your father experiences the spiritual side of this duality now. It is lawful for him to reject the material side.

— *What he said characterizes him, but he said it to me. I don't understand it. My experience is totally different.*

— Exactly. He is your dad. Our parents inculcate us with our personal program. One side of this program, paternal, will say one thing. Another side, maternal, will say the opposite thing. You will observe this parental conflict in every duality of your program. Your father has inculcated you with one side of your program; your mother—with the opposite side. That's how we acquire our inner duality, expressed in opposite assertions of our parents. We need to transform the interaction our parents had from conflict to partnership. This is our main task if we want to achieve Wholeness.

— *I understand the part of the program inculcated into me by my father very well, but I cannot see what mom planted in me. You have said that my father rejects the material side and experiences the spiritual side. In that case, my mom should stand for the material side. I got it. That's the fight they are fighting since the day they were married.*

— Exactly. What does your mom do in this conflict? She says to your dad, "You cannot make enough money. Your duty to your family is to make more money. You cannot fulfill your husbandly duty. You cannot fulfill your paternal duty." She oppresses him so harshly with this statement that he says, "I will go into the spiritual realm. I will not be stuck here." That's how he defends himself against her attack. He condemns her for her inability to understand that there are other things here aside from the material things. These two sides are in you. Their conflict intensifies now because you must pay for this webinar. Which side will you join? Taking your dad's point of view, you will say, "This is not a good webinar. I would only consider it to be good if I didn't have to pay for it." If you join mom, you don't know what she can say. She can say, "You have to pay for everything in life. But do you have to pay for this webinar? You better buy yourself a pair of shoes." Neither one of your parents answers your question. There is only conflict and fight there. Moreover, neither dad nor mom answers the question, "Do I need this webinar?" Wait a minute. Let me correct that. They answer it. They say, "You don't need this webinar." One of them asserts that people should not be charged for true spirituality. Another says, "You should not pay money for this garbage. You should pay for something palpable, something material."

We are dealing with a very important topic now. Your personality is a survival program. That's the way it was created. Your parents have inculcated two sides of this program into you—two modes of survival. Your personal program is a set of different methods of survival which were transferred to you by two people. These methods oppose each other. You, as a child, had to decide which side—paternal or maternal—to choose as successful. You had to make a choice about which part of the program to be conscious of, and which part to send to subconsciousness. These opposite parts fight inside you. This is a war between consciousness and subconsciousness, a war between two opposite programs of survival. These two halves can only answer the questions of survival. Their answers oppose each other and create a conflict related to survival in you. They do not lead you to Wholeness; only Supreme Aspect can guide you there.

Everyone who is present at the webinar today has a personal program. This program consists of two opposite modes of survival, neither one of which is interested in acquiring Wholeness. But you have come here. You are talking to me. You have read my books. That means something in you is interested in Wholeness. Where does this interest come from? It comes from your Supreme Aspect, i.e. from your Soul. That's where the difference between you and your parents lies. Your parents are not interested in the questions you pose, "Why am I here? What is my mission on Earth?" They cannot answer these questions. They can only answer questions related to survival, and their answers oppose each other. You will have to search for the answers to your spiritual questions somewhere else. You have come here to search for these answers.

— *Thank you very much. That was very important for me to hear. I have chosen my dad's side as the conscious side to survive. It's amazing. I have never thought of that, but now I understand where I am coming from when I speak to him. The conflicts between the aspirations of my soul and my survival program are the harshest conflicts I have ever experienced. What I just learned is very important for me: everything my dad has inculcated into me deals with survival.*

— I want to clarify something here. Oriented toward mom or dad, you receive conflicting answers in respect to the modes of your survival. This is the main suffering every personality deals with. These conflicts will prompt some personalities to start to ask questions which are not related to survival, questions such as: "Why I am here on Earth? What is my assignment? What is the meaning of my life?" We would not ask these questions if conflicts of our survival were not so severe. These conflicts are created by the program inculcated in us by our parents. Unable to regulate two opposite sides of our program, we start to ask questions that take us to the next level of consciousness, where we start to *see* the answers. This is the level of consciousness I speak from. You will need to find a consultant who will guide you through these higher levels of consciousness, as staying here, at the levels of consciousness you currently are, you will only experience escalation of conflicts of survival without any understanding of why they occur, why you need them, and what are the mechanisms that stand behind their appearance.

— *What is the relationship between the program of survival and intention that comes from the soul? Is it a conflicting relationship? Are they at war with each other?*

— Yes, they are at war with each other. Everything you see and deal with here is in conflict. Conflict is a collision of the opposites. We are living in the paradoxical world. We experience paradox here. This is a training ground, where we constantly deal with opposite tendencies. One side of you says, "Go South." Another side says, "No. Go North." This is a crude analogy, but it shows the dilemma we constantly deal with here.

A man who is not aware of himself tries to have everything good. He takes one point of view, and he says he doesn't experience conflict; he had chosen one side. If I am, "Yes," then I am only this "Yes," but if I also have "No" in me, I am "Yes—No." Then, I am paradoxical; I am in conflict. That's where we are and that's where the essence of our lessons lies. We try to take one side: everything is going to be good. No, everything is going to be both good and bad. You must understand that if you want to sort this mess out. People try to forget their negative experience. They use different methods to do that: alcohol, drugs, sex, shopping, work, etc. But you cannot escape yourself. You cannot escape your inner duality; it will follow you everywhere. You will always manifest your opposite side, and it will bring you suffering, unhappiness, anger, and aggression until you start to see and investigate yourself in duality, accepting your opposite side as the side that is equally necessary for you. That is what Wholeness is about.

The relationship between your Supreme and lower aspects is also conflicting and dual. Your Supreme aspect needs you to become whole, while your lower aspect simply wants to survive. Those are two totally different directions of movement. When you are on the spiritual side, you create another powerful duality, in which you will undergo some very serious challenges and experience severe stress. This stress will allow you to investigate yourself if you don't get off this path. But if you get off this path, you will continue to experience this stress. So, move forward. Use this stress, i.e. voltage potential to solve and to become aware of the conflicting, dual nature of your program.

— *Thank you very much for this dialogue. You are right, this stress is pushing me forward. My question is, "Who is pushing me? Is it my personality?"*

— You are being pushed by stress or voltage potential that appears because of the interaction of the dual sides of your personality.

— *I want to thank you for accepting money as a payment. The need to pay for this seminar allowed me to experience part of me that has a difficult time accepting anything. For a long time, I have been stuck in the giving part. I am trying the role of a teacher now. I am a yoga instructor. The role of a teacher is a difficult role to play. It's not a coincidence that the Indian word "teacher" or "guru" translates as "heavy." A teacher carries a heavy responsibility. The knowledge you transmit is difficult to appraise. From the standpoint of "to give—to receive," my conflict arises because I am in the receiving role. My personality resists that. I push away people who want to give me things. Moreover, I don't experience gratitude when people offer me their help or give me something.*

— Why are not you grateful for that? What kind of help do you reject more intensely?

— *I reject financial help. I reject the money. I push away men who try to take care of me. I discovered that men who give me money always try to take advantage of me.*

— There is an old Russian saying, "The one who pays orders the music." The one who pays the musicians decides which kind of music they are going to play. Men who pay buy you. They determine the way your violin is going to sound. That's what you are afraid of. You are not afraid of the money. You are afraid to be bought. If you take their money, you will have to perform certain services, which most likely have not even been discussed when money exchanged hands. You must predict what these men need. When a prostitute gets paid, everything gets discussed. A prostitute discusses the list of services performed and their prices. Your situation is different. You are given money for everything in bulk. Everything is included. Am I right?

— *Yes. I must listen and pay attention to him. I must manifest my positive side, only my positive side. I have a difficult time manifesting my negative side as it is. I have been in severe disbalance lately.*

— Look, every conflict is a marker of disbalance. We have just figured out why it is difficult for you to accept money from people. It is difficult for you because you equate money with total enslavement. "I have paid you. You have to do this and that." **Let's apply the basic tool of the School of Holistic Psychology here, the projection rule which stipulates that we always meet ourselves. When something irritates you in someone, it means you don't see it in yourself. If you don't see it in yourself, you don't know what to do with it.** A man gives you money. Then he insists you listen to everything he says. Then, he wants you to accompany him everywhere he goes to. Finally, he wants you to sleep with him. You don't know how to handle this, and you say, "I don't need your money! Get away from me! Let me be!"

You need to figure out why these people behave the way they behave. You can only do that by investigating yourself. They show you your own side, the side that you don't want to see. If you don't want to see it, you don't know it. If you don't know it, you cannot do anything about it. Imagine, you brought your car to a mechanic. You tell him, "Fix it." He replies, "I have never worked on this model before. I don't know how it works." You can use the tools our School offers to investigate your shadow side. In that case, you will have to accept that people, who try to buy you, reflect your inner side to you. When you accept this basic premise, you can move to the next phase—you can investigate these people. These people are very important to you. They will manifest externally what happens inside you. They will help you to investigate and to get to know yourself. This is the basic principle of self-investigation. We investigate ourselves using the help of others, using the help of the external world. This is our basic principle. How do you like that?

— *I like it a lot. It is very difficult to dive inside.*

— It is not that difficult, but one of your parts doesn't want to do that. It says, "Who the hell is Pint? What is he talking about? I don't like these people, and he says I have their qualities in me. Damn him!" But if you accept these people and start to look at the situations you encounter as an opportunity to investigate yourself, we will be able to get to this topic in the future and to look at it from a different angle. Presently, you are at this stage. I have explained what you need to do at this stage. When you choose to see these people as an important

37

element of your self-investigation, you will move to the next stage and come up with another question. Then, we will have another discussion. That's all I can say for now.

— I would like to discuss the results of my self-investigation and to get some comments from you. I have been observing the interplay of generosity and greediness in my personal structure. My mom is very generous. She showers me and everyone around her with presents. She is very active. She knows how to do everything, and she does it fast. When I see her work, I feel like a nincompoop. I have observed the interplay of generosity and greediness in many situations. I find myself on one side of this duality; another human being mirrors me my opposite side. Suddenly, I find myself to be very generous and capable with someone, while he manifests himself to be greedy and incompetent. When I started to observe that, a question appeared. When I meet someone, who shares a specific duality with me, I automatically flip and manifest the opposite side of the duality, the side opposite to the side he manifests. Why does it happen? When I started to connect two opposite sides of duality generous—greedy, I felt irritated by mom's manifestation of generosity. I could not manifest it. I thought, "Why do you have to dominate me all the time?" I wanted to dominate her. It looks like this interplay of the opposites is the opposite side of Wholeness. We must connect our opposite sides. Then, we will have a rheostat we can control.

— What does every woman hate? A woman comes to a party and sees another woman wearing the same dress she wears. Women hate that. Some women turn around and leave. In your story, both you and your mom pretend to be generous. As a result, you try to outdo each other in generosity. What does it tell us? It tells us that neither one of you accepts your opposite side. Why can't you enjoy your opposite side? This is a consequence of one-sided perception of yourself. You identify yourself with being generous, and you want to show everyone how generous you are. When another generous

38

human being shows up, you start to compete trying to prove to each other who is more generous. Why don't you use this situation and accept your opposite side? One of your sides is generous. The other, opposite side is greedy. Your mother is generous. She gives you something. That's the way she manifests her generosity. Take what she gives you.

Let's explore this situation further as it gives rise to many questions. What exactly does she give you? Do you want to take what she gives you? Why don't you want to take what she offers? Is it because you want to appear generous yourself or because you don't need what she gives you? For example, she brings you Tylenol and says, "I feel generous today. I want you to accept this big bottle of Tylenol from me." "I don't need Tylenol," – you reply. "Take it! Take it! I want you to have it!" – she insists. You must be specific.

— *I am afraid to accept her gifts, because I may never be able to pay her back. I am totally dependent on my Mom when it comes to money. She solves my every problem. The question that keeps popping up in my head is, "Why am I so weak?"*

— What do we see now? Generosity your mother displays is not a simple generosity. A generous man comes to a bar and says, "Drinks are on me! I pay for everyone today!" Everyone applauds him. Your mom says, "I will pay for you, but you will depend on me." One day, you will be asked to pay back.

— *"If you want me to do something for you, tell me how much you will pay me," I told her. She wants me to do things I don't want to do, and she gets upset when I don't do them.*

— These are the tricky grounds close personal relationships are built upon. When you walk into a store, you see a price tag attached to every item. You pay for a loaf of bread and you bring it home. You don't take anything else. You take what you have paid for. What

39

happens between relatives? Your mom says, "Take this. It's worth a hundred dollars." Then she says, "Why don't you do this, this, and that for me?" And she shows you a list of thirty items. When you express your unwillingness to do something written on this list, she gets upset, "How come? I gave you ..." No one remembers by now what exactly she gave you and how much was it worth, but here she comes now with a list.

— *Yes, the feeling of guilt appears. I feel indebted to her.*

— Exactly. You need to investigate these feelings. Relationships between family members are like a ball of yarn that has thousands of knots in it. You cannot untie these knots; you don't know how to do that. When you pull on one of them, you tie it even harder. You should do it step by step. Let's see how we can help you untie it.

— *I have started to untie this knot. We own a family business. We work together. I am not running away from her, even though everyone around me tells me that I will never be independent unless I leave her. I am afraid to do that.*

— Let's take a look at your main knot. You are afraid to leave your mom. You are afraid to do that for a reason. You are not sure about something. Imagine, you are ready to move on. What is it that you will have to do that you don't want to do now?

— *I will need to spend more time ...*

— You are uncertain of yourself. It is precisely this state of inner uncertainty that your mother maintains in you. She is self-assured, and she says, "You will not survive without me." She demands services from you and insists you provide them. To make a step in the opposite direction, you need to start to support yourself on your own. We are revisiting masculine and feminine modes of survival again. A woman's mode is to find a man on whose account she can survive. In your case, your mom plays a man's role. A woman finds a man who will take responsibility. A woman feels safe behind his back. He takes responsibility for everything. But in that case, he can ask from you, the same way a boss asks from his employee. It's a boss who takes responsibility. An employee simply does what he is told to do, but it is a boss who can control, order, and demand from his employee to do what needs to be done. If you become a boss, you will carry responsibility for what you do. Your mother carries this responsibility now. It's not an easy task.

— I started to do that. I feel great when she goes on a business trip or on a vacation. I can manage the firm during short periods of her absence.

— Parents go on a vacation and leave their house on three teenagers. Kids decide to throw a party. They do what they want. They invite a bunch of friends home. However, the responsibility for the house still lies on the parent's shoulders. Finally, parents return, and they see the mess their kids made. They ask, "What have you done?" These kids are pseudo owners who pretend the house is theirs. In your case, we are dealing with a similar situation.

— But I do make steps toward independence …

— You can continue to make these small steps for the rest of your life. That's what I call "An attempt to get up from a chair." A man is sitting in a chair. Suddenly, he says, "That's it. I don't want to sit anymore. I will try to get up!" And he tries to get up for one year, two years, three years… Nothing changes. He used to sit in a chair, and now he is screaming that he is trying to get up. He is still sitting in a chair. You need to get up. But you continue to sit in it. You should make a step in the direction where you will accept responsibility for something you do not want to take responsibility for. Otherwise, stay put and continue to do what she asks you to do. She does what she does because she must do that, as you maintain yourself in the position that allows her to do that.

Investigate your position. Don't just scream, "I am getting up!" Direct your energy to investigate what happens between you and mom. Learn how this interaction, during which she oppresses and controls you while giving something in return, occurs between the two of you. This is duality **"Employer—employee."** You have been offered a great opportunity to understand the position of an employee. You have been stuck in this situation for a while. That means it is important for you from the point of view of acquisition of this specific experience. Moreover, it means it has been written in your program. You will only be able to get out of this situation when you thoroughly investigate and understand it.

You will not be able to get out of the situation that irritates you until you investigate and understand it thoroughly. You and everyone who experiences difficult situations in his life have every necessary condition for investigation. So, start to investigate. Don't try to avoid your lesson. Try to figure out what is it you are dealing with and why. A man says, "I was locked in this room," and he starts to run around the room searching for a door or a window to jump out of. Why was he locked in this room? He doesn't ask this important question. In that case, he will continue to be there until he starts to ask questions he should ask and answers them.

— *I am afraid of getting married. I am afraid a man I marry will try to control me. I feel free now. I am on my own. I don't see Mom as a boss, because she is my mother.*

— Take a look at this mess. You think your husband will boss you around. You don't see your mother as your boss, because she is your mother. Start to look at your situations not from the point of view of the roles, but from the point of view of dualities. You will see that even though the roles in your show are different, your main role deals with the same theme. Whether it is mother and daughter who work in one firm or husband and wife who don't work together, you are dealing with one duality. The thought that appears in your head is the same, "Why do they boss me around?" For you to sort out and to get to know duality "employer—employee," you need to get to know both sides of it very well. It is not coincidental that you have found yourself on the side of duality called employee. You need to understand this side from the point of view of the opposite side, from the side of the employer. **You must accept this side. Why? Why is acceptance necessary? To accept is not just to announce, "I accept my enemy! I accept the man who raped me!" No. This is pride talking. In my dictionary, acceptance is the first step toward an investigation. What you don't accept, you reject. What you reject it, you will not want to look at. What you don't want to look at, you will not see. What you don't see, you can't investigate. This is an interesting chain as you can see. Acceptance is the first step on the road of self-investigation. You need to accept things to investigate them.**

Otherwise, you don't have a stimulus to do this work. You will say, "I am being oppressed. Why should I accept that? Go to hell!" When you have a stimulus to investigate, you accept every situation as a material for your self-investigation. This is the meaning behind your acceptance. You can conduct self-investigation in many ways. You can vest it with different meanings. And the efficiency of your actions will be different, depending on the meaning with which you will vest your acceptance. To conduct self-investigation, you need to accept a situation you find yourself in.

— *Thank you very much.*

— Thank you.

— *I have spent my entire life searching for love. Lately, I have flipped into the opposite side. For the past two years, I have tried to shower people around me with love. I have been nagging people, "Take my love. Take my love." But no one took it. Finally, it dawned on me that love I was offering had strings attached. I finally understood that to receive love, I must first give it to people. For two years I was giving love away, but I wasn't getting anything back. I understand now. I should just give it to people. I should not think about what I am to get in return.*

— I hear these words, "To give," "To receive," "To love," and a question pops into my head: What do you give and what do you receive? I see a box with the word "love" written all over it. You run around holding this box. You approach a man and you tell him, "Let me give you some love!" He gets scared and runs away. Another man opens your box and finds a pile of shit in it. He looks at you, "Is this love?" "Yes," you reply, "This is love. Don't you see what is written on this box?" He says, "Hmm? Really? Why does it smell so bad?" You reply, "That's how it smells." Let's sort out what exactly you try to pass on to people in this box of yours you call "Love."

— *I try to pay attention to another human being. I try to understand what he wants, and I try to give it to him.*

— Let's do it step by step. The first thing you have mentioned was attention. You approach a man, and you say, "Your fly is open!" You provide him with plenty of attention. No woman has said that to him before. Is this attention?

— *Well, in a way, it is attention.*

— Let's not hurry here. Or, you say, "Your tie doesn't match your shirt," or "Your shoes are dirty." Is this attention?

44

— *In a way, it is attention.*

— I have brought up three examples. Can you relate to them?

— *Yes, I do manifest attention this way sometimes.*

— What is the ratio between this "sometimes" of yours and the rest of the attention you manifest? Can you say that what you call love is good for this man?

— *I cannot say that.*

— Then what exactly do you offer when you open this box you call "love"? If you don't understand what you offer, you will not understand why people react to you in such a strange way. You say, "Our firm celebrates today! We are distributing love! Come and get it!" They come, and they say, "What is it? We don't need that." You say, "How come? We celebrate Love today! Take it!" They say, "We don't need your love!" You get upset.

Prior to starting a conversation about acceptance or giving love, we need to understand what love is. You can neither give nor take something if you don't know what it is. Do you really know what love is, when you use this word?

Let's figure out what exactly you offer in this box of yours wrapped up in paper with the word "love" written all over it. Open this box and start to sort out what is there. You will find many different things there. The box you call "love" contains many small boxes. You will find fear, condemnation, grudge, and dependency there. You pull out a small box out of the big box not understanding what exactly you have pulled out. You offer a man guilt, but you call it "love." You pull out a box called "condemnation" and you say, "This is love." Can you see what you have in this box of yours you call "Love"?

— *I am trying to discover that. I use people reaction to understand what I give them.*

— You are conducting a very interesting investigation trying to determine what you offer to other people under the name "love."

— *Another question is whether they need your so-called "love" at the moment. Perhaps they don't need it.*

— This is another topic for you to investigate.

— *So, prior to giving something to someone, one should think about what he gives. Then, one should think about whether his partner needs it or not.*

— You *think* all the time. You say, "I should *think* about what I give him. Does he need it or not?" Two months pass. He is gone. While you were thinking, he left. You *think*, but you offer feelings. Love is a feeling, but you keep thinking and thinking. The box that you call "love" is filled with *thoughts*, not feelings. This is very important for everyone to understand. You offer people *thoughts* that you don't fully understand yourself. You call it love.

— *I am describing my thought process with respect to feelings too. I can't say there are only thoughts there.*

— C'mon. I know you. I'll tell you more. When people who don't know you hear you speak they understand that you are an intellectual. Don't call it "love." I am not condemning you. I understand that you are at a certain stage of your investigation. I respect the stage you are at and I respect you. I am clarifying the situation for you.

You speak of love out of the intellectual center, but love is a feeling! If you were to offer us emotional states, we would have a different conversation. But under the title "love," you offer thoughts sprinkled with doubts. I will recommend you change the topic of your investigation from "love" to "thoughts about love." We have not heard anything about

46

feelings yet. You open a notebook called "love" and you write a totally different thesis. Everything gets messed up.

— Alexander Alexandrovich, you are a very special human being. I have attended many of your seminars. I came to this webinar to find out how you would conduct it in virtual space. You work is very difficult. When you answer one question, you answer many of our questions on different levels. I am grateful to you.

Now, to my question. I was struck by one student inability to understand where her desire to pay for the webinar was coming from. I am clearly stuck in the part that doesn't want to give. It is based on my inability to understand which part of me I am giving out from. Do I give to receive something for myself, or do I give out of gratitude?

— I am going to quote you. You have said, "I don't understand whether I give something to other people in order to receive something for myself or out of gratitude?" Let's sort this out in details. To give to receive is a question of profit. This is the main question in the matrix of survival. Whatever we do here, we do it to receive something in return. If we invest something, whether it is money, effort, emotional states or thoughts, we want to receive something in return, and we want to get more than we have invested. We want to invest five cents and receive a dollar. That's what every game related to the fluctuation of financial markets and exchange rates is based upon. Look at the banks that make money out of thin air. They want to minimize their investments and to increase their profits. The entire banking system is built upon this principle. But the banking system simply reflects our personality, i.e. what was inculcated into our survival program.

"Fool your neighbor" technique is the basic technique that allows us to survive. To receive something for free or to fool someone, i.e. to receive a profit is the aim of every personality. This is not a condemnation. I am not here to condemn. I am merely stating a fact. What kind of a thought was infused into this axiom? It is the thought of limited resources. We are short of everything. We are short of space. How much does a one-bedroom apartment cost in New York or Moscow? It costs a lot of money. The land is limited, and we are going to sell it at a high price. The more limitations you have and the shorter you are of something, the higher the price. Take advertising campaigns, "Only today! The last item!" Their aim is to have people run to the stores to buy these items—the stock is limited. That's how consumer interest is generated. The idea of SHORTAGE is the basic idea in the axiom of survival. If I have a lot of something, someone else has none or little of it. Therefore, I need to get as much of it as I can. But when I increase my share of this something, I simultaneously increase another man's shortage of it. That's where this constant competition, enmity covered by morals, and open hatred are coming from. This is the basic characteristic of the world of survival, i.e. the world of separation we are living in. Every one of us is familiar with this experience.

— *Let me clarify my question. At the current stage of my investigation, I clearly feel my spiritual pride. I am afraid of it. What do I pay for? I pay for something that no one else has. My pride is a pride of a spiritual man, who pays out of generosity and goodness. I don't understand what's going on.*

— Let's take a look at your pride. A man who is full of spiritual pride will not pay anything.

— *What if I belong to another group of people, to those who pay for something other people can never receive, for enlightenment.*

— You are *an exclusive* spiritual human being. You are in search of something unique, and you will pay a premium price for it. If we were to compare it to tourism, there are standard tours for average people, and there are exclusive safaris for very rich people. They cost much more. You belong to the second type of spiritual people.

— *I don't allow myself to go there.*

— What do you mean?

— *I had experienced these manifestations before, they always led to disenchantment. So, I am afraid to go there again.*

— Wait a minute. Where exactly are you afraid to go to?

— *I pay money to understand something. I pay to see something.*

— You don't pay to see things. As we just figured out, you pay for exclusivity. It is very important for you to have an exclusive package, "This package has been reserved for Uri! Don't touch!" You try to get things only for yourself. If you see that it is exclusive and only for you, you will pay for it. If, it is for everyone—you will not pay for it.

— *You are right.*

— I have been here before, "If Pint is only for me, perhaps I will pay. If Pint is for everyone, I will not pay, because in that case, I am not important. I am important when Pint works with me and only with me. That's the way you manifest your importance."

— *Where is this pride coming from?*

— This is a topic of a separate conversation.

— *Thank you. I got the answer. I have something to work with now.*

— *Uri was speaking about pride, and his words resonated with me. If I understand you correctly,* **pride is related to a disbalance in a certain duality and my strong identification with one of its sides.**

— Yes, one side of a seesaw ascends, looks at the opposite side and says, "I am important—you are not. I am good—you are bad."

— *I understand this. In the process of my self-investigation, I came to the conclusion that pride of the lower "i" exists.*

— The external world reflects our inner states very well. You are connected to the webinar, and I hear heavy static. Your words are muffled. I have said it to you before, and I will repeat what I have said again. This static and interference that we hear are related to the fact that your personality prevents you from understanding these questions. This is the second time you are asking a question related to pride and we hear static again. This is a state your personality is in at the present time. You ask a question, but you don't want to hear the answer. You want to remain where you are. You ask these questions to maintain the illusion of spiritual evolution.

— *I got it. Thank you.*

— *My question is about money. Let's say, I paid for something. It doesn't mean I am going to get what I wanted. Am I right?*

— I am not sure I understand your question. Please, clarify it.

— *Let's say, I spent my mental or emotional energy on something, or I paid money for something. Is there a possibility that I will not get anything back?*

— Okay. What exactly do you mean when you say, "Is there a possibility that I will get nothing back?" What do you mean, when you use the word "nothing"? What did you spend your energy on? Let's say you gave money to someone to do something, but he didn't do what was expected of him. Or, you gave money to someone to buy something for you, but he didn't buy what you wanted. Is that what you mean?

— *I gave my jacket to a friend. I never got it back. He behaves as if it is his now. Moreover, he has been treating me differently since that day.*

— I understand your question now. Let's take a closer look at it. You give something of a material nature to people. You expect them to respect you for this, but they don't. They take more stuff from you and they don't return it. You give them

50

something for a day, they keep it for a year. When I talk about profit, I talk about the profit of awareness. That's what important to me. You, on the other hand, talk about the exchange of material things. You give something to your friend and you expect to receive something of equal value in return. Looking at this situation from this point of view, you give something to your friend, he takes it from you, and he wants to take more. That's where your profit of awareness hides. To get it, you need to investigate this situation. What's your role in it? Where did you get out of balance? What is happening here? It *appears* to you that you are being used; something is taken away from you. It *appears* to you that the more you give, the more is being taken away from you. But look deeper. This situation indicates that your giving side is out of disbalance; it gives more and more. Consequently, it swells up. It accumulates importance and pride. But, your receiving or taking side gets weaker and weaker.

— *Yes. People offer me things, but I can't take anything. I cannot ask for anything either.*

— This is it. As a result, you will be used to the fullest. A statement is written all over your face, "He will give everything away." People read it. You will swim in this duality until this disbalance reaches its peak. Perhaps, you have come to this point already.

— *Am I the only one who can change it?*

— Of course, no one else can change anything in your world.

— *Why do I always insist that it is fate? This disbalance is inculcated in me. That means this is the way I am. I am not doing something right.*

— An old Arab proverb says, "Put your trust in God but tie your camel." Use the word "Faith" instead of "God," and you will have the same formula. No one will solve anything for you. Let's say, you have a broken computer. You are the only user. Until you fix it, it will not work. You can wait for a miracle or say, "This is fate. My computer doesn't work. This is fate." Someone came and took your pants, "This is fate." Okay. Live this way. It's your life. Your life is determined by your perception. If you think it is your fate to give things to people and not to get them back, continue to experience this. If you want to change your fate and come to harmony, you must start to reinforce your taking or receiving side. This work is not easy. Using concept of fate, you simply prolong what is habitual for you—people take things from you and never return them. Your entire life revolves around this habit. You will have to start doing something that you are not in the habit of doing. To make a step toward something that is not habitual for you is not easy and you don't want to make it. Not wanting to do that, you come up with a reason that explains your way of life—fate. That increases your disbalance.

— *I think that it is my friend who should do something about this situation, not me.*

— Yes, that's what you think, and you will continue to think like that for years. He will not do anything about it.

— *I understand. Thank you.*

— I want to thank all of you for this very interesting webinar. I want to remind you that this webinar is the first step on your way to enter the School of Holistic psychology. We will conduct another webinar next week. You will have to pay for it. That will be another test. Whether you pass it or not, you will receive a present of awareness. On the road to become aware of yourself, you will constantly receive presents of awareness. Sometimes, you will receive these presents experiencing very dramatic situations. When you start to see these dramatic situations as situations that hide the presents of awareness, their dramatism will diminish. They will suddenly change.

The School of Holistic psychology was created for people who have a strong *intention* to work. I will only work with people who are ready to conduct self-investigation daily. Our school offers this opportunity. I encourage you to attend as many seminars and webinars as you can. They will require additional effort from you, but they will accelerate your movement. Not everyone will be able to apply that effort. Not all of you will be able to handle School requirements.

The topic of today's webinar was "To give—to receive." Based on the conversations we just had, we can see that duality "To give—to receive" is strongly connected to the program of survival. It is one of the key dualities every personality contains. You either get stuck in the giving side and have everything taken away from you, or you want to take constantly. Stressing one of these sides, you increase the disbalance. The state of a disbalance that every personality here, in the axiom of survival, happens to be in, leads to multiple negative consequences. Your physical body suffers because everything that occurs in the mental-emotional sphere gets reflected in the physical body in the form of diseases, accidents, robberies, etc. If you don't understand that these so-called negative situations are connected to your disbalance, you will find other explanations for them, such as fate. But neither one of these explanations will explain the essence of the problem. Our work is to harmonize various dualities. The program of survival that the personality of most people operates on is built on the premise, "Take more and give less." From the standpoint of survival, this is the best option to survive. We will have to review it again and again, irrespective of the dualities we investigate. Your participation in school will cost money. You also need money to survive. I have already spoken about choice. Will you choose the road of survival or the road that leads to wholeness? Those are two different roads. You will always be tempted to stay on the road of survival. You are on this road anyway, but you will experience multiple obstructions that will prevent you from traveling the road of awareness. One of the strongest brakes will come in the form of thoughts, "I don't have enough money. I want to spend my money on something else." You will have these thoughts. If you want to walk toward wholeness, you will have to observe these thoughts and choose the direction of wholeness again and again. You will have to pay for it with the energy of money.

You will receive as much as you give; no more and no less. I want to thank all of you for this interesting discussion. I will be happy to see you at our next seminar, and I will be happy to see you as students of the School of Holistic Psychology.

CHAPTER 2

HOW TO STOP THE FIGHT OF YOUR PERSONAL OPPOSITIONS AND TO BECOME WHOLE IN THE DUALITY "DEPENDENCE—INDEPENDENCE"

•◆•◆•◆•◆•◆•◆•◆•◆•◆•◆•◆•◆•◆•◆•◆•◆•◆•

—The topic of our today's webinar will deal with dependence and independence. I will ask you to answer two questions, "What are your dependencies?" and "What do you want to do with your dependencies?" Most likely you want to overcome or to get rid of them. I will ask you *to feel* your relationship with your dependencies. What do you want to do with them? Have you ever won a fight against one of your dependencies?

Let's say, your answer to this question is yes. Has this dependency left you, or has it started to manifest itself in a different form?

Another question. Who is fighting whom when you want to overcome your dependency? You think you are fighting something external? Let's say you are an alcoholic, a compulsive shopper, or a sex addict. You think your dependency is external. You want to overcome it. It *appears* to you, you are fighting something or someone. It *appears* to you, this something or someone is not you. I will have to disappoint you—you are fighting yourself; you gave birth to this dependency, it appeared out of you, i.e. it is you.

So, why do you want to fight something you yourself gave birth to? This is an interesting question. Why does it happen? Why do we, thinking we fight a dependency, thinking that it is our right to overcome it, do not understand that we are fighting ourselves. This is a very common phenomenon. That's how most people view this situation. Why do they see it this way? Why don't they see that fighting this dependency, they fight themselves? They don't see it because they don't understand the dual makeup of their personal program. This dually made personal program gives birth and maintains the conflict between its opposite sides. That's how it is made. It is thanks to this program that we acquire the experience of separation here, the experience of fighting ourselves.

To exit this experience of inner separation and to stop this inner war, we need to clearly see and to become aware of the mechanisms responsible for the conflict that exists between dual parts of our personality. Our personal program consists of many dual parts. All of them are in conflict with each other. That's the inner relationships we are living in; they are reflected in the outside world. Every war we see outside reflects our inner world, the inner world of every one of us. My work is to stop the fight of the inner parts of our personalities and to transfer these relationships to the state of unity and partnership.

We are going to investigate duality "dependence—independence" today. What is a dependency? This word is frequently used by people to express dissatisfaction. They say, "I am dependent on …" and they experience inner tension accompanied by a desire to do something about this

56

dependency. The notion of "dependency" can be applied to everything that exists in this world. You can declare yourself to be dependent on everything that exists here, whether it is something people call "good" or something they call "bad." You can consider yourself dependent, for example, on alcohol, tobacco, gambling, junk food, etc. These activities or patterns of behavior are commonly considered to be bad. However, you can also be dependent on something that is considered to be good here: sex, money, attention toward your persona, etc. Explore your structure for the presence of some of these dependencies. Most people cannot see that all these dependencies have the same roots, the same causes that come out of dual makeup of their personal program.

Every personal problem and conflict you experience is written in your personal program. Every human being on Earth is a program. We have all been programmed. This is extremely important to understand. What you call fate is a program inculcated into your structure. Unless you understand your program, you will not be able to understand yourself. You may have your illusions and think you can do something or not do something. You may have your illusions and think you can get rid of something or attract something. Whatever you want to get rid of or attract is written in your program. Therefore, unless you understand and become aware of this program, you will not move a step closer toward understanding yourself.

So, how do dependencies appear and what do they point to? To answer this question, we need to understand the dual nature of our personal program. Dependency appears when one part of your personality starts to desire something. This desire is very important to this part. It wants to realize it. The opposite part of your personality wants something totally opposite; it wants to prevent the first part from achieving its goals.

Dependency points to the presence of a disbalance between two opposite tendencies of personality, or to the fact that two opposite parts of personality are in conflict with each other. They fight each other trying to realize their desires, which are opposite and, as it *appears* to us, mutually exclusive; they fight each other tooth and nail. If you didn't have a part that rejects what you call dependency, you would not have experienced inner tension about this dependency. You would not have developed a desire to get rid of it. You would just follow this dependency. You would not even consider it to be a dependency. You would consider it to be one of your desires. You would not condemn yourself for having this desire.

Every dependency is accompanied by the feeling of self-condemnation and guilt. When you do something that you consider to be your dependency, you condemn yourself for it and you feel guilty. Are you dependent on states of condemnation and guilt? You have many dependencies. Are condemnation and guilt on your list? Most likely, they are not. However, they are the real reason, behind the phenomena we call dependency.

What is condemnation? How does it appear? One part of your personality accuses and condemns the part that is opposite to it. The condemned part experiences guilt. Then, these two parts flip. This interrelationship exists between the dual sides of every personality.

What does it mean to bring one duality of your personality to wholeness? It means to stop the ensuing conflict between its opposite sides. How can you stop something that you don't even see? Do you think your dependency is a result of the conflict that exists between opposite parts of your personality?

If you don't think this is the case, you don't see this conflict and the resulting fight. Not seeing this fight, you cannot stop it.

For us to transform the relationship of the opposite parts of our personality, and to transfer these parts from the state of conflict to the state of partnership, we need to see and to become aware of every mechanism of conflict that was inculcated into our program. The personal program of every human being is unique; you will not find two identical programs. Therefore, even though the generic mechanism of these relationships is conflict, the nuances, shades, and characteristics of this conflict are different for every personality. You need to see and understand these inner mechanisms of your personality.

You will have to investigate your personal program on your own. This process will lead you to wholeness and allow you to transfer to the next level of consciousness. This is the task humanity is facing today. The Quantum leap, i.e. the Process of collecting ourselves in one, has started. This work to collect ourselves, to review every mechanism of conflict inside our personality works on is the basic assignment we are here to solve.

I have never transmitted this information before; it is new. It was preceded by twenty-five years of investigation of my own and other personal programs. **You will get to the next level of consciousness or fourth dimension as some people call it when you become aware of every mechanism of conflict your personal program operates on.**

To move toward Wholeness is the main task of every human being who came to Earth. This task consists of many steps. During each step, you will review and become aware of the mechanism of conflict that governs a specific duality of your personal program.

Let us explore the questions and situations connected to the topic of our current investigation, "Dependence—Independence," in a dialogue format.

— *While trying to sort out one of these mechanisms my mind works on, I experienced a sensation that I should not do that. I felt I would be completely lost if I were to stop this war. I was bombarded by thoughts, "Who should I trust? Should I trust my mind or my Supreme Aspect? Who will conduct this investigation: my mind or my Soul? The Soul has no mind. How can it investigate anything?"*

— That's right, the Soul doesn't have a mind. However, every personality is a continuation of the Soul. So, the Soul has personality; personality has the mind. Our task is to investigate this mind. The Soul is the investigator. The subject of its investigation is the mind, i.e. personal program.

— *Can the mind investigate itself?*

— This is a very good question. No. The mind cannot investigate itself. **You can only solve a problem by getting outside of a problem.** The mind is the problem; it creates problems on its own. How can we study the mind and the way it creates problems? You can do that from the spheres of consciousness that are higher than the mind. Let's get more specific here. The mind represents a certain level of consciousness. But there are levels of consciousness that are higher than the mind. One of these higher levels of consciousness I call the Supreme Aspect or the Soul. These higher levels of consciousness have nothing to do with personality. You will need to conduct your own investigation to understand that. In the process of your investigation, you will transfer to the higher level of consciousness.

As I mentioned already, we came to the world of survival. Most people associate survival with such needs as to make money, have a roof over their heads and food on their table. When I say that personal program is a program of survival, I talk about something else. Your personal program wants to preserve itself in its present form. In my terminology, to survive is to preserve something in its original form. In this case, it is a preservation of the personal program in the form it currently is, without any changes.

That's why your program resists. It doesn't want to be seen, as your observation and seeing it will start to change it.

— *Does the process of self-investigation kill personality?*

— Yes. That's how you may experience this process. We are dealing with death. You probably remember Russian fairy tales, in which sorcerers bring killed heroes to life by sprinkling dead water on them at first, and alive water next. To be reborn, you must die. This is the way to a higher level of consciousness and Wholeness. It must be experienced.

— *Does Higher Consciousness use some kind of an apparatus to investigate this reality?*

— Yes. Higher Consciousness navigates our machine or personality. However, a certain difficulty arises here, as the planet we have entered, Earth, is a zone of free will. Our personality is a carriage equipped with three horses. Each horse has a will of its own. They do what they want. Our Supreme Aspect must learn to manage these horses. These horses represent our three centers: mental, emotional, and physical. As Supreme Aspects, we should get to know and learn to handle these centers well. This is not an easy task. The School of Holistic psychology will help you to acquire this skill.

— Let me ask you an unrelated question. **My main dependence is suffering. I have a difficult time parting with this dependency. People around me suffer because of it.**

— I recall a slogan, which was popular during the Soviet era, "When people around me feel good, I feel good too." In your case, we can reverse this slogan, "When people around me feel bad, I feel bad too." This program was inculcated into each one us. The Soviet era is gone, but this statement has been deeply rooted in every one of us. We think if everything is good in our lives, people would condemn us. They will say, "Look at her. We feel bad, but she … She feels good." That's how they drag us into their wetland. This is the matrix of separation humanity has been submerged in for centuries.

The questions you have asked are very important. Your movement toward Wholeness will be accompanied by the need to review and to reevaluate many of your notions. One of these notions has just come up. **You have said, "If I feel good, people will condemn me for it." I am offering you a different axiom, which states that you only see your own reflection in the external world. Other people do not condemn you—your own inner parts condemn you.**

That what happens in the dual inner world of every human being. One part of us wants one thing, while the other, the opposite part of us wants something else. In your case, one part of you wants something that you call "good" to happen— we are not going to specify what exactly it is—while your other part wants something "bad" to happen. As a result, suffering appears. We are dealing with a dual assignment again. You are made of conflicting dualities.

— If this part were to die, I would have nothing to investigate.

— It cannot die. The entire history of human civilization can be expressed in one phrase: the fight of good with evil. The entire history of humanity is a history of conflict of dualities. For a short period of time, one part can prevail over another in this war. For example, communism prevailed for seventy years, but it has finally lost at the end of the last century. Irrespective of the nature of the process you investigate—cultural, economic, political, or religious—you will find this principle at work: temporary victory and temporary loss. The part that was winning for a certain period will lose for a certain period. One side cannot destroy the opposite side. It is impossible. Goodness will never win over evil. Now, let's look at how these global processes manifest themselves in every personality, as what happens in the macro world, happens in the microworld, and vice versa.

Sooner or later, every one of us will die. We die countless times every day. You were sitting in a certain pose. You moved. The pose you were sitting in has died. You have pronounced a word. It is gone. You have said another word. The word you have said before has died. You have taken a breath in and you have breathed it out. It has died. Our life consists of a myriad of small deaths. Why are we so afraid of death which is just one of many deaths we will experience throughout our life? Unless we experience all these deaths, we will not come to Wholeness. It is only by experiencing all these deaths that we will be able to feel and experience immortality.

For our Supreme Aspect death doesn't exist. Our Supreme Aspect is eternal and immortal. Our personality, however, is temporary and mortal. It undergoes multiple changes. It has been created to acquire experience and to understand the laws of the universe and the laws of duality.

— *Let me clarify something. Do I understand you correctly? I don't need to fight my personality. I need to investigate the mechanisms that suck my personality into the wetland.*

— Exactly. But who is it in you that fights your personality? Based on your question, I get an impression that there are your personality and some other you, who are fighting it. No. Your personality is a dually made structure. It has opposite tendencies. It fights itself.

— *This is very sly ...*

— It is very sly. I have sorted this slyness out. Now, we have the key that will allow us to understand what happens to us. We need to learn how to use this key. I had to experience a very difficult life to find this key. You must have passion, and you must apply strong effort to learn how to use this key.

— *The external world mirrors our subconsciousness to us. I want to get to know one of my parts. This part irritates me. It doesn't want to do anything remotely connected to spirituality. It doesn't want to talk. I am stuck. Is it me or a human being next to me who doesn't want to talk?*

— A human being who is next to you reflects your own inner part to you.

— *Does it mean I don't want to talk to myself?*

— Yes. Always search for duality. Let's tentatively call this duality "spiritual—material." One of your parts is spiritual, the other—material. Your material part is not interested in the spiritual part at all. **Can you specify what exactly irritates you?**

— *My friends and relatives are against my spiritual evolution. They insist I am wasting my time and money.*

— **You need to investigate these people. You need to understand their thinking process. What do they think when they say that? They will continue to say what they say, but you need to understand them. Talk to them. Ask** them questions. But don't do it to oppress them with your point of view, as they will only oppress you with their opposite point of view in return. Your task is to understand how this opposite part of yours thinks. What does it feel? What does it do? When you talk to them, you investigate yourself. People usually don't do that. They usually try to prove to other people that their way of thinking is right. Other people try to prove their opposite point of view in return: we are right. This is a war you wage with yourself.

I invite you to investigate. Don't fight! Investigate! When you investigate, you don't have to prove whether you are right or wrong. This fight is a mistake. When you understand that, you start to become interested in self-investigation. You start to explore and understand your opposite side. People will come, and they will mirror your opposite side to you. Don't fight them—investigate them.

— *I can't grasp this contradiction. How can I connect these sides?*

— It is not easy. Personality is a dual, paradoxical structure. Our task is to connect multiple contradictions. Our task is to investigate our opposite sides with a full understanding that both sides are ours. This is not a simple task. We have lived in a state of separation and conflict for thousands of years. It will not be easy to transfer to another level, but it is possible.

— *So, I have to accept both of these sides in me.*

— Yes. Every situation that arises in your life represents two actors show: one actor plays one role; another actor plays the opposite role. This show, played by two actors, one of whom, as it *appears* to you, is you, while another, as it *appears* to you, is another human being, is performed by one human being—you. You need to understand this show from the point of view of both actors, i.e. both of your parts. Then, you will see the situation holistically. Otherwise, your vision of the situation will remain one-sided; your inner conflict will persist.

— *When I observe both of my sides, I get confused. I don't know what to do. I don't know which side to act out of.*

— The question is not what to do and how to act, but how to investigate. **The task of self-investigator is to understand the situation from at least two points of view.** In the process of investigation, you will receive **gifts of awareness** which will help you move toward your aim, which is to see the situation Holistically.

When your aim is self-investigation, the situation you are in changes. Our first aim is to understand another human being and his point of view. We must stop being irritated by him. We must not condemn him. You will continue to experience these states in the dualities that are overstressed in you, but you will try to understand what he says, remembering that he is you. Otherwise, you will not do that. If you don't see a man across from you as yourself, why should you understand him? You may try to understand him to fool him. That's what many smart people do. They are smart, i.e. sly. Sly people understand what other people need and they fool them. This is temporary, however. Someone who is smarter than them will come along and fool them tomorrow. This war is eternal. I invite you to stop this war of oppositions and start to investigate it.

— *I want to express my gratitude for your work. My entire life is one huge dependency. I used to depend on everything and everyone. I understand now that behind everything I called love and acts of goodwill were fear and guilt. I got so enmeshed in this mess that I decided to sort it out. I started to read your books. You have opened my eyes. I started to look at myself from a different angle. Recently, I have experienced the side of duality I condemned before. This is something I was born into. I have always been decent and proper. I condemned those who were not. I had to experience everything I used to condemn in a very short time. It was not easy, but I am happy I have entered these difficult states, and now, looking back, I am grateful I did it. I also want to thank a man who is sitting next to me for helping me to conduct self-investigation. When I enter a duality and start to experience it, I go through an emotional rollercoaster. I frequently don't know what to do. He helps me to experience this hurricane. When he experiences his dualities, I help him. We cooperate.*

— That's what I call partnership in an investigation.

— *I see some of my dualities now. These opposite sides of me, which used to fight each other tooth and nail, are now having a dialogue. I come out of one duality and enter another one. This process helps me to understand myself. This is not an easy trip, but I have a feeling I am on the right track. It is very important for me to know where I am going and to have people near me who can help me walk this walk. To understand is to accept. To accept is to make another step toward Wholeness. I wish all of us to persevere on this path. As you said, it is not an easy path, but when one of my dualities comes to balance, I experience unbelievable kaif. Promise yourself not to give up!*

— Thank you. I want all of you to feel this emotional fervor. We must feel it to do this work.

— *I have experienced severe inner conflict in certain situations before. I don't experience it now. It seems to me, my inner war has ended. What is the reason for this drop in excitation? Is it because the conflicting sides became less active?*

— Every one of you has seen a lightning bolt during a thunderstorm. It is a discharge that occurs between the energy potentials accumulated in the clouds. When energy flows from a place of high concentration to a place of low concentration, we see a lightning bolt. It discharges, and everything gets calm for a while. But the fact that everything has calmed down, for now, doesn't mean the thunderstorm and lightning will not recur. You feel the war has stopped. It doesn't mean that duality that has manifested itself disappeared. No, its electric potential has been temporarily discharged. It will accumulate energy and manifest itself in conflict again.

— *During my self-investigation, I came to understand that when I enter a relationship with a man, I get financially dependent on him and make him dependent on me emotionally. At the same time, I experience a strong need to be independent. I yearn to break this relationship. When I finally brake away from him and I become independent, the opposite side of this duality gets activated. I frequently feel that I have overcome this duality already and can breathe easily.*

— This is exactly what I call sleep. While asleep, you may experience a nightmare or a happy dream. What we call life here is just one of many dreams experienced by your Soul. This dream can be different. At times it is stormy. Then, storm calms down, and it *appears* to you that it is over.

Let's take a closer look at your dependency and make sure we understand how it works. You have said you feel financially dependent on a man when you are in a relationship with him. Later, this dependency causes you to experience discontent because you feel you are too dependent on him. Look, you have been looking for a man based on the necessity to be provided financially by him. You have found such a man. Then, you start to feel that what you have strived for is turning into dependency. If he were to visit you every Friday, put some money on your table, smile, and leave, you would not call it a dependency. But he asks something from you. You must pay something. He wants to get something for his money. Am I right?

— *Yes. I feel I am being controlled. I get angry.*

— Okay. Let's sort this out. What exactly does he want for his money? What exactly irritates you?

— *The emotional contribution he expects for his money is more than I can handle. He wants me to pay attention to him all the time. He wants me to be close to him day and night. That's how I see it.*

— That's exactly how it is. It happens inside you. What you observe in the outside world, in your relationship with this man, reflects what is happening in your inner world. You need to sort out what is going on inside you, as it manifests itself in the outside world and will continue to manifest itself until you see it clearly. Are you ready to see this situation as a whole? If you are, you must investigate it in minute details. You have discussed your situation in a very nonspecific way. What kind of emotional contribution are you talking about? You don't say anything about it. Based on this fact I can make a conclusion that you don't understand it yourself. If you don't understand what is going on, you will not be able to change it. You don't know what needs to be changed.

— *You are right. I am confused. I feel a block. I don't know what is behind it.*

— Exactly. This situation is characteristic for everyone. Listen to the audio of our conversation and you will understand the specifics of this work. Our dialogue clearly indicates that you don't see what your man requires of you. This irritates you. This situation reflects the depth of your sleep. You don't even understand what dependency is.

The approach of a self-investigator is neutral. Self-investigator doesn't blame or condemn anyone. Self-investigator investigates and reviews things the way they are in minute details. This work is like an X-ray machine. You will start to see things inside yourself you didn't know existed. That's what I do. I X-ray you. But are you ready for such an X-ray? Doctors order X-ray to make a diagnosis. They need a diagnosis to order appropriate treatment. You need to

X-ray yourself to cure yourself. I am the X-ray machine. Are you ready to do this work? This is the question. Do you even want to see this X-ray film? Personality doesn't want to change anything. It wants to preserve itself in the present form, i.e. in the form of conflict and fight. It blocks every attempt to see itself. It prevents you from going through the X-ray machine. I encounter this situation every day.

— *I understand what you say. But when I go deeper, I feel that something in me resists this information strongly.*

— Exactly. It's not that "I don't know that." No, it is, "I don't want to know that." There is a big difference here.

— *Some kind of fear is there.*

— Exactly. There is fear there. Look, this is fear of fear. Personality generates fear. But it is not just fear, it is fear of fear.

Let's say, we speak of specific fear. For example, you are afraid of mice. You come to me, and you say: "I am afraid of mice. What can I do about it?" We have a subject to discuss. We will talk about mice and your fear of mice. But, presently, we don't even have a topic of fear to discuss. This is fear of fear. You come, and you say, "I am afraid." I ask you, "What are you afraid of?" You answer, "I am afraid that I am afraid." This is fear squared. This fear is so strong, it doesn't allow you to specify what you are afraid of.

— *Is there a connection between fear and program of survival? What will happen to me if I continue to move on this way? Will my program be destroyed?*

— I don't destroy anything. I help your personality to blossom. But your personality wants to preserve the inner conflict it operates on. It wants to preserve itself in its current form, i.e. it wants to survive. Survival is not just a war for money. Survival is about not allowing a change in the state of conflict that continues inside the personality to occur. Personality wants to preserve itself the way it currently is, as a structure that gets its energy and functions based on the conflict of its inner, opposite sides. And it comes up with this reaction—fear of fear. This is the way it protects itself from being opened by us. What do people consider to be most intimate? They say, "Don touch it. This is mine. This is too intimate for me to talk about." What do they consider to be so intimate that they cannot discuss? It is their suffering and pain. This is paradoxical, but this is the way it is. I know that very well based on my own self-investigation and based on my investigation of other people. It is precisely for this reason that personality doesn't want to part with its suffering. Moreover, when this opportunity presents itself, it closes even more and says, "Don't you get near me." And it reacts with fear of fear. Do you follow me?

— *Yes.*

— In the process of our work, we frequently get in touch with our intimate parts. I just explained to you what it means. I am not here to oppress anyone, I just show you things the way they are. I will only show you what you are ready to see. I will not break into your house screaming, "You don't see this! You don't see that!" I will only show you what you are ready to see. So, if you are not ready to proceed, have a sit. It's enough for now. If you are ready, we can go further.

— *I am ready. I want to proceed.*

— If you are ready, ask me a question.

— *Perhaps we can start where we stopped. I told you that I started to feel a strong inner resistance. This resistance is connected to my man's expectation that I will be heavily invested emotionally in this relationship.*

— You feel this is a dependency. Tell me more. Why do you feel that way?

— *I have a feeling I will have to stay with this man forever. I must do everything the way he wants. I must behave the way he likes.*

— So, he is buying you. Am I correct? As the old saying goes, "The one who pays orders the music." He will tell you what to sing. If you don't sing the song he likes, he will say, "What's wrong with you? This is not what I paid for?!"

— *Yes. Moreover, when this happens, I experience severe aggression. I suppress it not to get into a conflict. I am afraid to break this relationship.*

— So, you want to preserve this relationship. Let's look at why one of your parts wants to preserve this relationship. It wants to preserve this relationship because he provides for your material needs. You can say, "This is it. I am fed up with you. I don't want to ever see you again." But the opposite side says, "How can we say that to him? Where will we get the money to make ends meet?"

— *On one side, I understand I can take care of my financial needs myself, but my other part, which is very strong, doesn't want to do that.*

— Okay. Let's look at what was written in your program. It is written there that a woman must be with a man, and her man should take care of her. Is that so?

— *Yes. That's how my parents live. This is their program.*

— As I have said earlier, everything that happens to you is written in your personal program. This program was inculcated into you by your parents. That's why you and everyone who moves toward Wholeness must become aware of this program. The dilemma we face now is a consequence of something that was written in your personal program. This program consists of two opposite modes of survival. One mode tells you, "You have to find a man who will take care of you and keep him next to you." This is the feminine mode of survival. The second mode says, "I can make money on my own." This is the

72

masculine mode of survival. Which one of these modes are you conscious of? When you work and make money on your own, you act out of the masculine mode of survival. When you are in the masculine mode of survival, you don't need a man at all. Am I right?

— *Yes.*

— That's what happens to many business women. This is a common occurrence nowadays. As soon as a business lady starts to make money, she doesn't need a man anymore. But this goes against the other half of her program: "My man will take care of me." Fed up with every dependency, pain, and suffering that come with it, you say, "I don't need a man. I can survive on my own!" And that's where you face a dilemma. You can be with a man, but in that case, you will experience what you experience now. He will give you money, but he will ask a lot of you in return. Soon, you will get irritated with him, move to the opposite side and say, "I had enough of this!" And, if you have given birth to a boy, you might say, "All these men are not up to par. I will never find a decent man in my life. I will make a real man out of my boy." And you will proceed to make "a perfect man" out of your boy, placing him in the position of dependency.

Presently, you survive based on the feminine mode of survival. Every mode has its advantages and disadvantages, pluses and minuses. While in the feminine mode of survival, the necessity to do something for the money your man brings you is a drawback. But, if you start to survive using the masculine mode of survival, you will feel lonely.

Now, let's look at the way you put your question in the situation you happen to be in. I am following your questions. I am not here to take you out of the woods and tell you where to go. No. I ask you, "Where do you want to go?" Then, I explain to you what will happen if you were to take the route you want to take.

— *I got it. I can't live like this—thrown from one side to another—anymore. I must stop this endless, daily fight. I am ready to balance this duality.*

— Which duality are you ready to balance? We are discussing duality **"Man—woman"** now. At the moment of their arrival to Earth, people get segregated based on their sexual characteristics. This duality is physically expressed here in our being a man or a woman. This duality is also connected to a continuation of a human race. As all of you know, for a child to be born a man and a woman must have sex. But, it is in this interaction between a man and a woman that most dualities manifest themselves. Thus, achievement of the partnership between a man and a woman can be seen as a doctorate thesis of the investigation conducted in multiple dualities of separation. Unless you complete this work, you will not be able to move to a higher level of consciousness. As we can see, this thesis—a man and a woman—encompasses multiple other sub-theses, which investigate and sort out different dualities. These dualities manifest themselves in the form of conflicts that occur in the relationship between a man and a woman. In your case, we can see quite a few of these dualities. For your man and your woman to come to the state of partnership, you need to make many steps. These steps will investigate conflicting dualities that you see in the mirror of the opposite sex, i.e. in your man. Which duality would you like to explore now?

— *I would like to explore the duality we have started with: financial dependence— financial independence from a man.*

— First, **we have to define duality** and to see that it is out of balance. One side of you wants to receive money from

74

your man. Another side finds the fact that it is being oppressed emotionally unpleasant. In essence, this is the conflict that occurs between your centers. This is a very important idea to understand. A human being is composed of three centers: mental, emotional, and physical. We can see that at least two of your centers—emotional and physical—are in conflict. Your physical center needs and takes your man's money, but your emotional center must pay for it. One center spends, while another center must pay for this spending. This happens inside you.

— *I am not sure I understand what you said.*

— This work is not easy. I can see all of this because I have traveled this road myself. I have experienced everything I discuss with you myself. It is not easy for you to absorb everything I say, because I deliver my answer in a very concentrated form. Perhaps we moved too far. Why don't we stop for now? You need to digest what I said. Otherwise, we will look as a group of hungry people who, suddenly finding themselves in front of a table full of food, start to eat everything at once. We will eat and eat until we get nauseous. No, let's step away from a table while we are still a bit hungry. Let's stop this conversation. We have come to the point of being full. Try to sort out what you have been told.

— *Thank you. I can see now what I need to work on.*

— Thank you. You have brought up a very important topic.

— *I am not sure I understand how to enter duality.*

— Why do you need to do that? Why do you need to enter duality?

— *I need to do that in order not to suffer.*

— Why do you think entering duality will free you from suffering?

— I want to rise above all dualities.

— If you go to church, the priest will tell you, "Pray and you will rise above your suffering." If you go an esoteric group, you will be told, "Chant this mantra and you will rise above your suffering." Presently, you don't understand the difference between what Pint offers and what other places offer. That's why I ask you, "Who told you that entering a duality will free you from suffering?" We start from the very beginning. This is a very interesting situation. Every human being that shows up at our meetings with his questions is very important and needed. That's why I am grateful to every one of you, including you. Your presence here and your questions are useful to everyone.

The motivation you currently have is insufficient for us to enter a more detailed investigation of duality. Therefore, I will ask you to feel how important this path is for you and whether you are ready for it. If your answer is yes, you will start to read my books and listen to the audio recordings of my seminars and webinars. That will help you to come up with a specific question. I will *feel* your question and we will explore it.

— Thank you.

— I thought I freed myself from my dependency on the opinions of other people, but...

— You didn't free yourself from it. You think you did, but you didn't. What's your reaction to my words? I just offered you my opinion—an opinion of another human being. I have offered you a test.

— I agree with you. I think this dependency is still in me; it is hiding somewhere.

— People who listen to me usually react in two ways: they either agree with everything I say or disagree with everything I say. Both responses are conditioned reactions. What can we have instead of these reactions? For example, you just agreed with me when I said that you have not freed yourself from being dependent on other people's opinion. You could have disagreed with me. What else could you have done?

— I could have said that I both freed and didn't free myself from it at the same time. One side says, "I have freed myself from this dependency." Another says, "No, I have not freed myself from it."

— Exactly. That's how these sides argue with each other back and forth. This inner war between "yes" and "no," between "right" and "wrong" continues day and night. I have been doing this work for many years. What do you think I do when people tell me, "You are full of shit? There is no such thing as duality. There is no wholeness. We are not personal programs"?

— You agree with their right to have their own opinion. That's the level of understanding they are presently at.

— Exactly. But do I consider them to be right?

— No. Another reality is real for you.

— So, I follow a road that frequently disagrees with a public opinion. But, I don't lose my inner balance. What allows me to live in this society, and to maintain my inner balance while listening to the opinions people offer me?

— I think it is the experience you acquired that allows you to do what you do.

— The experience I acquired allowed me to open the matrix of dual consciousness. When I discovered it inside myself, I received immunity from public opinion. I want to remind you that the work I do is inner work. I don't reject, argue, or fight people who say that what I do is wrong. No. I accept them as my own parts, and I say, "Yes, I have these parts too." But my main part knows what is going on. It is in harmony now. Another part of me may try to hit it and say,

"You are not doing this right." The third part may scream, "What you do is right. You are a great man." I can lose my balance in both situations: in the situation when I am being attacked and, in the situation when I am being praised.

— *I am always surprised by your ability to balance. Listening to your seminars and webinars, I have noticed that you never lose your balance. Neither praise nor angry outbursts of some of the participants can get you off balance.*

— Exactly. Why do I discuss this now by using myself as an example? I do that because your question deals with this balance. I continue to work on your question, which deals with the influence of public opinion. Why don't you ask Pint, who is sitting across from you, to explain how he arrived at this balance.

— *That's exactly the question I want to ask you, "How did you come to this balance?" Your ego never manifests itself. You can use harsh, even foul language, but you never do it out of the ego. How do you do that?*

— I came to this balance by investigating and balancing multiple dualities of my personality. And trust me, my personality is very tough.

— *I can feel that.*

— This is not an easy work. Some of you say, "Pint is great. He walks down the middle—he never falls to the side." That's not true. I continue to balance my dualities daily. If you ready, we can review one of your dualities and bring it to balance.

— *I am ready to do that.*

— Which particular duality would you like to explore?

— *I would like to explore the duality **"Condemnation— Acceptance."***

— Does it deal with public opinion, too?

— *I think it is connected to my condemning something or someone.*

— Yes, you have started this conversation with the question, "How can I not be influenced by the public opinion?" When I asked you what it meant, you have said, "Condemnation." And now, let's look at how you get condemned by public opinion. How do people condemn you? This external condemnation is a consequence of your own inner condemnation.

— *I understand that.*

— "Do not judge and you will not be judged," Jesus has said. This formula was never deciphered. It is not clear how to apply it. People don't understand what it means. A man says: "I don't condemn people. Well, of course, occasionally I may …" However, when you start to observe, you understand that your daily life is full of condemnation. People are not aware of this. They are not aware of the fact that they are submerged in condemnation. They live with an impression they don't condemn anyone. It is great that you are ready to investigate this duality. What do you condemn people for?

— *I condemn people for not sharing my point of view. I think my point of view is the only right point of view.*

— That's what every personality thinks. Every ego stands for its truth and tries to prove its truth to other egos. This is what we call "formation and reinforcement of personality." If you can't defend your truth, people say you are a floor mop.

— *On the intellectual level, I understand that every man has his own truth and sees the world from his own vantage point, but I frequently find myself arguing with people about some stupid, minor issues tooth and nail.*

— Exactly. Moreover, you get angry. You get full of wrath and indignation: "Why can't you see that I am right?! How come you don't understand how important I am?! Why do you spit at me?" That's what stands behind your anger. Not only do I have to stand up for my truth and prove that I am right, I need to show everyone how important I am.

— *When I started to investigate my dualities, I came to see my main feature. My main duality is* **"Important—not important."**

— Where exactly does your importance lie? The reasons for this may vary. One woman may say, "I am very important because I am a good mother." Another will say, "I am very important because I can make a lot of money."

— *I have been living on my own since I was sixteen. I have graduated from college. I have brought up my son all by myself. That's where my importance lies.*

— You are smart. You can make money. You have brought up your child on your own. You are very important. So, what do you condemn people for?

— *I condemn them for criticizing me. No one should criticize me.*

— What exactly do they criticize you for?

— *They criticize me when I do something wrong.*

— What exactly do they criticize you for? A self-investigator explores the topic of his investigation in minute details and from every possible angle. This is the quality every self-investigator should acquire. You must be very specific.

— *I understand that.*

— Someone may criticize you for your shoelaces not matching this morning.

— *I understand. I used to get very irritated when someone called me stupid. Now, I am irritated by the fact that I don't do anything.*

— Are you lazy?

— *No, I just don't do anything. I haven't been working for a while.*

— So, you occupy yourself with doing nothing.

— *Yes.*

— Your business is to do nothing. Now, if someone asks you, "Why don't you do anything?" you can reply, "I am occupied with doing nothing." And I can tell you, it is not easy to do nothing. It is not that you don't do anything, you are occupied with doing nothing. That is a good way to maintain self-importance.

— *I like this approach.*

— Who prohibits you from using it?

— *Umbrage. I would take it as an insult.*

— They condemn you for not doing anything, and you support them in this notion that a human being should do something. If you don't anything, your life is meaningless. It is wasted. That's what bothers you. If you don't do anything, you degrade.

— *Exactly.*

— That's why I half-jokingly suggested you say you occupy yourself with doing nothing. It is equally difficult to occupy yourselves with doing nothing as it is to work. You satisfy the necessity of your opposite part: one part of you wants to do something—another doesn't want to do anything.

— *I just saw this part. It says, "Let me live. I want to manifest myself, too."*

— Look how these two dualities, "doing—not doing" and "important—not important," interconnect in your structure. When you don't do anything, you automatically lose your importance and become not important—you cannot accept that.

— *Yes.*

— **Not doing is one of the techniques used by the Yaqui Indian shamans. Carlos Castaneda discusses it at length in one of his books. People who live in the western culture are doers. They do, and do, and do. Try not to do anything for a change. The mere fact of not doing anything stresses the western personality greatly because** it sees *not doing* as an indicator of it not being important. We are dealing with the specifics of cultural programs. The specifics of the western programs will differ from the specifics of the eastern programs. For example, a program inculcated in New York will differ from a program inculcated in Calcutta. Your opposite side, the side that doesn't want to do anything, is very important and necessary for you.

— *I understand that now.*

— It is one thing to understand this mentally, and another thing to feel it. First, you must allow yourself to not do anything. Then, you must experience pleasure from it. Irrespective of what you do and what happens to you, you always satisfy a desire of one of your parts. At the same time, the part that is opposite to it condemns it. Do you see how interesting this situation is? One of your parts condemns another part, but it is you who experiences stress and discomfort. Irrespective of what you do, one part of you will always condemn you for doing it. For example, you are doing something. Your opposite part condemns that and says, "Why do you need to do that?" But as soon as you move to the part that doesn't do anything, this not doing part will start to hear the condemning voice of the part of you that wants to do something. In both cases, we are dealing with condemnation and suffering. That's why a man who happens to be in a state of sleep of consciousness, or fight of the opposite parts of his personality, is always suffering. You can clearly see how this suffering appears. When you see that, you understand the importance of knowledge I offer. You understand how important it is to transfer the interrelationship of these two opposite parts from the state of conflict to the state of

82

partnership, i.e. how important it is to stop this condemnation. There is no condemnation in the state of partnership.

— *Are you telling me I have to accept both sides?*

— Yes. However, as we can see, it is easy to say that, but not so easy to do that. For example, on the conscious side—you are *a doer*. It is with the help of this part that you graduated from university, learned how to make money, and brought up your kid. On the subconscious side, you are *a non-doer*. You must accept your subconscious side. This is not easy. Can you spend a whole day *not doing* anything? As soon as you start to *not do* anything, you will hear people scream at you. Your reaction—umbrage. In reality, it is not your father or your husband who is screaming at you—it is you. Your *doing part* condemns your *not doing part*. The external players simply allow you to see that.

— So, these are my parts. They reflect my own condemnation to me.

— That's good that you understand that. This is the first step. What do we do next? How can we soften these screaming voices? How can we bring the level of their condemnation down? As you start to accept your inner, subconscious part that we call *non-doer*, these loud screams will soften up. The level of your condemnation of yourself will get lower and lower. This will only happen when you start to accept this *non-doing* part of yours. **The external world will work as an indicator of the degree you accept yourself to.** If you were to tell me, "I have accepted everything, but for some reason, people still come to me asking why I don't do anything," I will say to you, "You have not accepted this part yet. You have an illusion that you have accepted it. This is just an illusion." To make sure you have accepted this part, you need to observe what happens in your external world. The moment your external world stops to condemn you for *not doing* anything will indicate that you have fully accepted this part. It will not happen any sooner, because your external world is you. The situations and voices that you hear from the external world reflect you to yourself. Without this mirror, we would not be able to investigate ourselves. Without this mirror, we would not be able to move toward being Whole. Without this mirror, we would not be able to understand ourselves. The external world is the indicator that helps us to do this work.

— *Thank you very much. I am shaking inside.*

— This is great. This shaking indicates that we have hit the mark of your inquiry.

— *Is there a way to classify these multiple subpersonalities?*

— Every classification, as the basic method of commonly accepted scientific work, is important for me from the standpoint of how it helps me to reach my aim. With this in the background, I will ask you: "What aim are you trying to reach? Why do you want to classify sub-personalities? What do you want to receive as a result?"

— *I want to do that to see the dualities I need to work on.*

— Okay. Then, I will offer you a classification I came to as a result of my self-investigation. What are we made of? A human being consists of the mental center—thoughts and images, the emotional center—feelings, and the physical center—sensations of the body and instincts (sexual instinct being one of them). Every one of these centers is dual. To every thesis, there is an antithesis. To every thought, there is an opposite thought. This is what happens in the mental center. In the emotional center, every feeling is opposed by an opposite feeling. In the physical center, every action is opposed by the opposite action. Self-investigation requires us to investigate dualities in every one of these centers. You can review sub-personalities in these arrangements.

I would like to add something in connection with sub-personalities and what I just said. These sub-personalities have mental, emotional, and physical components.

For example, **let's explore one specific role of personality: mother**. The role of mother is associated with certain thoughts. Relating to these thoughts, the mother experiences certain emotional states and performs certain actions. Opposite to the role mother is the role of a whore. The thoughts and feelings that this part harbors in respect to a man, as well as the actions it performs are totally different. For example, the mother relates to a man as someone she wants to conceive a child from. Later, she might ask him for money to support her child. What does a whore want? A whore wants to have sex. A whore looks at a man and sees an object of sexual attraction. She experiences corresponding feelings and performs corresponding actions. So, every subpersonality has three centers. Each one of these centers must be investigated in duality. This is the shortest route.

As we have discussed already, these dual sub-personalities are always in a state of conflict. We need to convert their conflicting relationship to the state of partnership. And now, in connection to our prior dialogue, I can tell you that your *doer*, as we tentatively called your subpersonality, has the opposite subpersonality—*non-doer*. Every one of these subpersonalities has its own thoughts related to the way life should be lived. The *doer* part says, "I have to do this!" It has its own notions why "this" needs to be done. It experiences certain feelings associated with these thoughts, and it carries certain actions related to these thoughts and feelings. The *non-doer* part has different thoughts that justify why "this" should not be done. The *non-doer* part has the corresponding feelings and carries the corresponding actions because of which it doesn't want to do what the *doer* part wants to be done. You need to investigate these subpersonalities in duality. Behind every duality stand two subpersonalities which must be investigated in all three centers.

We have just discussed a very important topic. Every duality should be investigated not as just a mental construct, but as a pair of two opposite parts of the personality, with an understanding that there are feelings behind thoughts and actions behind feelings. These thoughts, feelings, and actions of subpersonalities oppose each other.

— *I can see it clearly now. Thank you very much.*

— Thank you. We have reviewed a very important topic.

— *I have reviewed many of my dependencies and finally, I figured out which one of them holds me tighter than the others. I had to look deep down into my childhood.*

I started to transcribe the last webinar, and I asked my husband to help me. As soon as I did that, I felt nauseous. I started to investigate. What caused me to experience this sensation? It turned out when I am unable to do something on my own and must ask someone for help, I experience tremendous inner resistance to verbalize my plea for help. I recalled that this is exactly how my dad behaves. First, he inflicts his services upon another human being and makes him depend on him. For example, he has created a website for me. I have never asked him to do that. The website is difficult to navigate. He is the only one who can manage it. Now, I must depend on his help almost daily. When I ask him for help, he gets irritated. He tells me he doesn't have time to do it. I feel guilty. I experience this feeling because I have to depend on him. When I was a kid, I felt guilty for being born. I felt guilty for being alive and making my parents' life miserable. I learned early that they got married because Mom got pregnant with me.

So, my dad had created a dependency in me. I need him. I have created a similar dependency in my husband. I made him dependent on me the same way my father made me dependent on him.

— Let's review something very important here. You have said that your parents got married because you appeared. In connection with this, you experienced a feeling of guilt. But let's take a closer look at your parents. Your arrival allowed them to find a scapegoat and a reason to get married. They couldn't do it without you. They needed you. Look now at who needed whom? I am not saying that you didn't need them, but I show you the opposite side of the situation, the side that you didn't see. How much do they need you? They need you as much as you need them.

You have also said that your dad has created a website for you, and he is the only one who can manage it. When you ask him to help you with this site, he says: "I cannot do it now."

— *He gets irritated. He does what I ask him to do, but he gets very irritated and he expresses his irritation to me. He does what I ask him to do, but he clearly shows me that he does not want to do that. That's what upsets me the most.*

— Look at the way you appeared in this world. We are dealing with a similar situation.

— *Yes.*

— "She is born. She is here. What do we do now? She is here already—we will have to bring her up." And he manifests this attitude in his relationship with you. This is the program that was passed on to you and it manifests itself again and again.

— *I considered myself to be a victim when I was a kid. I savored this state of victimhood. I pitied myself. I thought other people should pity me too. I have entered this state now. Usually, I suppress it.*

— It is through the state of victimhood, that one can get to compassion. One cannot get to the state of compassion while one is in the state of an oppressor. It is very important to experience the state of victimhood to understand yourself. The state of victimhood doesn't guarantee this understanding. It is a necessary, but insufficient condition. I will tell you about myself. I went through the state of victimhood myself. I would not be able to understand what I discuss with you now without having experienced it. It was a difficult, but necessary experience. I want to emphasize that your Soul has chosen this experience. You have been born into these conditions so you could acquire this unique experience. This experience brought you to School of Holistic Psychology. Let's express our gratitude for this experience and to the Soul that planned it.

However, at present time, we happen to be at the next stage of our experiment, when we need to see and balance the states of victimhood and oppression inside ourselves. We need to see that the state of victimhood appears because of oppression. The state of victimhood cannot appear any other way.

An oppressor, who oppresses a victim, must be present. It's because of this oppressor that victim can feel as a victim. I want to help you balance these states now. I am showing to you that your father, for example, who you see as an oppressor, is also a victim—your appearance in this world was an oppression for him.

— *I am an oppressor. That's for sure...*

— When you start to see the situation from this angle, you start to balance and harmonize this inner, severely activated in you now duality.

— *I feel guilty again. I am an oppressor, but I am guilty anyway.*

— One cannot stop the train that moves very fast instantaneously. The force of its inertia is very high, and it will have to pass a certain distance to come to a full stop. The speed of your "victim" train is very high. It is carrying a heavy load of experience. Therefore, it will not stop at once. Your brake distance will be long. But, start to push on the brake. Start to slow this train down. I invite you to do that. I am telling you exactly what you need to do to stop this so-called "victim" train. I invite you to see your inner oppressor because this train runs at the same speed but in the opposite direction.

— *I need to see myself as an oppressor in relationship to my dad, a man I consider to be an oppressor.*

— Let's start with your dad, but you will have to see it in your relationship with other people, especially people who are close to you: your friends and relatives.

— *I can see myself behaving as an oppressor in relationship to people that are close to me. I make them dependent on me. Then, I push them away. I condemn them for taking my time. I condemn them for ruining my life. I can see where I behave as an oppressor.*

— Exactly. And you do that using the same mechanism. Why is it so important for us to see our mechanisms? You need to understand what I mean, when I say, "A mechanism." You have just described the mechanism using which your dad brings you to experience the state of victimhood. You use the same mechanism in relation to people that are close to you, and you make them equally dependent on you.

— *Yes, I can see this.*

— You have been taught this method and you successfully apply it.

— **Yes, I do that, even though it is not effective at all.**

— It is very effective. Why don't you give credit to your dad for teaching you how to use it? That's the reason you cannot experience gratitude to him for transmitting it to you. I, on the other hand, say: "He taught you to use this very effective method very well." If it was not effective, he would not have transmitted it to you. He transmitted the best he had to you. Look at this paradox. I offer you to express gratitude to your parents for something you presently hate them for. This should not be a simple affirmation, "Thank you, father, for this and that." You need to thoroughly feel this gratitude. That's quite a turn, ah?

— *Yes, on one hand, this is the case. But, on the other hand, I feel guilty. I feel guilty for mechanically applying this method.*

— This excellent method allows you to experience the feeling of guilt and to revel in the state of guiltiness.

— *I did that. I don't do that anymore.*

— Wait a minute. I have gone through the same experience. I used to revel in the state of guiltiness for decades. Who had taught me to use this mechanism using which I can experience this delightful and delicious feeling of self-pity? My parents taught me that. For this, I am grateful to them. Try to understand that if you enjoy something, you enjoy it thanks to your parents. They taught you how to do that. Thank them. And don't thank them formally. You need to feel this gratitude thoroughly. Otherwise, you enjoy this delicious state of self-pity, and you hate them.

— *On the conscious level, I hear the voice of my victim that says: "What are you doing, idiot? Are you pitying yourself again? It's your own fault. Get up!" My victim quietly continues to do what it does.*

— This is a manifestation of the inner conflict which rages between dual sides of your personality. We are witnessing a conflict between your inner victim and your inner oppressor. I suggest you transform this conflict and bring these two parts to a partnership. Can you do that if you continue to condemn yourself? How can you stop this condemnation if you think you are doing something horrible? Insisting that this is the case, one part of you will continue to condemn the other part. This conflict will continue indefinitely.

This is something that frequently happens in the spiritual communities. Under the slogan, "Love thy neighbor," people continue to condemn themselves. Do they get closer to God, or in my terminology closer to the next level of consciousness? No, they don't.

I am presenting you with an instrument that will allow you to stop this conflict. I invite you to feel satisfaction from something you call horrible. I invite you to feel satisfaction from your own victimhood, and your own condemnation. **You cannot investigate what you condemn. How can you investigate something if you don't want to look at it? You need to thank yourself for this experience and say: "Everything I experience and everything I do is right. I am not going to condemn myself for what I did." This statement will allow you to start the process of self-investigation.** It doesn't mean you are going to keep doing what you did. On the contrary, you will clearly see what you did. Your *seeing* it will change it.

That's the only way to wholeness, i.e. gathering and accepting yourself in all your aspects. You will not accept in yourself the qualities that you consider to be bad. This is not easy, but very important for us to understand. You must apply effort and do a lot of work to stop condemning yourself for the traits you consider to be bad. There is nothing bad in you. Everything you ever did, thought, and felt was right. You are on the way toward yourself. But if you continue to do what you do mechanically, your trip will take more time. You may choose to do that, but I invite you to take the shortest route. My way presupposes transfer to a different perception. You will not be able to investigate things you don't want to see in yourself because you consider them to be bad and ugly. I will repeat. There is nothing bad in you. There is nothing in you that cannot be respected. Everything that a human being contains was created by God and is good. Why would God create something bad and ugly? Would God do it to turn away from his own creation? No, creator loves his creation. That's why people say: "God is love."

We are in the zone of free will. This is a very specific zone, where God allows everything to exist. Do you think there would be anything "bad" here if God did not want this so-called "bad" to be here? Of course, not. God allowed it to exist; he had his reasons for that.

I am offering you a mental concept, but you need *to feel* it. You can't thank God for your being here, because you consider yourself to be bad. In that case, you will blame your creator for creating you this way. But he didn't create you to be bad. He created you exactly the way you need to be to move toward next level of consciousness.

By locking yourself in the domain of the ego, which constantly condemns itself, you will never see the light at the end of the tunnel. You will never feel grateful to your parents for inculcating you with your dual program. You will never feel grateful to your Supreme Aspect who sent you here to acquire this program. You will never feel grateful to the Creator who created everything that exists. This chain can bring you to experience the state of gratitude. However, you will not be able to feel gratitude to God, unless you experience gratitude to your parents.

Your work here will allow you to become aware of your personal program. That will lead you to experience the state of gratitude. This emotional state will signify the completion of your work on becoming aware of yourself. We are walking toward this state and this is not an easy walk. Later, we will face another assignment. Believe me, we will not be left without assignments. But no one will be able to jump over or skip an assignment here. Until you solve your current assignment, you will not be given another one.

— *I got it. Thank you very much.*

I would like to ask one more question that might be related to the topic we discuss. I noticed an interesting tendency. I create dangerous and harmful dependencies, which I then battle relentlessly and unsuccessfully. Now, I understand why I do that. I do that to be in a victim state.

— Exactly. And until you understand that you need to be in the victim state and that you receive kaif from being in it, you will continue to recreate these situations.

— *Yes. This work is interesting. So, I have to return to that childhood state, where, as I remember, I had experienced pleasure from suffering for the first time. Growing up, I condemned myself for experiencing this state. I started to deny this state.*

— Yes, your structure started to crystallize. That's what happens to people as they age.

— *Thank you.*

— *When I am in a relationship with a man, I lose myself. Being close to a man, I sense what he experiences very well. When that happens, I forget myself completely. I experience every emotional state and every physical sensation he experiences.*

— And how do you manage to forget yourself in the process?

— I don't know how it happens, but I disappear completely.

— You have brought up a very interesting question. Let's review it. There are two modes of survival here: masculine and feminine. Similarly, you can perceive yourself and the world around you out of two modes: masculine and feminine. From the standpoint of the feminine mode of perception, there is no me; only the external world exists. That's what you just said. You start to search for verification of your existence in your relationships with other people. In the process, you feel these people, their thoughts, feelings, and physical sensations strongly. You dissolve in these people. But at the same time, you don't understand who you are. "Why do I feel these people the way I do?" you ask yourself. This is one way to perceive yourself and the world around you.

Another way to perceive reality is to perceive it from the standpoint, "There is only me." Other people are just a context. Your thoughts, emotional states, and physical sensations are the only things that important to you. You use other people to achieve your goals. In that case, you are only oriented on yourself.

The duality "altruist—egoist" shows these two opposite types of perception well. It appears you are suffering from a disbalance. Where is it? Between which polar sides of your personal program do you see this disbalance?

— I am not sure I understand your question.

— Okay. Let me clarify it for you. You experience thoughts, feelings, and actions of your man in their totality. Are you satisfied with these states of affairs?

— No. It appears to me I understand the experience of my man, but this experience is not really mine.

— Let me use an example. You happen to be close to a man, and, having a sponge-like quality to absorb everything, you understand him very well. If I understand you correctly, you become him. What exactly do you feel and think, when you say that you feel and think like him?

— *I don't think I turn into him.*

— What can you say about a man after you have absorbed him?

— *I can see the mistakes he made during his life. I can see the world from his point of view. He is unhappy and miserable. That's why he treats me the way he does.*

— What can you say about him? **Life brought you face to face with your own part.** What can you say about this part after you have spent some time with it?

— *It is a very egotistical, picky, and demanding personality.*

— Is this personality opposite to your personality?

— *Yes.*

— What is your attitude toward it?

— *I pity it.*

— What if we were to use the axiom I constantly remind you of, **"There are no other people. Every human being around you is a mirror for you."** If we were to use this axiom, you, after getting to know this part of yours, come up with a verdict: this part deserves pity. Am I correct?

— *Yes.*

— So, this part is not worthy of gratitude. You can only pity it.

— *No, that's not exactly true.*

— According to what you just said, this man is very demanding and harsh. It *appears*, he is oppressing you. You experience the state of victimhood, but you get out of this state by feeling pity toward him, i.e. you start to project the state of victimhood onto him. You have said: "He is unhappy and miserable. That's why he treats me the way he does." But, he is you. You pity yourself. How do you like this state of pity?

— *It's a heavy state.*

— What is pity? How does it appear? What's the opposite side of pity? Can you answer these questions?

— *No.*

— A very old technique can help us here. Let's say a man screams at you. You are offered to feel how bad he feels and to take pity on him. He hits you—you pity him. He hits you on the right cheek—you offer him your left cheek and you say: "Hit me again. You feel so bad, you need to do that."

— *Okay.*

— When you see a poor, old, dirty bum on a street corner, you give him alms out of pity. You do that because you think: "God forbid I experience what he experiences." You look at him and you think: "Wow! My troubles are nothing compare to his." You walk down a street. Your boyfriend just dumped you. And you see this poor, legless bastard, who screams: "Give me a dollar!" You look at him and you think: "His situation is much worse than mine. Thank God, I have legs."

What is pity? I compare myself to someone and because of this comparison, I feel better. He feels very bad. I don't feel that bad. But is this a clear vision I call you to? No. This is a continuation of a delusion: you don't see other people, you only see yourself and you pity yourself. You think he feels bad, but it is you who feels bad. Can you grasp the idea that this man is you, or do you still think he is someone separate from you?

The opposite side of pity is to see things the way they are. This is not an easy concept to grasp. **Pity is an illusory perception of the world.** If you experience pity, your

96

perception of the world is illusory. You are seeing an illusion, but you perceive it as reality. This illusion gives rise to the state of pity in you.

— *I frequently feel pity for the people around me.*

— You always feel pity toward yourself, but you project this feeling onto the external world. **The pity you feel for someone is self-pity.** This pity stems out of the illusion that something is not the way it should be, that something is wrong. It points to the fact that you don't understand the world you are living in, you don't understand why you came to this world, you don't understand the nature of the assignment you came here to solve.

You should start seeing this world as a training playground and dualities as training machines. You were sent here by your Supreme Aspect to acquire a certain experience and to solve a very important assignment. When you start to see that, you will start to see yourself and other people in a totally different light, and you will experience totally different states.

What is the difference between pity and compassion? In a state of compassion, I see a human being as someone who goes through an experience I know. I understand the situation he is in and I know what he experiences, but I don't pity him. Do you see the difference?

— *Yes, I do.*

— This is a very important difference. Why do I *see* what is going on with you and other people so clearly? I *see clearly* because I know what you experience. But it doesn't mean I pity you.

But what does your ego want? It wants somebody to pity it.

— *It looks like I live in a state of victimhood.*

— Yes, you want someone to pity you. I am talking about something else. In my world, pity turns into empathy. **To empathize with people is *to clearly see* and understand the stage they are at, and to be able to show them where they are.** A man who wants pity from me will not progress on the road of understanding himself. What happens when one human being pities another? Does either one of them move on the road to wholeness?

— *I don't think so.*

— They stay in the dark. My task is to disperse this dense fog and to show you what is going on. Self-pity is one of the most common states people experience here. There are three main states here: condemnation, pity, and guilt. These states give birth to every illusion. The constant fight between dual sides of our personality gives birth to these three inner states, which in turn give birth to all our illusions and suffering. This mechanism maintains suffering and pain, which are kaif for the ego.

These states—condemnation, pity, and guilt—are narcotic producing states our ego uses to survive. As you know, a drug addict needs a small dose of narcotic at first. Then, tolerance develops—he needs to escalate the dose. By increasing the dose of these narcotics, we intensify our suffering. Every life situation we experience is potentially a narcotic producing situation. Your ego creates these situations, escalates degree of their intensity, allowing you to experience more condemnation, more pity, and more guilt. Your ego holds on to these states the same way a long-term drug junky holds on to his drug.

— *I had a desire to find a similar man, who would do the same thing to me, but now I want to change this situation.*

— This is a paradox. People go to prison for physically abusing other people. Now you know that someone who was physically abused not only wanted to be abused but searched for and attracted his oppressor, according to the degree of victimhood he or she wanted to experience. That's the game people play here. Nothing happens without a reason here. Every victim will attract an oppressor and not just any oppressor. A victim will attract a specific oppressor who will provide it with the necessary level of oppression.

— *I want to experience greater and greater suffering. I want to move from cocaine to heroin, so to speak.*

— Yes. Sooner or later every ego-personality starts to escalate the dose of a narcotic it uses. This is not surprising. Until you understand that, you will not develop the passion necessary to continue this work of collecting yourself in one Whole.

— *So, what do I do now? Which direction should I work in?*

— Every word of mine is a pointer that will point you in a certain direction. Every dialogue with me will provide you with a pointer. If you really want to move toward Wholeness, you need to become aware of what you are doing. You need to see what every action of yours leads to. When a drug user takes another dose of a drug, he shakes, in anticipation of feeling better. Does he think of what will happen next, when the drug will stop working and cause him to experience withdrawal? No, he doesn't think about that; he searches for the next fix. Until you see yourself doing that, you will continue to do what you do. You need to see the consequences of your emotional drug addiction. That will be a step forward.

— *Thank you.*

— The road to wholeness is not an easy road. The vast amount of knowledge I have accumulated during my self-investigation can only be transmitted in a stepwise fashion. You will not be able to absorb it at once. I have a barrel of water. You come to me with a small glass. I can fill up your glass. I cannot give you more than you can carry. You can only accept what you are ready to accept. The more you do this work, the more you will be ready to accept what I have to offer. How much can you carry? That depends on you. To assimilate this knowledge, you need to work in three complementary directions.

You need to read and listen to school materials: books, audio and video recordings of our webinars and seminars. When you start to do that, you will start to understand and feel what I say. This work will activate a certain experience in you, which is necessary to investigate the questions you come up with. We have discussed stress and increase in voltage potential today. This is a necessary part of our work. The work that each one of you does in School—transcribing the seminars or working with audio files—is a very important work. You can do it at home and feel its effect and usefulness. Your attendance of seminars and webinars is of utmost importance, too.

As you can see, this work is not easy. You will experience strong resistance during each step. You will experience resistance reading our site materials. You will experience resistance going to the webinars and seminars. This resistance is very important, too. It creates a voltage potential you need.

CHAPTER 3

HOW TO STOP THE FIGHT OF YOUR PERSONAL OPPOSITIONS AND TO BECOME WHOLE IN THE DUALITY "LOVE—HATE"

We are going to discuss a very interesting topic today: love and hate. Relating to it, I recall my childhood. As kids, we would get in front of a TV every evening, asking adults what kind of movie we were about to watch: was it about love or war? Boys wanted to see war movies. Girls wanted to see movies about love. Today we are going to learn that love is war.

I will ask you two questions. What do you mean when you say you love someone? What do you mean when you say you hate someone?

What is love? Who do we love? We love those who we find likable. Who do we find likable? We find likable those who we find useful. What is their usefulness? Their usefulness is in their ability to satisfy our needs. It might be financial needs, sexual needs, a need for respect, and so on. Moreover, they need to satisfy these needs the way we want them to be satisfied. If at some point, they stop satisfying our needs, we start to

101

experience the opposite state that ranges from slight irritation to passionate hatred.

So, what determines our feelings? It appears that our feelings are determined by the profit that is appraised by our personality. If another human being reinforces our conscious personal pride, we love him, if he does not—we hate him. I will remind you that pride appears in every one of our opposite personal parts. For example, there is the pride of the personal part which we can call respectful. But there is also the pride of the personal part which we can call worthless. The question is which one of these parts we are conscious of, and which one hides in our subconsciousness. **For example, if you consciously consider yourself to be worthless, you will attract a human being and love him for constantly supporting the notion of your worthlessness, i.e. pride of the worthless part. Every part has its own pride.** It seems to you that your pride is based on the fact that you are good, but you are also full of pride on the account of being bad. I purposefully chose this example so you can understand why you can fall in love with people, with whom, as it *appears* to you, you should not fall in love.

To understand how and why states of love and hate arise, we need to understand the makeup of our personal program. Secondly, we need to change the level of our consciousness, as at the level of consciousness which I call "sleeping" and which is predominant here, dual sides of our personality are always in conflict. It doesn't mean that with a change in our level of consciousness duality will disappear. No, duality will not disappear, but the relationship between its opposite sides will change from conflict to partnership.

While in the "sleeping" mode of consciousness, a chronic conflict rages inside the personality; every part of us fights its opposite part. We don't feel this pain, because it is chronic. The part that is winning at present time not only gets stronger, it also reinforces its pride. In other words, every personal part of ours hates the part that is opposite to it. Now, you can understand why hatred in all its manifestations and a broad diapason—from irritation to aggression—is so common here. Initially, we feel slight irritation and dislike. Then, we experience hatred, malice, vengeance, and wrath. The diapason of love manifestations is similarly broad.

Why does the feeling of hatred arise? It arises because the opposite parts of our personality, having totally opposite desires, get irritated by and start to hate each other. You can ask: "What about the state of love? When does it appear?" It appears when we project onto another human being, the one we say we love, those of our qualities that we consider to be good. It turns out, we can project what we don't accept in ourselves as well as what we cherish in ourselves. The external world and people around us reflect our positive and negative qualities as screens. In other words, when you project the qualities you don't like and don't accept in yourself onto someone, you hate him. I will remind you again that hatred has a broad diapason of manifestations. When you project the qualities you like and accept in yourself onto someone, you love him or her.

That's why when you accept yourself totally, you love everyone. **It is precisely by accepting and starting to love the qualities you have considered to be your negative qualities, that you will get to love everything.** This is what mystical, unconditional love is about. In reality, we do not love or hate other people, we love and hate ourselves. It only appears to us that we love and hate other people. And it is because of this *appearance* that we constantly try to change other people. We should investigate, understand, and accept ourselves. That's the work we are doing here.

Love and hate are two forces that attract us to the lessons assigned to us. Those are not easy lessons, and without these forces attracting us to them, we would not have completed our assignments. The stronger the power of love and hate we experience, the harder the assignments we need to solve.

But is this the way you look at love? Do you understand its real meaning or just want to prolong the pleasure associated with it? What will happen when this pleasure end? Will you hate the human being you loved, grind your teeth at night, or scream at the skies?

This is the topic we are going to discuss today. Let's explore this topic in dialogues now. By recalling your own life experiences, you will come to understand that love is a force that attracts you to your assignment to understand yourself as a whole.

— *I will start with the second topic—hate. A few weeks ago, I was walking down a street listening to an audio file of the last webinar. My earplugs in, I was totally absorbed in it. Suddenly, I heard a word, which was thrown in my direction: bitch. I turned around and saw a young woman walking behind me. She appeared to be angry. I asked her whether her remark was directed at me. "Who else?" she replied in a voice full of hatred. I understood that she was not herself. She did not know me, but for some reason, she tried to insult me.*

If this situation were to occur a year ago, I would have thought: "What a strange girl?" and forget her fast. But now, I turned off my iPod and I started to think: "Perhaps my bitchy part is getting ready to manifest itself. Perhaps this is a warning?" I got home and resumed listening to the webinar. As I listened to it, I realized that one of the female participants irritated the hell out of me. I did not like anything she said. The webinar was about to end when suddenly, a thought popped into my head in relation to that woman: "I hate you, bitch!" I took my earplugs out and attempted to sort out where such malice was coming from. I felt it in every cell of my body. I sat down and started to explore my feelings, sensations, and thoughts. It didn't take me long to write down nine points for which I disliked her. As soon as I did that, I found them in myself, too.

— Did you sign it, "What a bitch I am?"

— *Yes, I did. My question is, "Which one of my parts has pronounced this word?" Was it my inner bitch who insulted my nice girl for not allowing her to manifest itself? Or was it my nice girl part, which called her opposite part a bitch and told her it hates her? I can't figure out which part of me have said it. I must get to know this part. I didn't want to see my angry part before. As soon as it will start to manifest itself, I would hide it. I want to know it in all its beauty now.*

— It is beautiful. But what's the difference who said what to whom? Perhaps God has sent you this woman to make you think about this subject. I think it is much more important for you to sort out what's going on with your inner "bitch." You finally saw it. You need to rejoice and observe this part.

— *I am happy I saw it. I want to thank this woman on the street who pointed me in in the direction of my "bitchy" part.*

— Yes, this was a divine intervention. Some angel spoke through this woman's lips and instructed you to work on yourself. I can also tell you that most men like bitches. They scream: "You are such a bitch!" and they try to get close to you. Or, they say: "You are such a bore. I am tired of you." You might find this "bitchy" part of yours to be very valuable in a situation when you want to keep a man next to you. How does your "bitch" do that?

— *She insists she knows everything. She disagrees with her man on every topic.*

— She invites him to be her sparring partner. When two boxers come to a ring, they scream: "Come here! I am going to get you!"

— *Yes. Moreover, I calm down when he gets to the ring.*

— You have someone to fight. That's great. You have a partner to fight.

— *Yes, I can always find a sparring partner in my husband.*

— Great. When your partner dies, you will become depressed, "I fought him my entire life. We had so many good fights. Where did he go? Why did he leave me?"

Okay. So, how does this "bitch" fight? Does she do it with pleasure? Is she interested in it? A "saint" fights a certain way. A "bitch" uses different tactics.

— *I think my "saint" irritates my husband more than my "bitch." "Why do you always have to be right? Why are you so smart? You think you know everything?!" he says.*

— Why? Let's take a look at this very interesting situation. Let's review Jesus story. He caused people to experience great hatred. While they were dragging him through Golgotha, he was saying: "Forgive them, God. They don't know what they are doing." People were screaming: "Take a look at this saint! He cannot even save himself!" They threw stones at him. They hated him with passion. The huge gap that existed between them and Jesus caused them to crucify him. So, sainthood is a very strong weapon, while a bitch is the same as everybody else. Bitch doesn't insist on being on a high pedestal. She is down low, bitching and arguing with everyone. She is common, while a saint is not of this world. Nobody can reach a saint.

— *I want to accept this part of mine.*

— Let's accept this part together. It must be accepted piece by piece. Tell us about the qualities of your "bitch."

— *She is angry.*

106

— For which of your qualities do people call you bitch?

— *My husband says: "Why do you try to boss me all the time?"*

— Okay. So, you are a boss-bitch.

— *Yes, I am a boss.*

— What is your rank?

— *If I was in the army, I would be a general.*

— Hmm ... you are a high-ranking bitch.

— *He calls me a dictator. He doesn't do everything I say, but most of the times he complies with my orders.*

— This is interesting. A drill sergeant orders his platoon to march around a square. They sweat. They curse him. They don't like it, but they keep marching day and night. Ten years later, they recall that day with a smile: "Remember how we marched?" So, it *appears* to them they don't like it, but in reality, they do like it.

— *Yes, this is probably the case. He is not aware of the fact that he likes to be ordered around, but subconsciously he likes it.*

— It *appears* that he resists you, but in reality, he brings it on himself. He found a high-ranking bitch to experience what he experiences with her. As you can see, nothing is coincidental. It may *appear* to you that you are a bitch and he is a nice guy. "How did he wound up with me? What does he need me for?" you may ask. But let me tell you, he needs you very much.

— *Sometimes I ask him: "Why don't you order me around?"*

— And what does he say?

— *He doesn't say anything. He sits there with his lips tightly sealed.*

— He has not mastered the art of giving orders yet. That's the reason he is with you. He is learning about your art. Do you see how useful your "bitch" is?

— *When we argue, I always insist on my point of view. We fight all the time.*

— Is that when he screams "Bitch" again?

— *No, he never calls me that. The worst word he can use is "dummy."*

— So, he never uses the word "Bitch," ah?

— *No, he doesn't. But in our relationship, I am always in command.*

— You are fighting for leadership. Look at the army, where rank determines who is giving the orders. Every soldier strives to rise up the ranking order to be in command. A platoon cannot function without a commanding officer. It will be a herd. Someone must be in command.

— *By the way, I am not against him taking the throne. I understand he is a man. But he never shows any initiative.*

— Perhaps he is a woman?

— *His mom is very powerful. His dad plays a subservient role. I can't say that my husband is in the subservient position in relation to me, but the maternal program he inherited manifests itself strongly. My dad, who was very powerful, fight his, equally powerful mom. It happens all the time.*

— Exactly. Let's take a closer look at this situation. When he was a boy, his mom was in command. He grows up and he finds a woman with similar qualities.

— *I have absolutely no relationship with his mom, by the way. We cannot communicate. She had never accepted me.*

— **Because you are similar. She sees herself in you. Not accepting herself in you, she rejects you. The situations that happened in the family he grew up in and in the family, you grew up in, continue to play themselves out in your family now.**

Performing a role of the mother in command, you assign the role of subordinate father to him. That happens without any awareness; the script simply plays itself out. His paternal subprogram requires a strong maternal

subprogram, which gets projected onto you. **Take a closer look, conflicts that occurred in your family and in his family, are playing themselves out between two of you now.**

I have clarified the situation. Do you have any other questions? What else do you want *to see* here? If you don't have any other questions, we can stop here.

— I don't have any questions related to this topic now. I have to think this through. But, I have an unrelated question.

Based on the prior discussion, I understood that in order for me to start doing something three forces are necessary: active, passive, and neutralizing. The active force will help me to investigate myself. The passive force will manifest itself in my reluctance to investigate myself. What about the neutralizing force? What is it? What do I need to start this process?

— Personality is made of the opposite sides. We can call them positive and negative, or active and passive. We deal with different dualities, but all of them are opposite, i.e. dual. **For you to start to investigate these dualities, you must develop the Observer.** That's the third point. We are dealing with a triangle. At the bottom of this triangle, in two corners, lies a duality. At the top is the observer, which can investigate them. That's what I do. I investigate dualities of my personality. A "sleeping" man is submerged in the conflict of these dual sides; he cannot see anything else. He projects one of his sides onto someone and starts to fight. There is no investigation there.

The work we are doing is not known here yet. Self-investigation is an exclusive process in the reality of "sleeping" people. The only thing people experience here is the mechanical fight of their opposite sides.

— I got it. I need the observer who will observe different parts of my personality.

109

— Are you asking me how the investigator appears?

— *Yes.*

— Ah. Unfortunately, I cannot say anything with certainty here, because this process starts not in *this* world. It starts in *That* world. It is determined by our Supreme Aspects. I came here with this assignment inculcated in me.

— *Are you saying it is inculcated in the personal program?*

— Yes. It is inculcated in our personal program. In particular, it was inculcated in my program. I had to come to this point. And for my personage to come to this point, it was shaken from left to right and back so hard, that it came to become aware of itself.

Has it been inculcated in your personality and other personalities present here? How was it inculcated? Who inculcated it? I cannot answer these questions at present time.

— *What can stop one on this road of self-investigation? It looks like personal programs of many people were inculcated with a message to wake up from the sleep of illusions, but not many of us get far on this road. One man starts on this path and walks all the way, another stops a week later. What stops us? Is it fear? Is it laziness?*

— The ego-personality does not want to be seen. It doesn't want to see itself. It cannot see itself. It can only do one thing. It can see one of its sides from another, opposite side and condemn it. Let's say, you happen to be on one side and you condemn your opposite side. In the meantime, you don't understand that you condemn yourself, you think you condemn somebody else. Later, a change might occur—you will move to the side you used to condemn and start to condemn someone, who reflects your opposite side now.

That's the only thing that happens here: condemnation, followed by the feeling of guilt. Nothing else is available at the level of consciousness I call "sleep." When you start to observe

110

that, you will understand that the passion to stop the conflict comes out of the Supreme Aspect. How strong is this passion? You are the only one who can answer this question. My passion is very strong. Personality creates resistance to this passion; it doesn't want to open itself up. Personality fights for its survival. And this is not a common survival the way people understand it, in terms of money, status, etc. No. The meaning of survival here is different—it is a preservation of the ego-personality the way it is, i.e. in the sleeping state, in a state of conflict, in a state of condemnation and guilt. That's what survival means here. This survival wants to preserve condemnation and guilt. That's what creates the main resistance.

If the power of your observer, experimenter, Supreme Aspect is strong, you will slowly slough off this resistance, i.e. condemnation and feeling of guilt. This is a slow process. I do not know how long it will take you to complete it?

— *What about you? Do you still experience these feelings: condemnation and guilt?*

— Yes, they pop up here and there and prompt me to investigate: why, how, and for what reason did they appear now?

— **In my case, the feeling of guilt is enormous. I think it comes from my childhood. This feeling usually manifests itself in my traumatizing the left side of my body. I cut and burn myself almost daily. There is a deep feeling of guilt behind these injuries.**

— **So, you traumatize your left side—your feminine side. When we feel guilty, we attract punishment. Guilt demands punishment. When we feel guilty, we punish ourselves. Your inner woman is in a state of guilt, and she demands punishment.**

111

— *Yes, my inner woman feels guilty.*

— What exactly does she feel guilty about?

— *Perhaps there is more to it, but I think I feel guilty because I don't work. My husband works, but I don't make any money. It is hard for me …*

— But why do you feel guilty? You do not work now. That's a fact. How do you create a feeling of guilt out of this fact?

— *That's exactly what I don't understand.*

— Okay. **Every answer lies in your program.** Your personal program has been inculcated with a directive: those who don't work should feel guilty. Who, when, and how inculcated you with this directive?

— *My problem is I do not remember my childhood.*

— These things are hard to get to. You must dig deep. I repeat, this work is not an easy work. Imagine, you decided to run out of jail. You may spend years digging your way out of it. The door will not open immediately. Your questions are very important. They will point you in the right direction. They will work as a jackhammer.

— *What is the right way to formulate a question?*

— **You will need to learn to do that. You will need to learn to formulate and ask questions. You will never receive an answer to a question you never asked. If you get an answer, it will be an answer to a question you have asked. Moreover, it's the strength of your question that will determine the degree of your understanding of the answer you will receive. I am talking about questions related to your personal program. You will need to master the ability to pose these questions, keep them burning inside you, and track down the ways answers come. Next, you will need to pose new questions, and again track** down the ways the answers come. Your ability to pose questions is of the utmost importance in our work.

— *I need to learn to do that.*

— Yes, that's a skill you need to master. That's the key feature of our school. Other schools offer you techniques. We work with questions.

— *I tried many different techniques. They don't work.*

— And they will not work. People perform these techniques mechanically. They don't want to work on themselves. They don't want to understand themselves. They don't want to elevate the level of their consciousness. They want to take a magic pill that will resolve all their problems. These techniques will not help you elevate the level of your consciousness, which is what Quantum leap is about. Most people think some supreme force will pull them out of this reality. No. This Quantum Leap is different from any other Leap experienced by humanity. People will have to work and elevate the level of their consciousness on their own.

Many people think they can hide from Quantum Leap. They think they can wait it out and continue to live the way they lived. No, this will not be possible. You will need to transform yourself. That's what we do here. We work and transform the level of our consciousness. No one will do this work for us.

What does it mean to work on one's consciousness? Not many people understand that. People are expecting a messiah to come and tell them everything. That will not happen.

— *Thank you very much.*

— *During yesterday's meeting, I asked my soul to talk to you. I listened to your every seminar, and I noted that many participants asked the same question: "Who do I talk to? Do I talk to the personality or do I talk to the soul?" When I formulated my question yesterday, I wanted my soul to talk to you. When I started to talk, I felt something very unusual. I felt air moving, and then I saw you and your soul. I forgot about my question completely. It is only in the middle of our conversation that I realized what I was saying. I was very emotional. My soul is learning to speak.*

— It is learning to speak through your personality.

— *Yes. I saw how much love you give to every student. I feel grateful for that. I would like to ask you to excuse me if I said something wrong; I am learning. I felt the unconditional love I have never felt before. I felt happy and sad at the same time, "Where am I? What is happening to me?" Later, I realized this was my soul talking. Perhaps incoherently but my soul has started to talk. It was afraid and silent for so long.*

— This is great! I am grateful to you. What happened yesterday was very important for me and for everyone here. We are working with the intellectual center a lot. You have experienced a new and very important emotional state. Hold on to it. This state is very important. Everything we do here is done to feel this state. You need to feel it thoroughly.

— *I want to come to the state of acceptance we discussed yesterday. I want to experience the state of inner calmness I feel you are in during seminars, the state of unconditional acceptance. I want to come to this level of understanding and acceptance of myself and through this state accept everything that comes into my life with gratitude. I want to thank you.*

— Thank you.

— *On my way home yesterday, I saw a dead dog. It was a big, grey dog. It was tied to a fence head down. Blood was dripping from its neck. An old, rusty grill was standing next to it. Somebody was getting ready to skin and cook this dog.*

When I get home, every single light in the house is on. My dad is there. It's my younger brother's birthday. Dad doesn't live with us. We seldom talk. Mom lives in Europe. My brother gets up and shows me a new gun—dad's present. I get angry and I express my anger: "What's

114

going on?! Why is light on everywhere?" I have told him many times to turn off the lights where he doesn't need it. We need to cut down our energy bill.

I observe myself, and I see myself getting angry. He gets upset, and he tells me that I upset him. I start to apologize. I ask him to show me the gifts he received. I asked him about his day. I hug him. He is still upset. I am not on speaking terms with dad. We fight all the time. Dad gets up and walks out. My brother threatens to shoot me. I think of running out. The gun he has in his hands is not a real gun, but he can hurt me. I continue to observe myself and the situation that unfolds. My brother gets hysterical. His face gets red in color. He spits at me and runs out of the house. He runs after dad and complains to him. Dad returns saying, "I had enough of this. I will beat the crap out of you."

I just stand there. I don't know what to do. I feel fear. I am afraid for my body. I realize I need to do something to get out of this mess. I explain to dad what I was trying to do. I explain to him that I want all of us to live in peace. He feels I am sincere. He calms down and leaves.

I observe another fear. Now, I am afraid of him coming back to beat me. I don't feel I am out of the woods yet. I am afraid of him screaming at me. He used to scream at me so loudly, my ears were hurting for days.

I cannot sleep because of this fear. I get out of the house. I call my girlfriend. I don't know what to do. She tells me to go back and to hug my brother. She advises me to express my feelings to him. She explains that he didn't receive love the same way me, my father, and my mother didn't receive it. She advises me to visit my dad and to express my love to him, too. I go back into the house. I hug and kiss my brother. Then, I go to dad's place. I tell him I love him. We go back home, and we talk quietly until midnight.

— Wow! That's some story. The dead dog was not a coincidence.

— *Yes, both of us—my dad and me—are dead in this life scenario. We are big. We are gray. And we are dead.*

— Two key moments that you have brought up are the dead dog and the light. You started to scream: "Why is light on everywhere?" Our discussions bring light into the darkness of our inner house. For you, to have light in every room of your house is too expensive. You are afraid you are not going to survive.

— *Yes.*

— The physical reality reflects what happens to us and manifests itself in signs. I am glad you could switch to another side. If you were to continue to move in the direction of the war, you would have skinned and eaten each other.

— *I wanted to run away and hide somewhere. I am glad I was able to talk to dad.*

— You need to manifest love which everyone here is short on. None of us received enough love. People are angry with each other because of it. They try to avenge themselves. Instead of giving each other love, people deprive themselves of it even more. There is nothing but anger, hatred, and aggression around us. I am glad you could feel and share your love.

How can you find whether you have unconditional love in you or not if you don't manifest it? You need to manifest it to find whether it is in you or not. You try to take it from others, but they don't have it. They cannot give you anything but anger. It is habitual for us to scream, spit, and beat each other for not being loved, right?

— *Yes. One of my parts is active. It observes itself and it receives answers. Another part says, "Why do we need so much light? It is way too expensive."*

— Exactly. You need to observe all that. It was not easy to observe the states you experienced yesterday, but you did it.

That's what it means to accumulate awareness. It needs to be accumulated.

— *Yes, I need to accumulate it. Otherwise, it will be the end of me.*

— Sometimes, one can start a fire with one match. Perhaps what you have experienced yesterday is enough to start the fire of your awareness. One man cannot even light a match. Another man's match is burning, but he cannot start a fire. The match of the third one has started a small fire. The fourth man's fire is burning; he throws firewood into it. The situations you observe and the dualities you investigate and become aware of are the firewood you need for your fire to burn. This fire must always be maintained. You have started a fire, You need to feed it. To do that, you need to attend our seminars and webinars. Otherwise, your fire will burn out soon. Remember, dualities are the firewood you need for your fire to burn.

— *Thank you very much.*

— *I have noticed I punish myself. I physically hurt myself. I was walking down a busy street yesterday when a thought pop into my head: "I cannot see my dualities. I want people who see them to hurt me so I can see them." It was immediately followed by an afterthought: "This is so stupid. There should be another way." As soon as I acknowledged these thoughts, a tough looking young man approached me. He told me he needed money to buy gas. A minute later his facial expression changed, he grabbed my arm, and said: "Give me your wallet!" I realized I was about to be beaten and robbed. Just a minute ago I entertained a thought about being hurt, and someone, who was about to hurt me instantly materialized out of thin air. It's funny, as soon as I want to hurt or punish myself, someone is always ready to come to my service.*

— Exactly. When you feel guilty, you attract oppressors who will punish you. The level of guilt each one of us carries is enormous. We do not see that. Then, we get surprised when so-called "bastards" beat and rob us in broad daylight. But, we attract them ourselves. Until we see how and why we attract these oppressors, we will continue to attract them.

— *Thank you.*

— *I read in one of your books that a man gets formed in solitude. Can you elaborate on this topic, please?*

— I cannot recall the context of the book you read, but let me explain it. A man's task is to survive on his own. A woman's task is to survive on the account of her man. So, it's important for a woman to become very sensitive. A woman should feel her man very well. She must understand what he needs very well. So from the get-go, a woman is oriented on her man— her survival depends on him.

A man survives on his own. He must feel solitude because he is on his own. However, his opposite side is connected to a woman. He is attracted to a woman, who feels what he needs.

— *Thank you. Let me ask you another question. We frequently read and hear people on TV say, "Life is a game." Quite frequently, it is successful people who say that. Can a paralyzed man say that? I have never heard a paralyzed man say that. Is there pride there?*

— We are dealing with different shades and connotations of words. I frequently use the word "game" to mean a show, a script, or a gym, but many people carry a different notion when they use the word game—something not very serious, something like game children play on a school playground. Kids play in a sandbox—their game is not serious. But the game politicians play is serious; the lives of many people depend on their game. That's why politicians don't use the word "game." This word is being used in connection with "a playful mood." The more serious the situation is, the less people are inclined to use the word "game." If you were to tell a disabled man that he is *playing* a disabled man, he would not be happy to hear that. The more serious a people's situation is, the less they are inclined to call it a game.

Nevertheless, we are dealing with a game. This point of view comes from a higher level of consciousness, which sees us as personages, playing a game in a kindergarten sandbox. Yes, some kids play rough here. Yes, fights and wars do occur here. It appears to us, we can kill and main each other, but from the standpoint of a higher level of consciousness, from *over there*, whatever happens *here* is a game, a virtual game.

— Do we take what happens to us here so seriously because we do not remember our Supreme Aspects?

— Yes, you take yourself so seriously because you do not see yourself as Supreme Aspects. Why can I say what I say? I can say what I say because I say it out of my Supreme Aspect. When I talk to people submerged in a sleeping mode of consciousness, they often don't understand what I say. Some of them get angry with me. They cannot connect what I say with the way things should be according to their notions.

We are dealing with a Soul and its personage here. A Soul is much more important than a personage. We are dealing with two types of perception—the perception of the Supreme aspect, who sees things from *There* and perception of the personage, who is *here*—they frequently do not see things eye to eye.

— I would like to ask you one more question. When while asleep we see dreams at night, we are not aware of ourselves. Irrespective of how unreal the events in our dreams may appear from the point of view of our daily life, we take the events that occur in them seriously. On awakening, we think, "What kind of a gibberish was that?" But while asleep, we take whatever happens in our dreams seriously. Many people practice aware dreaming nowadays. My intention is to become aware of myself in my dreams. If I achieve that and start to perceive my dreams as a game, I

will not perceive them with such a grave seriousness anymore. I will have an opportunity to investigate these dreams. Am I right?

— Yes, but which dream do you consider to be your main dream? The subject of aware dreaming was brought up to our seminars many times. Let me ask you a question: "Why are you so interested in your dreams? Why don't you concentrate on your main dream—the dream you take to be your reality?" We are presently submerged in a dream. How do you react to this dream? This in the main dream I am in; all other dreams I have while asleep at night are pointers that help me to figure out what's going on in my main dream, i.e. in my life.

This is very important to understand. When you realize what your main dream is, you start to apply effort to wake up in it. When you start to do that, everything and everyone around you starts to help you to do that. I remember things that happen in my dreams, and I treat them as prompts that help me to do something or not to do something in my day life, i.e. in my main dream.

— *Thank you.*

— *My personality doesn't allow me to understand everything you say. I cannot pay full attention to what you say now. I don't have enough energy to walk down the path of self-investigation.*

I want to share with a group what happened yesterday. After the seminar, I experienced a state of total acceptance. I accepted things I could not accept for many years. I heard and felt many of my screaming parts. I am still in pain. I didn't see these parts before. I suppressed them. I didn't understand they belonged to me. I cannot stop crying.

— **This is good. Keep crying. Do not hold anything in.**

— *I cannot hold it anymore.*

— You don't need to hold anything inside anymore. Allow the energy that was confined in you to come out now.

— I have been to your seminars before. I was always able to understand what you say. Something is off today. I cannot understand anything you say.

— You were able to understand things mentally. Now, you are dealing with feelings that force themselves into your heart. This is the prison where the pain is located. Suddenly, all your prisoners-feelings start to come out.

Imagine a concentration camp. Its prisoners have spent years behind bars. They can barely walk. Suddenly, they see the doors open. Full of fear, they wander outside. They are afraid to be beaten by those who are there to liberate them. That's the state of your prisoners-parts. Of course, they will cry from happiness. Of course, they will cry from pain.

That's what every human being experiencing now. I understand, and I respect you and what happens to you. Your perception has shifted from intellectual to emotional. This is a very important shift. Allow this energy to come out. That's the way it comes out: with pain, tears, and shakes.

— I don't understand what is going on, but I want to thank you for your support.

— Allow yourself to manifest everything that comes out of you. Do not ask any questions. Allow yourself to experience the state you are in.

— Thank you.

— I can't stop crying, too.

— It's okay. Do not hide your tears. Do not condemn yourself for them. Allow yourself to manifest every feeling that tries to come out.

— I am sorry.

— You are not guilty of anything.

— I have been dating a young man for two years. We were supposed to be at the City Hall today, but instead, I am here, talking to you.

121

Yesterday, we got into an argument and broke up. I moved to my parents'
house last night. He doesn't accept my parents. He thinks they are
responsible for my being in debt. Every credit card I have is maxed out. I
spend all my salary to pay the interest. He has been paying my debts while
we were dating. I cannot accept the fact that he doesn't accept my parents.
Yesterday, I gave him an ultimatum. I told him that unless he comes to
my parents, I will break up with him. He didn't show up. How can I
understand this part of my personal program?

— He doesn't accept your parents, and you gave him an
ultimatum: "If you don't come to my parents, I will leave you."
**Now, recall the axiom I keep returning you to: There are
no other people here—only you, reflected in different
mirrors.**

So, he reflects you what you ask of him. Look, along with
the part that accepts your parents, you have the opposite part,
the part that doesn't accept them. He reflects you this part.
This is your fight, your inner fight. These two parts do not want
to talk to each other.

Tell us why you don't accept your parents. This is not bad.
When you start to understand the dual nature of your
personality, i.e. it's being composed of the opposite sides, you
start to understand both sides; you start to understand that all
of them are you.

It is precisely your not accepting your part, which we can
call "not acceptance of my parents," in yourself, that causes
you and your boyfriend to repel each other. This happens
inside you.

— *I understand that all these problems are in me. Do I have to accept*
my parents the way they are?

— First, you need to understand what is it that you do not
accept in them. Otherwise, you will not have anything to
accept. Accept everything. Then, one part of you, the accepting

part, will tell you to accept everything, another part, the part you don't even want to listen to, will tell you what exactly it doesn't want to accept. Then, we can review your dilemma. Otherwise, I don't know what to review.

— *Perhaps we need to review my financial situation?*

— Of course. Every financial problem you encounter is an assignment. When a problem appears, you start to think: "Why do I have to deal with this problem?" You try to get rid of this problem as soon as you can. But this problem has been given to you to solve. I find these assignments interesting; I like solving them. **You need to start seeing your problems as your assignments.** Every problem is an assignment; you are the one who is interested in solving these assignments. I help you solve these, as we can see, not so easy to solve assignments. People hurt, rape, and kill each other in this reality. Those are our assignments. Let's solve them with interest.

— *I have accepted the fact that there is no relationship between my boyfriend and my parents. I could not accept it before.*

— You have accepted this, but you did that grinding your teeth. That's not what I asked you to do. For me, to accept is to investigate. While investigating something, you start to understand what you need to accept, instead of just pronouncing the word "accept."

Your enemy is standing across from you. He is cursing you. He is spitting at you. Suddenly, a priest shows up and tells you: "Accept your enemy!" Will you fill up with love instantly and accept him?

That's not what I invite you to do. I say: "Let's look deep and investigate. What don't you accept?" Tell us exactly what you do not accept. That will allow you to see what you need to accept and guide you how to do that.

— I do not accept my parents, because they have tried to start a business a few times, but they were never successful. To tell you the truth, I have accepted that.

— No. As the rest of the people who come here, you are in too much of a hurry. You just found out there is such a thing as acceptance, and you immediately scream: "I accept everything!" Do not hurry. What exactly irritates you in them? Discuss everything that irritates you in them in minute details and discuss it with pleasure. Share the given conditions of your assignment with us. I will not think bad of you on the account of your assignment. But you consider yourself to be bad because of it, and as a result, you do not want to tell us about it. Am I right?

— Yes.

— Share the given conditions of your assignment with us, and we will help you to solve it. If you think your assignment is bad, you will not want to talk about it. If you don't talk about it, you will not be able to solve it. Do you understand?

— I am irritated by the fact that my parents don't have any money. They are still renting an apartment. At the same time, I am in the same shoes. I work, but I am not happy with my salary. I wish I was paid more.

— You are irritated because your parents don't have money. Let's think this through. Your parents don't have money. This is a fact. This is just a fact. But you condemn them for creating a situation where they don't have money. Let's talk about that.

— I don't condemn anymore.

— This is not true. I don't believe you. You continue to hide the given conditions of your assignment. Let me try again. I am a seasoned self-investigator. I am interested in every assignment, but you hide your assignment from me. I keep asking you the same question: what are the given conditions of your assignment? If you are not ready to discuss these conditions, we will not discuss them. This is my approach.

— *So, what do I do with my boyfriend?*

— You will not figure out what to do with your boyfriend until you solve your assignment. This is your assignment. Do you understand that? You have not said anything about the given conditions of your assignment yet. You do not even know what you need to find. You are not ready to start working on this assignment yet.

— *I am ready. I think I said everything to you.*

— No, you have not said anything yet. You have said that you don't like the fact that your parents don't have any money. Then, you mentioned that your situation is similar. Now, I ask you: "Are you irritated by the fact that your parents, together and separately, do not have money? What is it about them that prevents them from having money?"

— *I am irritated because time passes but the situation doesn't change.*

— It will not *change*. Why would it *change*?

— *They work and they try their best, but they are not successful.*

— So, they work, but they are not successful. Perhaps, they are not working in the right direction. Why don't you try to determine the reason they don't have any money? Why does it happen that they work but don't have the money? What is the reason for that?

— *I don't know. Perhaps, they don't work in the right direction. Which direction should they work in? That's not easy to determine either.*

— But look, you are stuck in the same situation yourself. That's why I recommend you investigate your parents' situation. By using this route, you will be able to sort out your own situation. Unless you sort out your parents' situation, you will not be able to sort out your own situation. You will keep doing what they do. You are doing that already. That's what investigation is all about. You are facing the dead end now. You cannot do anything. You repeat what you have done; it only exacerbates the situation. Am I right?

— *Yes.*

— Therefore, we need to look at the situation from another angle, as everything you do now just makes the situation worst. You come up with a question, to which I give you my self-investigator vision. You don't understand my approach, and you ask me again: "What do I do?" I keep telling you what to do. You need to sort out the given conditions of your assignment because unless you sort them out, you will not be able to do anything. The situation will only get worst and worst.

The situation that happens in your parents' life arises in your life too, because the program was transmitted to you. These situations bring people whose personalities want to be rich, want to have men or women next to them, want not to be insulted or thrown out of their apartments here, to the place where they can expand the level of their consciousness. But your personality doesn't want to do that. That's the basic contradiction. What I discuss here can help you to become aware of what your soul wants. You, on the other hand, are interested in what your ego wants. But your ego, striving toward what it wants, came to a dead-end. The only way to untangle this problem is to self-investigate.

Your personality may say that it doesn't want any investigation. It may say it just needs some help to regulate the relationship with a boyfriend and to have some money. I don't know what is going to happen in your case. I don't impose anything on you. I am just showing you what I see. I don't know what you will do with this information.

This is a continuation of our conversation on what a soul needs and what an ego-personality needs. We can see a wide discrepancy here. The ego-personality doesn't want to understand that it is the Soul's messenger. The soul has sent it here. The soul has its own intention on its agent being here. The ego-personality says: "What is a soul? There is no such thing as the Soul. I need to survive. I want to eat well and to sleep well. I want to have money in my pocket and boyfriend by my side." However, it finds itself short of money and lacking a boyfriend. It experiences a tragedy and it comes here crying, "Pint help me!"

But it is only through these tragedies, as you will see later, that substance of consciousness can be changed. This change in the substance of consciousness is why we are here, in this world.

I am not a psychotherapist. I am not here to give you directions. I will not tell you what to say to your boyfriend or to your parents. That will only obstruct your understanding of the situation. Many people don't understand why they are here. They will continue to do what they do until they understand what the situation they are in offers them. Our process is not fast. I don't hurry you, but unless you understand the given conditions of your assignment, you will not be able to solve it. That's how I see the situation. If you also see it this way, you must start to sort out these conditions. That's what we do here.

— *Thank you.*

— *I am not sure whether we should address my question now or later. I felt horrible when the case of the dead dog was discussed. What does this cruel relationship with animals show us? Why do we see these situations?*

— Do you think people are cruel to animals only? Don't you see how cruel people are to each other?

— *I will only speak about myself. For some reason, I react strongly when I see people treating animals harshly.*

— It tells us how you react to being treated harshly yourself. **The external world always reflects what is inside us.** The external world provides us with signs that help us conduct self-investigation. So, you are very sensitive to cruelty. Am I right?

— *Yes, I am.*

— In the end, everything boils down to you and you alone. **Irrespective of the topic you discuss or who you speak of or to, you always speak about yourself.** So, the question of cruelty interests you.

— *I am not sure I understand you. I don't feel people are cruel to me. Does it mean I project the cruelty I feel I am exposed to onto the animals?*

— Exactly. That's the way people live in a sleeping state of consciousness. They think they pity a sick child or a legless beggar on a street corner. They think they pity a dying man. In reality, they don't pity these people—they pity themselves.

— *But I don't feel pity. I feel pain. I think I can separate between these feelings.*

— Okay, the pain it is then. What exactly concerns you in these situations? It is not the pleasure that you experience when you witness these situations. Let's say, you see a dog being beaten. You don't encourage the guy beating the dog to beat it harder. You don't have a smile on your face. No. Something else happens in your case. What is it?

— *I think the duality I manifest in this situation is "loyalty— betrayal." Animals trust us. They are part of the planet. They are part of us. But we kill them.*

— Great. Now, recall and explore similar situations you have experienced in your life. Recall a situation where you were loyal to someone and beaten in return.

— *I have experienced situations like that a few times.*

— Of course, you did. And that is what is bothering you. But you don't speak of these situations directly, you project them on animals. I keep explaining to you again and again that regardless of the topic a human being is talking about, he is always talking about himself. I invite you to talk about yourself. When you do that, we will be able to see this duality in you. We need to bring this hurting part of you to the surface. We need to see the duality. We will not get anywhere if we continue to talk about dogs, cats, and rabbits.

— *I got it. I need to find this duality inside myself. When I find it, I will see how this situation relates to me.*

— You will see what's behind this situation. Our main task is to see the reason that causes us to experience inner conflict. What happens in the external world happens not because it is bad, but because our inner parts are in conflict. The external world reflects this conflict. The situation you brought up and the situations brought up by other students confirm that. The roots of this conflict and of every negative phenomenon you see around you are inside you.

You need to modify your inner world. Then, these situations will stop to recur. When you do that, the external world will reflect a different picture to you. The external world is a mirror. When an ugly man gets in front of it, it reflects an ugly man. When a handsome man gets in front of it, it reflects a handsome man. A mirror simply reflects the object that shows up in front of it. What does this mirror show you? It shows you yourself. "What's going on? What is this?" you scream seeing your own reflection. You are seeing yourself! If you want to see a different picture in the mirror of the external world, you need to transform yourself.

— *I see. So, I don't accept my own cruelty. I don't accept the fact that I cheat and betray others.*

— Yes. You think those are bad qualities. You insist you do not have these qualities in you. "I am not cruel! I do not betray people!" The pride of your personality is built upon these statements. Your personality says: "I am better than those who betray! I am better than those who are cruel!" Every time you see someone who you appraise to be cruel or hear of someone betraying someone, you feel you are better than them. You feel good. You feel like you are a saint. You feel important. That's your gain. That's the profit your personality gets. That's why you attract and see these situations repeatedly.

— *What if I don't feel that I am better than these people?*

— It means you do not allow yourself to feel, either. Do you see the depth of your sleep?

We don't understand what is going on. We are submerged in fear, but when we ask a man what he is afraid of, he says he is not afraid of anything. He can add: "It is Pint who is crazy. He is talking about fear all day long. His place is in a nut house. I am normal. I am okay." I've heard this response many times. That's a very high level of self-forgetfulness. These mechanisms are known to me. You will not be able to fool me in this respect.

— *I did not try to fool you. I truly want to figure out this situation; it causes me unbearable suffering.*

— This suffering is connected to the fact that one of your sides says: "I am not a traitor. I am not cruel." Do you see the mechanism I keep showing you all the time? I keep talking about it every day: our personality is dual.

— *Yes, I understand.*

— So, you have two parts. You need to define them. How will you call them?

— *Can I call them: empathetic and cruel?*

— Don't ask me. You need to learn to define them on your own. There is cruelty, and there is something that is opposite to it. What is it?

— *Empathy?*

— Empathy or pity?

— *Empathy.*

— Okay. What is the difference between empathy and pity?

— *I think, when one feels empathy, one tries to do something about the situation.*

— What do you do when you see cruelty?

— *I get involved and I try to prevent it whenever I can.*

— How do you get involved?

— *I try to help. I try to talk to the one who is cruel.*

— Okay. Let's be specific. Describe the last situation when you witnessed cruelty and tell us how you got involved in it.

— *There is an old house next to our house. It was remodeled last winter. Every morning, I would see a big dog tied up to its porch. Someone was leaving this dog outside for the whole day. It was a very cold winter. Finally, I got a hold of the owner and I explained to him that this was cruel to the dog. We had a nice conversation. He heard me.*

— I don't see a conflict in this situation. You will have to recall a more conflicting situation.

— *The situations I deal with do not appear to concern me directly. For example, the situation that one of the students brought up earlier, the story of the dead dog that was hanged on the fence didn't concern me directly. I didn't witness it. It happened far away from me. Nevertheless, I felt pain.*

— Okay. This shows the level of your understanding of yourself. You maintain a very long distance with yourself, and because of it, it is very difficult for you to apply this situation to yourself and to see your inner conflict. You walk around the bush so to speak. Until you dive deeper into yourself, this pain will only get worst. **Pain is an indicator.** Without this pain, you will not pay attention to these situations, you will not investigate these situations, i.e. you will not investigate yourself. You are keeping your distance, you do not want to enter these painful situations. You are not ready to see these cruel men and these dead, hanged dogs in yourself.

— *How did you come to this conclusion? How can you say that I am not ready?*

— I came to this conclusion because you are not answering the question I ask you. I invite you to see your inner dualities, but the cases you bring to the table are weak, "I spoke to him and he heard me." The appearance is being created that everything is okay with you. But if everything is okay, where does pain come from?

A patient comes to a doctor and says: "I am hurting bad!" The doctor says: "Disrobe. Let's look at you." The patient replies: "No, I will not get undressed. You don't need to examine me. Let's just talk." The doctor raises his eyebrows: "But I need to examine you."

— *I don't understand why I keep avoiding your questions. Perhaps you are right. Perhaps I am not ready to discuss this part of me yet.*

— Yes, you are not ripe yet. You cannot jump here.

— *Thank you.*

— Thank you.

— *I came to your seminar in 2002 after reading your book "Love— Hate." You signed it for me. You wrote on the cover, "Accept your inner man!" Prior to reading your books, I was totally dependent on my husband. This dependency turned into severe conflict and I left him. I am free of this dependency now—I live alone. But what if I were to become dependent on a man again? Will the part that was active while I was living with my ex-husband pop up again and start to reject dependency?*

— This is a great question. You have said you were dependent on your husband. Then, you separated, and now it *appears* to you that you are independent. It *appears* to be so. We live in the world where everything *appears* to us. First, it *appeared* to you that you were dependent on him. Then, it *appeared* to you that by leaving a man, you were dependent on, you became independent. I want to emphasize that these two things just *appeared* to you. Neither one of these *appearances* is real. Why?

There are a woman and a man inside each human being. You, for example, have a physical body of a woman, but it doesn't mean you don't have an inner man. This inner pair is always inside you. You are this pair. Therefore, when you get close to a man, he starts to reflect your inner man. You started to experience a conflict between your man and your woman, which manifested itself in the external situations. Then, these situations started to escalate, and you left your external man. It *appears* to you that everything has been resolved. Nothing has been resolved. The conflict between your inner man and your inner woman continues. Irrespective, whether you physically have a man next to you or not, the conflict continues.

Where does your stress or excitation come from? It arises out of a conflict between your inner man and your inner woman. This excitation is the indicator that this assignment has not been solved. The most important thing I want you to understand is that when you leave a man, your dependency doesn't leave you; it continues as an attribute of the relationship of your inner "man—woman" pair.

— *So, what do I need to do?*

— If you were to come to a witch or a wizard, they would have told you what to do.

133

— *I have been everywhere. You are my last hope.*

— This last hope keeps telling you: "Conduct self-investigation!" Use my seminars, webinars, and books. They will show you what self-investigation is about. However, people keep asking: "Pint, what do I do now?" What do you expect from me? Do you expect a prescription?

— *No.*

— That's what people expect. They go to a doctor, and the doctor prescribes them some medicine. They take this medicine, and their pain diminishes. Then, it resurfaces. I am not a doctor. I tell you: "Investigate yourself! Get to know yourself!" You don't understand why you are here, on Earth. Your assignment is not to have a nice, handsome, rich man next to you. Your assignment is not to be comfortable on this planetary trip. All of this is temporary. You will not take anything with you to the grave. Why did we come here? How do you answer this question? Do you even ask this question?

— *I need love.*

— So, you came here for God to give you love. You didn't have enough love where you came from. Why did God send you to this world? Why did God send you to the world where love is so strange? Why did God send you to the world where people oppress and hurt each other? Why did God send you to the world where people beat animals? Do you really think you came here in search of love? It would be like you coming to a grocery store looking for a cat. You walk around the produce department, thinking: "What's wrong? Where are all the cats?"

People do not even ask these questions. It *appears* to them that they came here to experience love. They keep praying:

134

"God, give us love!" God gives them love. They look up, and they ask: "What is this? Is this love?"

You don't understand why you came here. Until you understand that, you will continue to have this surprised expression on your face: "Where am I?"

— *I got it. Thank you.*

— You are welcome.

— *I have been practicing self-investigation for two years now, but I still cannot figure out my main conflict. Only recently I understood how important your seminars are and how important it is for me to be here.*

— Yes, you can read a hundred books on the subject of driving a car, and never get behind the wheel. Let's say you have read fifty books on the topic. You still don't know how to drive a car, because you have never driven one. That's the situation you are in. Please, ask your question.

— *I have read many esoteric books prior to discovering your website. After reading your books, I become interested in self-investigation. I started to investigate myself because I felt physically unwell. I asked a question: "Where do diseases and negative physical states come from?" I was not interested in the reasons people break their legs or develop pneumonia. No. I was interested in the state of the organism I call fatigue. I felt as if I was ninety years old. I was tired and dizzy all the time. I could barely get out of bed. No one could tell what was wrong with me. I was examined by the best doctors. All of them insisted I was healthy, but I felt horrible. My question is: "How did I come to this state?" I have been working on this question for many years now, but I still cannot figure this out.*

— Okay. Let's review your situation. Our body contains indicators which are related to physical and emotional spheres. They point toward our not understanding of ourselves. Our not understanding of ourselves leads to the disbalance in our personal structure. The greater our not understanding of ourselves is, the more severe this disbalance gets.

Unresolved disbalance in the intellectual sphere spills into the emotional sphere. If it cannot be processed on that level, it spills into and starts to manifest itself in the physical body. Diseases, traumas, accidents, and other negative physical states are the indicators that point out to this disbalance. This fatigue of yours is the indicator of your not understanding of yourself. You can go to a doctor. Most likely he will give you medicine, which will only muffle your symptoms and send you to a deeper sleep. When not understanding the reasons behind your symptoms you try to alleviate them, you exacerbate the state of your disbalance. If this disbalance manifests itself on the emotional center, you get more anxious and depressed. Contemporary medicine has invented antidepressants. After taking these pills, you feel even worst. The physical state you are in points to a certain disbalance in your personality. Eventually, everything points to this disbalance. Irrespective of what you investigate, you will always come down to this disbalance. Every negative state you experience points to disbalance in your personality. To resolve this fatigue, you need to investigate your personality.

— *I understand that. I am scared. I have a difficult time expressing what I want to express. My main problem is self-humiliation. How is it connected to my being fatigued?*

— One part of you is a victim, another—an oppressor. Both parts were inculcated into your personal program by your parents.

— *I have figured that out on my own. I am strongly connected to my mom.*

— If you were to figure that out, we would have a different conversation now.

— *I got stuck somewhere along the line. I cannot see any further. I have been sulking in this not understanding for more than a year.*

— Are you ready to see it? If you are ready, you need to start talking about it. Personality doesn't want to talk about most intimate things. The most intimate thing for every personality is the pain it experiences. It says: "This is my pain. Mine! Don't touch it." How do I discuss Pint with you? I always discuss him in the third person. Who is it that talks to you about Pint? Can you talk about your personality in the third person?

It is not easy to start to dismount one's personality. Personality doesn't want to reveal itself. It wants to survive the way it is. It thinks: "If I say something now, it will be used against me."

— *I feel I am ready to talk, but the minute I open my mouth all my thoughts disappear.*

— That's right. That's how personality defends itself. "I am ready to talk, but I don't know what to say."

— *That's what I am dealing with.*

— It defends itself a thousand ways.

— *Prior to our conversation, I had some thoughts in my head. They are all gone now.*

— You sort of asked a question, and you need to continue the dialogue, but suddenly another level of personality defense pops up: I don't have any thoughts in my head, I don't know what to say. Behind this level of defense is another one. That's the way ego-personality is structured: defense on top of a defense.

— *Is this about my inner impulse to understand myself? Perhaps this impulse is not strong enough? I am so tired of this game.*

— If you are tired of this game, you have to start to unravel this defense system. The impulse of your personality to defend itself and to hide your program is stronger than the impulse of your Supreme Aspect to unveil your program. That's what we are dealing with.

— *Yes, I am hanging in the middle of this stalemate.*

— That's correct. You cannot bypass this defense system.

— *I understand that mentally.*

— That's right. You understand that on the intellectual level, but on the emotional level, you do not accept that. I know these programs very well. That's my job. I hack human programs. I started by hacking and opening my own program. By doing that, I have acquired the skills I need to see other programs. You investigate a drop of water, and you wind up understanding the structure of the entire ocean.

So, you got stuck. You cannot move forward. Unfortunately, I cannot help you here, it is your choice. I am not going to force myself into your program.

— *I have felt this self-humiliation since childhood. It was difficult for me to see it. It took me a while to figure out how it works. I project this self-humiliation on other people. I look at myself through the eyes of other people.*

— You don't look at yourself through the eyes of some hypothetical other people. You look at yourself through the eyes of your mother and father. Look at the way this self-humiliation manifests itself in the relationship of your parents. Who humiliates whom there? Does your father humiliate your mother or is it your mother who humiliates your father?

— *My situation is analogous to my dad's situation. He has a similar program. My mom is an oppressor at home. He does everything she wants him to do. She manipulates him by making him feel guilty.*

— Okay. So, you need to see how your mother controls your dad. What kind of mechanisms does she use to make him do what she wants him to do? That will help you to open the part of your program you have called self-humiliation.

138

— *He doesn't like himself, too. He hates himself.*

— No human being likes himself here.

— *Wait a minute. Wait a minute. I thought one can self-identify with a good side or with a bad side. Usually, people self-identify with a good side—handsome, smart—and feel proud. When one self-identifies with a bad side—ugly, stupid—one humiliates himself. Is there pride associated with being in a bad side too?*

— Of course. You are talking about the same pride. Someone says: "I am the smartest here! I am the prettiest here!" And she swells up with pride on the account of being the smartest and the prettiest. You took the opposite side, "I am the ugliest! I am the stupidest!" That's how you nourish your pride. Until you understand the profit your personality extracts out of this situation, you will not understand your program. That's what you need to do. It *appears* to you that self-humiliation is bad. That's not true. It is the opposite side of aggrandizement. Some people move up, others move down, but as paradoxical as it may seem, the level of satisfaction we are dealing with here is the same. What kind of satisfaction does self-humiliation offer? It is the same satisfaction one gets from praising oneself.

— *I don't allow myself to manifest my states. I am all fear. I have been sitting at my house for thirty years. My life is black and white. I have never been with a woman. I can't even approach a woman. I don't allow myself to be near women.*

— Your personal program contains a silent subprogram that you are not even aware of: "Do not get close to a woman." This subprogram was inculcated in you, but you are not aware of it. When a subject shows up, which this subprogram should eliminate, it eliminates it. You work in Information Technology. You should find your program interesting to investigate.

— *I see my program, but I cannot understand myself.*

— Okay. Imagine, you have encountered a new program. You are interested in it. You want to get to know it well and you want to use it. You wake up next morning, and you feel you hate this new program with a passion. You tell this program: "Go to hell!" You throw away the manual that describes how it operates. Will you be able to understand, install, and use it? No. This self-humiliation is part of your program. But you don't even want to look in the direction of your program. You rebuke it. Why do you rebuke it so hard? If you do that, you cannot investigate it. Start to feel that this subprogram is your subprogram. Become interested in it. You came to this world and you asked for this program to be installed in you so you can understand it. You will not be able to understand it if you continue to rebuke it.

— *Yes, you have said it before, "What you don't accept, you can't investigate."*

— Start to feel the pleasure these states offer. You do experience pleasure from being humiliated, don't you? You do experience pleasure from being alone, don't you?

— *Yes, I do. I used to wallow in self-pity before. When I observe myself doing it now, I detach, and I ask myself: "Why do you wallow in it again?"*

— You have to move from wallowing in self-pity toward investigating it. You could not do it before, because you had to experience this energy. You have experienced it plenty. You can start to investigate it now. Acknowledge that you have been getting pleasure from wallowing in self-pity and start to review the mechanisms you have been using to create this pleasure by feeling self-pity and loneliness. Get interested in these states. Investigate them as good, positive states. You came here with this assignment. Your soul longs for it.

Start to investigate positive aspects of these states, and their mechanisms will open similarly to a manual of a new computer program. If you say, "This book stinks" and throw it away, you cannot read it. If you see that a book is interesting, you start to read it. So, start to look at your self-humiliation as an interesting and exciting topic your soul is interested in. Otherwise, you would not have work on this topic for so long.

— *I will have to overcome a powerful force of inertia. I have identified so strongly with the state of fatigue, I don't want to do anything.*

— I understand that.

— *I feel I am sitting in a wetland. It is horrible.*

— You must act. Otherwise, you will only feel worse. To start feeling a different state, you need to start doing something. Your opposite side resists that; it wants to experience this heavy physical state. It gets pleasure out of it. It says: "I am not just an old man. I am a very old man."

— *You are right. This state of fatigue is getting worse and worse.*

— It will continue to get worse and worse. Imagine a train. It was running in one direction for many years. It needs to start moving in the opposite direction now. To do that, it has to start to slow down first. Then, it will start to move in the opposite direction. Of course, it is not easy. You are in a similar situation. You must start moving in the opposite direction. To do that, you will need to apply effort in the opposite direction. Right now, you are applying effort to feel like an old man, and as we can see, you are succeeding in doing that.

— *That's my physical state. I look like a young man, but my physical state ...*

— Yes, this is a paradox. I want to repeat what I said. You need to redirect your effort. It seems to you that you are lazy. You are not lazy. You are actively moving in the direction of aging. You apply strong effort in the direction of aging. You need to change the direction of your effort. That's the only way to correct your disbalance, which at present time is very strong.

— *Thank you. I do feel that I need to act.*

— Thank you.

— *Today's webinar raised a storm of feelings in me. I have shed a few tears listening to my fellow students. I observed and investigated my own program while they were talking.*

When I asked you a question last time, I was terribly scared. I was afraid to say something wrong. I was very rigid. I do not allow myself to be the way I am. I observed people who spoke today. Every dialogue was very emotional. Some of the students cried. Their words were not perfect, but they were real. They were natural. I cry now because I don't allow myself to express myself so openly. I feel an enormous tension. I must correspond to some perfect image of me all the time.

— Why don't you try to not to correspond to any image now? Why don't you tell us to go to hell? Do it. Tell us: "Go to hell you stinky bastards!"

— *No! I can't say that!*

— Okay. Say that you love us.

— *I love you all.*

— I don't feel you love us.

— *I love you.*

— Tell us how you love me.

— *You caught me off guard. I was about to complain, but you are spinning me in the opposite direction.*

— You have prepared a speech. Put your speech aside. Tell us how you hate me.

— *I don't hate you.*

— C'mon. What can you hate me for?

— *I don't know.*

— Okay. Who do you hate? Do you hate flies?

— *I am getting angry with you now. You keep interrupting me. I don't understand why you are doing this.*

— The funny thing, I don't understand it either.

— *I am trying to be rational. I am trying to figure out what is going on.*

— Drop your rationality. Tell us how you hate a fly that is sitting on your sandwich.

— *Ugly fly. I hate you.*

— Tell us about something that caused you to experience a strong emotional reaction in childhood.

— *I don't know. You started to talk about a fly, and I felt such hatred, I wanted to get up and kill it. Moreover, there is some sadistic twist to it. I don't just want to kill this fly. I want it to suffer. Perhaps, it is not even a fly.*

— Who is it then?

— *I don't know. I just recalled my parents' divorce. I recalled a haircut I was given when I was a kid. I didn't want my hair cut. I got very upset. I got into a bathroom, and I cried for two hours. I didn't know how to show my face to people.*

— Were you afraid you will not be beautiful anymore?

— *Yes, I didn't know how to live with myself.*

— You could only be seen in public if you are beautiful, right?

— *Yes. I have to be beautiful. If I am not beautiful, people will not talk to me.*

— What would happen if you were to go outside when you are not beautiful?

— *I don't know. I don't want to experience this. I will run away. I will not say anything. I will forget every word I know.*

— Imagine, you are standing in the square. There are people around you. You are not beautiful. Everyone is looking at you. Somebody is screaming: "She is not beautiful! She is not beautiful!" What else would they say? Tell us.

— *I want to run away.*

— You cannot run away. There are many people there. They scream. What do you hear? There is a drunk man there. Here he is. What is he saying to you?

— *He says I am ugly. He calls me stupid. He laughs and makes fun of me.*

— Tell him something. He is so drunk, he can fall. Say what you want.

— *You are an idiot. You are a fucking idiot. You are a piece of ... garbage. Stop insulting me.*

— What does he say?

— *He opens his eyes, and he says: "Let's have a drink."*

— And what do you do?

— *I share a big bottle of beer with him.*

— Okay. What do you feel now?

— *I am getting brave. I want to say something bad to him.*

— What else will you tell him? Do it fast. He may fall any minute.

— *I tell him: "What do you know about my life? Do you know how hard it is? Why do you say these words to me?"*

— Give it to him now. Let me help you. "Hey, you, drunkard. Why do you insult this woman?"

— *I don't understand why I need to insult him.*

— Okay. In that case, why don't you praise him?

— *I don't understand anything now.*

— You don't need to understand anything. Just feel it.

— *I want to hit him.*

— Hit him.

— *He falls down. I kick him in the face. I kick him in the stomach.*

144

— Great. People have gathered around you. They say: "Wow! She is a strong woman. Look what she did to this idiot!"

— *I keep beating him. I get tired. I sit down on the pavement next to him.*

— What happens next?

— *I feel better. I am not so important anymore. I am down to his level.*

— People around you are happy, "Finally, she got down to our level." People congratulate, hug, and kiss each other.

— *Yes. I've been there before. I cannot allow myself to behave in such a simple way. I must explain everything. I can't just tell someone to go to hell or punch someone on the nose. I can't do that. I must be a smart ass.*

— You are a victim of polite society. You are the last polite woman in Russia. People here are simple. You are dealing with factory workers. They are simple people. They want to get drunk at night after a hard day work. But you sit very high. People cannot be drunk and carefree in your world. They get upset: "What the hell is wrong with our Queen?"

— *People don't understand me.*

— People say: "Why can't she understand us?" When will she come up with a law that will help her working-class subjects?

— *I am a queen. Great! I will force all of them to start practicing self-investigation.*

— You will cause a revolution. Perhaps you want to reconsider.

— *Shall I offer them free food and drinks?*

— Good idea. Let's start with a free shot of vodka for everyone.

— *This will cause a revolution in my world.*

— Great! That's what we do here. We are revolutionaries.

145

— *Okay. Free shot of vodka for the factory workers.*

— What about peasants? They are watching you. There is an expectation in their eyes.

— *Let's give them some land.*

— Land? They say, "We have been there before. Lenin used to promise us land. Then, he sent us to GULAG. No, give us something new. Allow us to have sex in the fields? We work hard plowing your fields. We are tired of this work. Let us have sex in your fields.

— *Okay. You can have sex in my fields.*

— Great. The first couple that will have sex in the field can give this field their names. We'll have a bronze plate. It will say: "Masha's and Peter's field."

— *What are you doing now? You speak about these things in such a matter of fact tone of voice … I have not accepted these people yet … I used to condemn them … I thought they were low, dirty scumbags … and now you make them normal. Should I acknowledge and accept these parts of me?*

— You have to respect your subjects. Otherwise, they will rebel.

— *I don't even know my subjects. I don't allow myself anything of the sort … and I don't allow anything to my people. I want to kick their asses.*

— That's not good. Why don't you give them a lecture? Tell them the process of self-investigation is great. Every newcomer will get a free shot of vodka. People will come.

— *I feel I need to sit down with my people. I need to listen to them. I must understand what they need. I have to feel myself in this role.*

— Yes. That's what you need to do.

— *Otherwise, I behave as a Snow Queen. I keep telling them things, but I don't understand what they say to me. I don't know my people. I don't hear them.*

146

— And people don't hear you.

— You are on the brink of a revolutionary situation: the upper classes cannot maintain the lifestyle they have maintained for centuries, while the lower classes don't want to live the way they lived anymore. If it wasn't for today's conversation, you would have gotten yourself a revolution tonight. You would not have awoken in your palace. You would have awakened in jail and sent to the guillotine.

— *Hmm, they are ready to depose me, ah?*

— Yes, they are tired of you. But, you can appease them now.

— *Do I need to befriend these people?*

— Perhaps you should.

— *Thank you.*

— This work to collect your parts and pieces in one whole requires a constant effort. A constant effort! Look at yourself. It was very difficult for you to come here. You didn't want to pay for this seminar. Your feet didn't want to bring you here. I understand you very well. But, I also understand another part, which says that you will not get a fish out of the pond unless you work hard on it.

What kind of effort do you need to apply? You need to start reading the books we have published. You need to listen to the audio recordings of our seminars and webinars. That will offer you a taste of self-investigation.

You need to attend webinars, i.e. apply more effort.

You need to pay for these webinars. How do you feel about that? You will start to experience inner tension. That's what you need to do to move in the direction of wholeness. Moreover, you need to understand what you hear and read. The fact that you are reading and listening to me doesn't mean you understand what Pint is saying. If you do understand, how much of what I am saying do you understand?

More effort will be required of you. You must attend seminars. We are dealing with a ladder: getting familiar with school materials, participation in the webinars, attending out of town seminars. Where do you find yourself on this ladder? Eventually, you will need to organize a seminar in your hometown. You will have to pass through many steps to do that.

Most people think they will achieve something by reading a couple of my books and by attending a few webinars. No, this will have a very limited effect. To increase the effect, you need to apply constant effort not only to understand yourself but toward yourself as a Whole, toward ascending to your Higher Aspect.

You need to apply two types of effort. You need to walk using both of your legs. The first type of effort is directed toward asking and starting to figure out the answers to your questions. The second type of effort relates to your work at the School of Holistic psychology. We have not discussed it yet. I am introducing it now as a very important condition.

What does work in our School entail? We have many types of work, and we will discuss it with those of you who understand the necessity of this work and are ready to take it on.

Why is this second effort necessary? You read books and you listen to the seminars and webinars. That's great. But at some point, you will get tired of it. Your attention will wander off. That's when you need to work in a different direction and start to use your other leg. As I said, you need to use both of your legs and you need to spread your weight evenly. We can call it balancing the dualities. So, I will ask those of you who feel the impulse to do this work to let us know that you are ready.

I would like to add one more thing. To collect yourself in one whole, you need to attract your own parts, i.e. people who will reflect you your own features. That's what I do when I conduct my webinars and seminars. You are parts of me, parts I accept, investigate, and teach. You need to start doing the same.

How can you do that? You need to disseminate the knowledge I pass on to you. Perhaps some of you have already started to do that. This is an important part of our work, too.

You need to tell people about Holistic Psychology and of your investigation in this field. This is not an easy work. People will react to this information differently. Some will reject it. Others may behave aggressively toward you. Those are your parts. You need to see and investigate these parts and the way they react to the idea of this work. Do not oppress them with your knowledge. People frequently oppress others with what I call their "awareneshness." You will experience that. This is a normal course of events—observe it. You need to get to know their reactions to what you say, i.e. your own reactions. This is what practical work is about.

I have created a playground and I will continue to expand it—many more of my parts will join in. We might see thousands of these parts; humanity is one unified whole. In essence, our work is to gather ourselves, all seven billion of us, in one whole. Start to discuss school ideas with your friends. You need to start feeling the taste of this work. Ask them to come to the webinars. This is important. Don't ask them to come because Pint needs them. No, you need them. Pint needs them too, because you are part of Pint, and all of us are parts of one Whole. Attract the parts which will reflect you the best.

149

Talk to these people. Observe their reactions. Those who are ready will come. That's the way to create a group in your city.

Where will it lead to? Eventually, it will lead you to organize a seminar in your city. Why is it important? It is important because your city is your nest. It represents the coordinates of your position on Earth. It carries the energy of your personal program. That's the place where you can see your program with utmost clarity. You will not be able to do that with such clarity anywhere else. It doesn't mean you should not attend seminars in other cities. But the seminars conducted in your city will offer you the best presents of awareness. Those who will organize these seminars will have to apply extra effort, and it is precisely due to this extra effort that they will receive these presents.

I want to emphasize that it is very important for you to be present at the seminars where you feel an impulse to be. Our site publishes information about the location of monthly seminars a year in advance. Don't just read it—feel where you need to be. It might come as a surprise—you will feel where you need to go. Questions will appear: "Where is that? What kind of place is it? How much will the trip cost?" Doubts will come, "Why should I go there?" You will need to investigate your doubts—do not just yield to the desire of your personality not to reveal itself. How strong is this desire? As you have seen during today's webinar, it is very strong. If you feel the impulse to be at a seminar, enter and explore this feeling. Your personality will oppose the desire to be there. You will have to become aware of these two forces. This is extremely important. This awareness and the stress that appears in connection with it are preparation for a seminar. You will not get anything out of a seminar if you come to it free of stress, i.e. excitation. **The higher the level of your stress or excitation, the stronger**

is your opportunity to become aware of your program; awareness is a result of the voltage potential that appears between dual parts of your personality. Don't be afraid of this voltage. Personality creates this voltage potential. Then, it calls it fear and gets afraid of it. Learn to work with this excitation. Learn to work with this fear. That's the basic skill we acquire here. This capability to work with fear, stress, or excitation points to the level of your self-investigator, to the level of your ascend to Wholeness.

I want to thank all of you for today's webinar.

CHAPTER 4

HOW TO STOP THE FIGHT OF YOUR PERSONAL OPPOSITIONS AND TO BECOME WHOLE IN THE DUALITIES "BETRAYAL—FAITHFULNESS" AND "BETRAYAL—CHANGE"

Do you consider yourself to be a betrayer, or do you think you are the one who always gets betrayed? Do you understand that the one you have betrayed wanted and contributed to the situation that was created? The pain of which betrayals have you experienced stronger: pain from being deceived, pain from you deceiving or breaking up with someone, or pain from close people dying?

What people call betrayal causes serious changes in their relationships with people, who they think betrayed them, or, who, they think, they have betrayed. In a situation in which you suppose you were betrayed, you wanted and expected one thing, but something of the opposite nature happened. Something happened that presently you cannot accept. You call it betrayal or cheating, and you experience pain.

When you think that it was you who betrayed, you feel guilty. You can't get rid of this feeling. You do not understand, and you do not accept your inner betrayer, who did not behave this way coincidentally; the person your inner betrayer betrayed stimulated him to act this way, even though you do not see it yet.

What is behind this pain? If the feelings of guilt, pity, or reproach are behind it, you might not be ready to see this situation as a whole yet. It is seeing your dramatic situations as a whole that allows you to remove the conflict and to stop the fight between the opposite sides of your personality, harmonizing the situation. Only then your pain will transform into a full, holistic understanding of yourself, allowing you to see what really happened to you.

Are you ready to see your inner "betrayer" part and its fight with its opposite part, with the part that considers itself betrayed? Are you ready to understand the motives of THE *** behavior of these dual parts of yours or do you want to continue to revel in the tragedy you have created?

Every scene or act of your life show is staged in the strict correspondence with the scenario that has been written in your personal program. Therefore, everything that happens to you in life happens as a physical realization of your personal script, the script that was inculcated into you by your parents. While in the sleeping mode of consciousness, you do not understand that and cannot become aware of that. You perceive this show from the standpoint of one of its actors—from your own standpoint. However, every man is an entire show, with all its actors, scenes, decorations, relationships between the actors, and changes in the plot.

So, what does our task, the task of beings who go through their lessons on Earth, consist of? Our task is to expand our consciousness. Our task is not to be limited by a one-sided and fragmented perception of our life show. We must start to see our life and our experience here as a whole, i.e. we must start to perceive everything that happens in our external life as a reflection of our personal program or our internal world, which is dual and paradoxical.

Equipped with this understanding of your task on Earth, you will be able to see that the pain you experience, which in this case is connected to betrayal, is an indicator pointing to the fact that you do not perceive what is happening to you holistically.

You separate yourself from other actors of your show. You don't see them as your own projections. You don't see that you project the shadow parts of your personality onto them.

Are you ready to become aware of your projections? Are you ready to stop blaming other people or yourself mechanically?

You can only understand your shadow parts when you refuse to continue the inner war that goes on inside you. If you do not have *the intention* to stop this inner conflict, the opposing parts of your personality, not even understanding what's going on, will continue it. You will continue to live in fear and its three derivatives: condemnation, pity, and guilt. You will not be able to see the whole picture, because in the state of separated perception you cannot understand your opposite parts. You do not understand that you play all these games with yourself. Other people simply support you in this game, playing the parts your personal program allocates them to play.

In case of every betrayal, every participant involved in the show, not just one of them, committed the act of betrayal. If you think you have been betrayed, you should understand that you have contributed to the act of betrayal too, i.e. one part of your personality wanted this betrayal to occur. But do you know this part? Do you know why it wanted this situation to unfold?

You have betrayed someone. You suffer because of it. Do you understand that the person you have betrayed also wanted this situation to happen? Why did he or she want it to happen? You will only be able to understand that if you investigate it. So, stop feeling pity for yourself. Stop blaming yourself. Start to investigate the situation!

If you continue to insist that you or some other party is guilty of betrayal, you will not understand yourself and your show. Blaming the external player or yourself for what has happened will not allow you to see the mechanism of the fight of the opposite sides of your personality impartially. Blame will prevent you from becoming aware of your personal program. An impartial investigation will allow you to understand and accept your shadow parts. It will allow you to stop the never-ending conflict inside you. So, what will you choose: to continue to blame or to start to understand and accept yourself as a whole?

I invite you to investigate duality "Betrayal—Faithfulness," "Betrayal—Change."

— *As soon as the topic of this webinar was announced, I got into a situation of betrayal. Questions connected to loyalty, fidelity, and betrayal arose and have caused me to experience habitual for my personality state of excitation. I have been investigating my personal program for a long time, and I have learned to talk to my inner parts, parts which create these situations. I can see how I create these situations. However, I am still unable to see my program in full. And the question arose: What do I do with this feeling which appears as soon as I understand that the program is about to replay itself? This feeling gives rise to a wave of negativity inside me. I see now that this negativity is a replica of my maternal script. I experience it the same way she had experienced it. I can conquer negative thoughts using mental reframing, but when feelings are involved, my mind is powerless.*

— As we have discussed already, a personal program of every human being forces him to fight. This fight starts and continues because the personal program is an assembly of mutually opposing parts. The only thing these opposing parts can do is fight each other. One of the consequences of this fight is a situation people call betrayal. Betrayal, treason, unfaithfulness are terms that show the degree of a conflict that occurs inside us, in our inner world. This conflict is reflected in the external world. However, a man who is asleep does not understand this. He perceives this as something given—people betray and cheat, and in these situations, they should experience pain, suffering, and hatred. These negative states have been accepted by humanity. They have been inculcated in our common human program as guidelines: we don't need to think anymore, we know how to react to these situations. The autopilot is on.

Our school will teach you to approach the phenomena of betrayal from a different angle. We will see these situations as lessons given to us to expand our consciousness. We'll see these situations from at least two sides: from the side that was betrayed and from the opposite side, from the side that betrayed. We usually identify with one of these sides, but irrespective of the side we identify with, we feel pain.

A man who is not familiar with our methodology will look at betrayal the way people commonly look at it here, "I was betrayed. I condemn the man who did it," or "I have committed an act of betrayal. I condemn myself for doing that."

We will approach betrayal by using the holistic method of perception now. We already understand how this method works on the level of knowledge. It turns out that knowledge alone is not sufficient here, because the program has been recorded on three levels: mental, emotional, and physical. As you have rightfully said, you know what's going on intellectually, but you react to the situation emotionally as if you did not know that.

— *I am experiencing a severe conflict between my intellectual and my emotional centers. My mind cannot solve everything. Feelings come first, understanding follows. The understanding I have doesn't remove these negative feelings—pain persists.*

— Duality "betrayer—betrayed" we currently investigate reflects the fight that occurs inside us. We will see this fight in a different light, depending on the parts and participating centers we investigate. Let's look at this situation from the point of view of two centers which participate in this fight: intellectual and emotional. **This is something we frequently call "a man and a woman." From the standpoint of Holistic psychology, a man represents the logic of the mind, while a woman represents the logic of the feelings: two completely different logics.** The most painful betrayals are connected to the betrayals on the grounds of love, on the grounds of relationships between opposite sexes. Physically, these opposite sides are expressed as a man and a woman. Metaphysically, however, a man represents the mind, while a woman represents the feelings.

The fight we are dealing with is the fight between the feelings and the mind, and our main question deals with our *intention* to stop this fight. This *intention* is extremely important. Without this *intention*, you will not even understand what I am talking about. It will *appear* to you that you understand what I am talking about, but your understanding will be different from mine, and you will continue to fight. All our earthly lessons deal with the transformation of the relationship between our inner parts: from conflict and fight to unity and partnership. The roots of this conflict are buried deep in our conflicting program. Thus, every question pertaining to this conflict is extremely important for someone who conducts self-investigation and moves toward wholeness. We are going to touch upon other aspects of this conflict that you are not aware of. Please, proceed.

— *It is good that my mind cannot suppress these feelings. I am going through a painful change now, which is connected to my intention to stop this inner war.*

— I want to direct your attention to what you have just said. Pain and other negative states you experience are extremely important for the personality; these painful, negative states are kaif* for the personality. (Kaif — a pleasant state of drowsy contentment commonly experienced by narcotic users)

— *You are right. These states excite me.*

— These states excite you and everyone around you. What is excitement? It is a drug. The war on drugs continues in the external world. But how many people understand that a human being is a factory that manufactures narcotics? Every human being is a walking factory that manufactures drugs. Those drugs are not registered by the external world. They don't come prepackaged in the form of tablets or capsules. They are chemical neurotransmitters that are being secreted into our circulatory system. When we experience conflict, cortisol, adrenalin, and other neurotransmitters get released into our bloodstream. They create this excited state that personality uses the same way a drug addict uses heroin.

— *Yes, I have started to observe it; I receive my hit from every emotional situation I encounter.*

— Moreover, you must constantly escalate the dose, because tolerance develops.

— *Wow. It may sound crazy, but I find myself jealous of the emotions someone else experiences, emotions I don't have. I am cold and reasonable. Suddenly, a woman appears. She carries the states that are unknown to me, and my male friends get attracted to her. In my scenario, this is the reason to experience jealousy and excitation.*

— Human beings use different drugs. Each one of us uses his own cocktail of choice: a shot of cortisol mixed with two shots of adrenalin, two shots of cortisol and a dash of dopamine, etc. We can compare these cocktails to the new drugs pharmaceutical companies come up with every year; our inner factories release these neurotransmitters nonstop.

— *My factory works according to my maternal program. I keep doing exactly what my mom did, one to one. Her script gets superimposed on every situation I find myself in, causing me to experience great excitation.*

— Let's investigate this topic from the standpoint of sexuality. We know that behind sexuality people praise so highly is excitation. No movie or TV commercial can be released today without nudity and sexual content. For sex to be good, we need strong excitation. **Our physical body can get excited, our emotional body can get excited, and our mental body can get excited.**

Sexuality has many different aspects. What is platonic love? At first glance, it appears that it only turns on the emotional and mental bodies, leaving the physical body uninvolved. We think of romantic love as the purely emotional state. What we call "a bang" or "wild, animal sex" primarily involves the physical body, but certain parts of mental and emotional bodies are involved in it too. We like this rough, animal sex—the sex of a fight.

Have you ever observed animals having sex? Do they feel guilty? No. They jump at each other and when finished, they part and go their separate ways as if they have never seen each other. Look at people around you, and you will see many similarities. Those are three main kaifs of the third level of consciousness: excitement or excitation, sexuality, and drugs. Do you think you can easily refuse these kaifs? Your functioning here depends on them. You don't even understand what it is you depend on.

And the question is not that you don't understand what to do with this annoying, terrible phenomenon. It turns out, you find it pleasant. It is kaif. Here is the paradox of our inner makeup. On one hand, you scream: "I can't take these conflicts anymore. I am sick and tired of these dramas. I can't experience betrayal anymore. I can't betray anymore." On the other hand, we want to experience these negative emotional states, which are connected to the roles we play according to our scripts.

— *Yes, and the more sophisticated we are, the less physical actions we need to experience this excitation. My boyfriend writes a letter to a woman, and boom—I feel jealousy. My excitation level skyrockets.*

— You can just imagine him writing a letter. That will be enough. The soil has been well prepared. A man screams: "It's midnight! Where are you going? You are cheating on me!" A woman is taking a shower, getting ready to go to bed, but in his dream, she is sneaking out on him to go downtown to have sex with her ex-boyfriend. He wakes up sweaty, full of excitation. We need to understand that what is a horror for one of our parts, is kaif for our other, opposite part.

160

Until we experience this kaif and see it as kaif, in other words consciously feel that what we call horrible is also kaif for us, no transformation is possible. We'll continue to be stuck. One side screams: "This is horrible! I can't take it anymore!" Another, subconscious side, silently realizes what it wants to realize, getting its kaif. It pertains to everyone. Look at the kaif you get when you betray someone, or someone betrays you. There is kaif there! Unless you understand that, you will not understand why nothing changes inside you. You have tried many different techniques. You repeat affirmations day and night. Nothing changes. Why? I am explaining the reason nothing changes to you.

I want to summarize. You must be fed up with pain and suffering. You must get nauseated with it before you begin to understand that **these states are the indicators** that point you to see that your vision of the situation is incomplete, i.e. not holistic. Then, you will understand that these negative states are as necessary for you, as the car dashboard indicators are necessary for a car driver to see that some parts of his car are about to break. If a car's dashboard indicators are silent, the shortage of gas or oil can lead to an accident. With this understanding, pain, suffering, and other negative states we experience become important to us. They allow us to better understand what's going on.

— *When I started to feel my two opposite sides, my eyes opened. I know where to look now. I know what to do next.*

— I repeat, all these difficult, negative, painful states you experience are the indicators. They point you in the direction of wholeness. We need them. Without them, we cannot see where we are going. But only a man who consciously moves toward wholeness can understand that. The one who is asleep desperately wants to rid himself of these states but is unable to do so.

— *I have been suffering from these feelings all my life. I am happy I did not get rid of them.*

— It is impossible. You can't get rid of these feelings. While we are alive and here, all the lessons and indicators of our partial understanding of ourselves will manifest themselves in the form of pain, suffering, and uncomfortable situations. No one will be able to avoid them. If you experience one of these states, it means one of your dualities is out of balance. Do not rush. Don't say you have reached wholeness already.

— *I can't concentrate on your dialogues with other participants. I experience very strong tension. Where does it come from? Am I the only one who experiences this problem?*

— As you prepare to go to the webinar, a question arises. You run around with this question as chicken runs with its egg. You cannot hear anything that is said here. You need to unload your question. Afterward, tension drops.

— *I can't get back to my normal self for hours after I unload my question.*

— Imagine you are using a machine gun for the first time. It may take you some time to get back to your normal self after you are done: your shoulder is hurting; your ears are plagued. Your reaction is normal and appropriate. Your question produces a strong inner tension. To be precise, you create a serious tension by exploring this question. But what does personality want? It wants to create a strong tension and to dump it. We can look at sex as an analogy. All of you have experienced it. Everyone will understand what I mean.

The higher the voltage—the higher is your sexuality. Until voltage drops, you will experience sexually charged, excited state. When you experience this sexually charged state, you

162

start to search for a partner to have sex to drop this voltage. As soon as you drop this sexual charge, you start thinking how to get it back and where to dump it again. We are dealing with a similar process here. You don't even care for your question to be answered. You want to acquire this voltage, or excitation and to dump it as soon as it reaches its peak. We cannot talk about any understanding here. When your question pops up, it is like an erection. As soon as you get a hard-on, you start running around thinking where to insert it.

— *Yes. If we use this analogy, asking a question is like an ejaculation. I am done now. I can relax.*

— Yes, now you can relax. Everyone has experienced these moments. This is how this mechanism works. Being conscious of this mechanism, you will see your questions differently. You will not experience a very high level of tension you need before having sex. You will get into a mode conducive to the understanding of a topic we investigate, and your perception will not be narrowly focused on your erected penis, i.e. on your question. It will be broader. That will allow you to listen to and to hear the important topics other students bring up and discuss with me.

— *I will ask the organizers of this webinar to record it so I can listen to it in a different, not so galvanized state.*

— You can listen, but will you hear? You listen to what is being said, but how much of it do you hear. How much of it do you process? In the state you are in, you can process only a fraction of information that is being discussed.

— *Just a small fraction.*

— That's why it is so important for all of you to participate in these webinars. You can understand something only by experiencing it. Entering this experience, contemplating on it, and getting to know it will allow us to move forward.

— Okay. Let me ask you the question that got me so excited. We are discussing duality "fight—no fight." The state of unity is a state of "no fight." It is nice to think of some Supreme "I," who without my personality knowing anything about it brought me to your webinar, to the knowledge you pass on, for me to come to unity. However, when I observe myself and think about my actions, I see that my aims and behavior are geared toward one thing only—toward being more successful in society. If that is the case, can we say that if my Supreme "I" has a strong intention to be in a state of "no fight," my personality has a strong intention to be in the state of "fight"?

— Who are our Supreme Aspects? We don't know that. Perhaps it is a group of souls that is passing its own lessons. This group had its own goals and meanings to send us, their parts, here. We were sent here to pass through a certain experience, and to acquire a certain understanding based on this experience. Our Supreme and lower aspects are strongly interconnected. Our lower aspects reflect our Supreme Aspects.

What happens with our personality here? Why is it the way it is? The reason it encounters certain situations and receives certain life experience is connected to the lessons your Soul, i.e. your Supreme Aspect is trying to solve. Therefore, a solution of these lessons by the Supreme Aspect is directly connected to a solution of these lessons by your lower aspect, i.e. by your personality.

Personality gets inculcated with a program of conflict at the moment of inception. Everyone here gets inculcated with a program of conflict. To understand what we discuss here and to transform this program of conflict is the main task of our Supreme Aspects. These lessons, the most important lesson for our Souls, can only be solved through us. Therefore, our movement in this direction is movement in the direction of our Souls.

— *Can I get to the state of "no fight" if my "fighter" is weak?*

— No, if your "fighter" is weak, this idea will not even enter your head. You will only want to become a stronger fighter. If your personality is weak, you will try to get stronger and stronger. Only a strong personality can get to the state of "no fight." My personality as a good example. I have spent many lives here as a fighter until during this incarnation I came to experience the meaninglessness of this fight. This fight is totally meaningless—you are fighting yourself. I have not seen it before.

— *But it did not happen to you right away during this incarnation either?*

— Of course not.

— *Was your "fighter" getting stronger and stronger?*

— My current life was very interesting. A program was inculcated that allowed me to go through the extensive experience accumulated by my Supreme Aspect very fast. The states of a brutal fighter and of complete hopelessness were lived through and experienced by me so vividly that I felt as an old man. Everything appeared meaningless. Eventually, these states made me realize that I was fighting myself.

The process of giving up weapons took many years. It was a very painful process. I have been incarnated as a Viking once. Viking's ideology postulates that only death with a sword in hand will allow a man to meet Odin, God of War. I have been incarnated as a Japanese samurai and as a fighter in a Mongol's horde, for whom to give up weapons is an unacceptable act. I came to the dead end. I started to give up my weapons. This was a difficult and painful process.

— I was married. My husband died six years ago. A week later, I learned that he was unfaithful to me. I have tried to explain his behavior to myself ever since. I spent the last six years in pain. Now, after you have explained that pain is kaif for the personality, I understand that this suffering was giving me pleasure. The man died, but resentment remained. I could not solve my issues with him as he was physically absent. There was another concern: I was never unfaithful to him. I pondered the question: "How could he do that to me?" I can understand and accept why he did what he did. I would never do to another man what he did to me because I understand how painful it would be. Currently, I choose not to be in a relationship. I am more comfortable on my own.

After reading your books, multiple dualities have surfaced in me. However, something is still unclear to me. I accept and try to be grateful for everything I experience. I don't get involved in conflicts. However, I am still afraid to enter a new relationship. I am afraid to experience what I had experienced with my husband again.

— Allow me to comment on what you just said. This is a typical situation for many people. People try to use spiritual groups and religion which say: "Accept and love everything the way it is." I stand for something else. **I say that our main task on Earth is to become aware of our personal program.** This personal program has been inculcated into us as a program of conflict. From the point of view of awareness, we must study the mechanisms using which our inner parts fight each other. Religion and many esoteric traditions advise you to accept, to love, to forgive, and to repent. The most important step without which you will not be able to accept and to love yourself is to become aware of the mechanism of conflict inculcated in your program. Unless you understand this mechanism, you will not understand why and how this inner fight of yours occurs—it will continue to proceed silently. Do you understand?

— *Yes.*

— This is very important. And what did you just say? You just told us, "I don't get involved in conflicts." You have covered your eyes saying, "There is nothing there. There was a man. He betrayed me. But he is not here anymore. It would be great to solve my problems with him, but I can't do that now because he is not here. I didn't solve it with him, and I would not be able to solve it with anybody else. I will not deal with men from now on." That is how I see the situation. But let's take a broader look. You did not leave this planet. You are still alive. Do you think betrayal is only sexual in nature? This point of view is commonly accepted here. If you were to have a sexual encounter with someone outside wedlock, you would consider yourself to be a betrayer. What if you were to meet someone and to feel emotional or mental attraction toward him. Would that constitute a betrayal?

— *No, that would not constitute a betrayal. What I call a betrayal was him living with me and hiding his affair from me. He should have discussed it with me, but he did not. The fact that he did not leave me and was lying to me for all these years is what I call a betrayal.*

— Why do you think he was lying to you? He has been with someone, and you think that because of this he should have left you. "If he is with me, he cannot be with anyone else." Is that what you think?

— *I thought we had a relationship. This relationship satisfied me. I wanted to have a reciprocal treatment. If he had lost interest in me, why did he continue to live with me? Who needs that kind of a relationship? Perhaps, that's why I cannot build another relationship now. He should have been honest with me. He should have told me what it was that didn't satisfy* him.

— Wait a minute. "What was it that didn't satisfy him?" It could have been many things. For example, you could have

167

been unhappy with his taste in shoes or the way he walked. Were you satisfied with the way he walked? Were you satisfied with the way he smelled in the evening? Were you satisfied with the way he drank his tea and the produce he used to bring from the grocery store? I can continue this list indefinitely. Why is it that the only factor that concerns you narrows down to the question, "Did he sleep with another woman or not?" Is this the only concern you had in this relationship? Did other things concern you?

— *Well, everything else satisfied me.*

— You were satisfied with everything, but him sleeping with another woman. Then why do you disregard everything that satisfied you? Why? Why do you insist he had to leave you when there were other things you were satisfied with? This is a very interesting topic. Really, this is the key feature here: did he have sex with another woman or not? I understand you very well. It does overshadow everything else.

Why do you cross out and disregard everything else? Why can't you feel how important everything else was? Why does this part outweigh everything else?

— *It is not what he did that I can't take. I still don't understand why he had to stay with me. Why did not he leave me and go to her? Later, he decided to leave, but it was too late. He died. I still can't sort this out.*

— Take a closer look. The fact that he died points to the colossal level of guilt he carried. He did not just leave you—he left this life. I've seen these situations when a woman is afraid that her husband will leave her for someone else, and the man just dies. He died because he could not solve this equation. He died because the level of guilt he carried was tremendous. That's why he left you. That's how he left you—through death.

— *Yes, that was my familial maternal program at work. Every man in my family dies young.*

168

— Yes, but who inculcated this program into him, and why was he punished so severely? I am not going to discuss his experience as he is not here. I am discussing this situation as it pertains to you. He had a very harsh program. He had to die. Try to feel the level of guilt he carried. You, on the other hand, are still alive.

— *Yes.*

— You have destroyed him. This is the war that occurs between a man and a woman here. Sometimes it leads to death. It occurs everywhere, and until you understand the mechanisms of this war, you will continue to fight. Closing your eyes in meditation, repeating affirmations, reading spiritual literature will not stop this war. Until you understand that this is war and create a strong *intention* to stop it, you will not transform your program. You don't even see this program. Your *intention* will allow you to see, investigate, and get to know your program and the mechanisms of war it operates on.

We are about to see something very important now. To persist in the illusion of sleep, pretending not to have a relationship with a man, pretending not to have a man in your life, pretending no one can betray you is to continue the fight. You need to investigate this situation. You need to see where and when you behave the same way your deceased husband behaved. You behave the way he did. He was reflecting your own side to you. I am saying it without judgment or condemnation. I am saying it as one self-investigator to another. This investigation is your road to yourself. Do not be afraid of it. Do not close your eyes on it. You need to investigate and start to see this situation from both sides. You will not be able to see what's going on here using a commonly accepted here point of view, "I am good! He did me wrong!" That stand will indicate that conflict continues. This conflict

169

can take many forms. You can use different weapons to fight this war. Are you ready to investigate this battlefield and every move you and your opponent make on it? That is the only way to accept your shadow sides. Our dialogues will help you to investigate the ways this war is being waged.

— *Thank you.*

— Thank you.

— *After reading your book, I realized I did not accept my inner man. I used to reject him. I am aware of him now. He helped my inner woman to confront the opposite sex. Prior to meeting you, my friend's husband told me that he could not deal with me. He said I was a man in a skirt. I was very upset with him, but after reading your book, I understood that it was my inner man he was referring to. This man of mine is very strong. I have decided to accept my masculine side.*

— This is the first step.

— *However, I still cannot allow any man to get close to me.*

— It's your inner man who does not allow any man to get close to you. Inside a human being, whether it is a man or a woman, both masculine and feminine energies are present. The relationship that develops between two people has four connections. Four, not one. When considering yourself to be a woman, you meet a man, it looks to you that you have only one connection with him: I am a woman, he is a man. Suddenly, you start to see that there is a man inside you. But the man you just met also has a woman inside him. Who does your inner man react to when he deals with this external man? Does your inner man react to his man or his woman?

— *My inner man sees men as his friends. He sees my girlfriends as potential sexual partners, and he fights their boyfriends and husbands. Now, I understand what I have intuited before; I play a weird role in my girlfriends' lives. My inner man fights my girlfriends' boyfriends. My inner man wants to possess my girlfriends.*

170

— Exactly! It's not that you are not doing something right, you just don't see what you are doing. When you start to see what it is you are doing, you will see that you do exactly what the role you are in entitles you to do. Your girlfriends are your men; there are a man and a woman inside you. While in a company of men, you may find yourself fighting for a certain man, who happens to be a woman in a man's body. Is not it interesting?

— *It is very interesting. Will I have to experience these roles until I am bored with them or do I have another choice?*

— This is a question someone deeply submerged in a sleep of consciousness would ask. "Should I experience these roles until I am bored with them?" The aim of an investigator is to investigate, to learn, and to become aware of herself. A self-investigator will never ask whether something is boring or not. How will Pint answer such a question? He will say: "You decide." When you find something interesting, you investigate it until it stops being interesting to you.

— *I must understand the mechanism I am working with. Why did this situation appear? What kind of a lesson do I have to solve?*

— Exactly. Why are we here? Why are we on Earth? We are here to go through certain lessons. Most people don't understand that. The outlook most people have on life here is totally different. They think they are here to satisfy the desires of their personalities. They try to do that, even though they have absolutely no understanding what these personalities represent. **Every personality represents a set of given conditions of an assignment.** You have been sent here by your Supreme Aspect to solve this assignment. But because you don't see your personality as an assignment, you don't even attempt to solve this lesson. The only thoughts that appear in your head are: "Boring—not boring, Should I—should I not, right—wrong, betrayed—didn't betray, good—bad." That's what people work with. They don't even have an inkling that they are here to solve their assignments, not to satisfy their personal desires. People don't have a clue what personality represents. This is my vision of reality, and it determines the direction of my movement. Let me repeat: **your personality represents a set of given conditions of an assignment you came here to solve.** Can you solve this assignment if you don't know and don't investigate the **given conditions** of your assignment, i.e. your personal program?

— *We should start to understand why we experience the situations we experience.*

— The first condition without which there will be no investigation, no movement to Wholeness is to understand, at least on the level of knowledge, that your **personal program is a set of given conditions of an assignment you came to this reality to solve. The meaning of your presence here is to solve this assignment. I just expressed the essence and meaning of your being here, on Earth in two sentences.** How many people share this notion? How will people react to this notion?

— *I want to ask you one more question. Recently, I started to feel that people don't accept me. Up to a certain moment, they find the school information I share with them to be interesting. Then, something changes, tension develops between us. Does it have anything to do with my assignment?*

— Absolutely. The assignment that I call personal program is vast. As you solve its initial parts, you will move to the next level. The way people react to what you say is part of your assignment. Everyone around you is your projection. These people are your parts. They show the absence of rapport between your opposite parts, one of which is represented by

172

you, another is represented by them—your projections. Now, start to think what kind of a lesson it is and what do these people reflect you? **Which duality are you solving?** Every assignment here is an assignment on duality, an assignment to transform the relationship between opposite dual parts of your personality from conflict, rejection, feud, and war to the relationship of mutual understanding, unity, and wholeness.

— *You keep repeating that we need to stop the fight. Do you mean we should not try to change a situation we are in physically but search for an internal solution?*

— Saying no to fight is the first and the most important step on the road of self-investigation: you cannot investigate something you fight. Actually, you do investigate it, but you do it mechanically. You are not aware that this is not a fight, but an investigation. We have spent thousands of lives in this state, accumulating the experience of war. Imagine, you have a strong enemy. You fight this enemy tooth and nail. Eventually, you become this enemy. We understand another human being from two sides: through so-called friendship and so-called feud. People say that if you don't have a real friend, your life is meaningless. They also say that if you don't have a real enemy, you don't have a strong personality. Those are two aspects of our discussion.

— *Should I start my self-investigation with my clan, my parents?*

— Yes, the assignment is introduced through two clans: paternal and maternal. Your inner conflict originates in the conflict between these two clans.

— *I didn't know my father at all. He was never physically present in my life.*

— How can you say, "He was never physically present in my life," when I have a pleasure of talking to you?

— *I have never seen him. My mom divorced him before I was born.*

173

— Okay. But do you understand that the genetic material that came from him is in you? Without his sperm penetrating your mother's ovum you would not be born. So, how can you say, "He was never physically present in my life"?

— *I meant I remember my mom and what she did, but I don't remember my dad. I don't know what he did. I don't know anything about his relationship with mom.*

— What does it mean? It means the conflict between your parents, i.e. between your masculine and feminine aspects is severe. It is so severe that the only thing your father could do was to impregnate your mom. Then, he disappeared from her and your life.

— *Yes, there are no men in my life.*

— You find yourself in this situation because one of your ancestral lines is fighting another to death. That's why your husband died. That's why your father disappeared after your conception. Those are your roots.

— *Roots, ah? My grandfather was killed during the war. My stepfather died when he was forty-three. Yes, this is a war.*

— Your Supreme Aspects are groups of souls of your paternal and maternal clans. Remember Romeo and Juliet? Two kids fall in love, but their clans hate each other. Transfer this situation to these higher worlds and you will see the same situation there. It is extremely important for them to solve this assignment. That is why they send their representatives—you are one of them—to Earth to solve it. This is the reason you came to Pint. You can contact these two clans and ask them to explain to you why you came to Pint now. If your channel is open for contact, they will answer your question. They may tell you that their main task is to solve this conflict, and you were sent here to accomplish this mission.

You carry this conflict in you. This conflict is an assignment you came here to solve.

— *I hope I am solving it as we speak. I just gave birth to a boy.*

— Do you think this is the solution?

— *This might not be a solution, but I am on the right path to solve this problem.*

— Whether you are on the right path or not is a question for you to answer. The appearance of the boy, however, points strongly to the issue we discuss—this assignment will not leave you until it is solved.

Now, I will tell you what birth of a boy represents in a situation when a woman rejects men. A growing up girl wants to be loved by boys. Then, she starts to wish for more. After being betrayed by boys and men many times, she comes to the conclusion that all men are bastards, and being with a man would not do her any good. The idea of romantic love is gone now, and she says: "I will give birth to my own boy! He will be my man!" And she brings up this boy to be her man. In the process, she ties him to her very hard. Neither one of them understands what is going on. The conflict she wanted to run away from, saying: "I am not going to have another relationship with a man," is transferred onto her relationship with her son now.

— *Oh, my God…*

— Yes. That is how it is. How old is your boy?

— *He is seven years old.*

— You cannot even imagine what awaits you. You will experience a hundred and eighty degrees turn in your assignment. You think not having a relationship with a man solved your assignment. You are mistaken. A man showed up in your womb, and he is running around your house now. **You cannot walk away from your assignment, no one can.**

175

— I got it. Thank you very much for your answer.

— Thank you for allowing us to review this very sensitive and important topic.

— I recently saw how my personality uses School's webinars, seminars, and the knowledge you transmit to us. What does my personality do? A very high level of tension develops in me, followed by a desire to get to the seminar and to be close to your energy. My personality gets energy here, in School. It accumulates this energy and it uses it to fulfill its own one-sided desires. Betrayal of personality consists of taking the energy of awareness you transmit to us and spending it on its own illusions. When I saw that, a question arose. One part of me wants to understand what my Supreme Aspect wants me to do, but my personality obstructs everything. It does not want to hear anything. It does not want to feel anything. The only thing it wants to do is to continue its game. I cannot stop this fight. The pendulum swings so hard and so fast, I cannot do anything.

— Everything that happens around us in the physical reality reflects what is happening inside us. Notice that our conversation is muffled by static and echo.

— Yes, I hear an echo, too.

— I don't hear what you say. I can only hear myself. You have removed yourself. You've done something because of which I hear myself instead of you. That's a very interesting situation that relates to your life. You have said that you have a question, a situation which increases your tension, voltage, or excitation. **Every excitation produces energy that will be spent by the personality to continue the fight. And it is not accidental that your questions and intentions of spiritual nature escalate your excitation. Excitation is energy that is being saved in anticipation of a fight, and it will be spent toward the fight. You must observe your states. You must learn to discern the state of excitation**

176

you are frequently in from the state of the investigator. The state of the investigator is different. Look at me. Do I conduct this webinar in a state of excitation? What is my state? Try to define it. Try to see the difference between the state of excitation you know and the state I conduct this webinar in.

— *You are focused and collected.*

— Two boxers get to a ring. They are facing each other. One of them is focused and collected, another relaxed. They manifest their preparedness for a fight. They got on a ring to fight. Which one of them is going to win?

What I discuss is different. Imagine me getting tense and excited about your questions. Do you think I will be able to answer them? And what kind of a relationship will I have with a student whose question got me so excited? I will fight him. It will only appear that I explain something, but, we will fight each other. We will exchange blows. That's what happens when you are in an excited state. Do you feel it? I want you to feel it. We are touching the domain of feelings now. People find it difficult to become aware of their feelings. To become aware of our feeling is more difficult than to become aware of our thoughts or logic of the mind. The logic of feelings is different.

Let's review emotional states again. I will ask you to feel my state. It is very important for you to be able to do that. **Pay attention to my words and to the way I conduct the conversation, but direct predominant part of your attention to feel my state. Feel my state!** You can only feel the state of another human being through your emotional center. It is your emotional center that perceives the emotional center of another human being. If you try to define my states, you will have to use your intellectual center. That's not what I ask you to do. I ask you to feel my state. I ask you to feel what

177

I feel. In other words, you need to find the emotional state I am in your emotional center. Can you do that?

— *I can't do that now.*

— Here is the answer to your question. You cannot feel me. That means your state is rejecting my state. It is in a very excited state, i.e. in a state of conflict. I, on the other hand, am in a different state right now. It is because you cannot feel this state, as you just said, that your emotional center rejects mine. Therefore, it continues to be in a state of war. And it is because of it that you said you don't know what to do—it *appears* to you it is impossible to exit this state.

I have invited you to exit this state instantly, but you said: "I cannot feel it." Try to feel it anyway. This will be your first step getting into another state. Afterward, you will be able to compare. This is very important. You can get to your emotional center only through your own experience. There is no other way to navigate the emotional center. You cannot operate a car if you are not in a car.

— *After ten years of investigating my life on my own and after being involved in a serious accident, I discovered your books. I found them to be very interesting. I want to compare my observations with yours. The way I understand it, our fate is the quintessence of thousands of lives we have lived through before. All these past lives create a certain algorithm. Certain situations repeat themselves until negative aspects that traumatize the common field are brought to balance. We are dealing with a certain cumulative mass here. The situations we find ourselves in and the personalities we meet as we go through our life journey are lessons we have not solved in previous incarnations. As all these situations get resolved, everything comes to a state of balance and harmony which governs this world. I would ask you to comment on this point of view.*

— Okay. Is this incarnation a culmination of all your incarnations? It may be so, and it may not be so. If the Supreme

Aspect continues to work through and accumulate the experience that has not been accumulated fully, this incarnation may only realize and accumulate the experience or energy that is required. To approach the final incarnation and the assignment of wholeness one must live through many lives. This is not an easy process.

Does harmony rule this world? As all of us know, Satan rules over this world. Satan is not a negative character for me. I respect and admire the devil for his work. He does it impeccably. His job is to get people out of balance. This disbalance or temptation is necessary for the soul to make its choice and to determine the direction of its movement. This direction may be negative or positive. Devil cannot create a soul, but he can seduce and take a soul created by God. That's how he accrues his eparchy. We have descended into the world of separation, the world of war ruled by disbalance, where the work to become aware of ourselves is of utmost importance. Balance and harmonization is our main work.

There is one more important point here. The personal program of every human being gets inculcated with a subprogram called "get better." What does it mean? I am not talking about specific parameters one needs to work on to get better. These parameters were determined by one's parents and they are different for every human being. But the mere fact that a man must get better presupposes he needs to clean up, improve, and fight his bad side. What is it, but not a disbalance? Thus, every slogan you are surrounded with, which calls you to improve and perfect yourself, prolongate this disbalance. That's why I say that this world is ruled by disbalance. That is why it is so important to understand what is behind this disbalance and to investigate the dual parts and the war they wage in your personal program. That is the only way to come to balance. However, at present time, this task is virtually unknown here.

— You have mentioned sexuality. Is it also dual? What's opposite to it?

— Opposite to sexuality is impotence.

— What about women?

— Frigidity. Everything here is sexual in nature. It is said that God is love. People usually see love as being sexual in nature. Why do people find incidents of betrayal so painful and dramatic? Whenever betrayal is discussed, people immediately assume that the situation involved sexual contact. These situations are our main assignments. We are present here as physical creatures and physical sexuality is the main gauge of our assignments.

Many cases of betrayal, or cheating, occur not in the physical but in the emotional and mental realms. People experience different types of love, and it would not be correct to say that everyone here is concerned with who got into a sexual relationship with whom only. For some people, the way their mates react emotionally to other people is more important. Let's say, a woman notices that her husband or lover suddenly starts to exhibit a strong attraction to another woman. He does not have sex with her, but his emotional reaction toward her is very strong. Are we talking about sexuality here or not? The way I see it, everything here is of sexual nature.

Let me bring up another example. A woman starts to listen to another man. In your case, you are listening to me. Would you say that our interaction is sexual in nature?

— Yes, I would. When I started to read your books and listen to the recordings of your seminars, I noticed that one part of my personality appraised and approved of you as of a potential sexual partner. Does this

fact in combination with my interest in the knowledge you pass on to us speaks of my trust in you? Have I accepted you on all three levels—mental, emotional, and physical?

— I will put it differently. Does your desire to possess me physically indicate that you have accepted me as a teacher? No. But this desire indicates that your physical center is interested and has been galvanized. What it can lead to is another question. These impulses and reactions that appear in our mental, emotional, and physical centers are manifestations of our assignments. That's the way our assignments present themselves.

Sexual energy is a very strong energy that points us in the direction of our assignments. I have said earlier that God is Love. We can also say that God is sexuality—everything and everyone here is in sexual contact. You are drinking a cup of tea. Is not it a sexual act? You are caressing a cat. Is not it a sexual act? You are driving your car. Is not it a sexual act? I am offering you an alternative point of view on your life now. Someone may say, "He is a sex junky." No, I am not. I am a self-investigator—this is my point of view.

During the period of adolescence, when sexuality starts to awaken in teenagers, boys and girls start to get attracted to each other. Usually, boys experience the physical aspect of sexuality stronger than girls; girls experience the emotional aspect of it stronger. That's when canalization of sexual energy occurs.

The whole world starts to feel sexual to a boy in love: the wind, the sun, birds chirping. But soon, sexual energy gets channelized and directed toward certain objects, certain people with whom he will go through the lessons he is here to go through. How can we attract one human being to another for them to go through a lesson together? We need to have a strong force to do that. Sexual energy acts as such a force. It attracts us to people who will go through our assignments with us. Without this force, we would not be attracted to anyone. We would not want to interact with other people. This is a very important function of sexual energy.

— *Observing my reaction to you, I realized that the personality of every human being always appraises another human being as a potential sexual partner. Sometimes we are aware of this and sometimes we are not. Why do we do that?*

— Why does our personality appraise the sexual attractiveness of another human being?

— *Yes.*

— That is the way we are brought up. Being born into a body of a man or a woman, we get inculcated with stereotypes connected to our belonging to male or female sex and gender. These stereotypes get downloaded into every personal program. They are very strong. You can only cognize yourself as a woman in a relationship to a man, and vice versa. You can only feel as a woman in relation to a man. Without men, you will not exist here as a woman. Your reactions to the opposite sex are indicators of your *identification* with a role of a woman.

— *Thank you.*

— Thank you.

— *I have experienced a betrayal ten years ago from which I still cannot recover. I will start with my parents. My mother was faithful to my father. He was unfaithful to her. An impression was formed in me that a woman should be faithful to her man. I thought my wife was faithful to me. I loved her. One day, after we have been married for ten years, she told me she was living. She told me I was not a good match for her. I took it as an act of betrayal, and I experienced it heavily. I was unable to create a new family. I think I suffer from a subconscious fear. I am afraid this situation will repeat itself. That old betrayal doesn't allow me to live my life.*

182

— Tell me please, what did she mean when she told you that you did not match? What parameters did she appraise you on?

— *She said I was a tyrant.*

— You were a tyrant, and she did not want to be a victim any longer, right?

— *Yes.*

— How did her words influence your perception of yourself? Why can't you create a family? How does this so-called betrayal prevent you from having a relationship with another woman?

— *I am unable to have a relationship with another woman because I am afraid to be betrayed again. What she did, traumatized me to my core.* **Perhaps, the reason I was betrayed is that I carry a lot of hidden betrayal in me.**

— Let's look at this situation from a different angle, from the angle of oppressor—victim duality. There is an oppressor and there is a victim in this situation. Finally, the victim says: "I can't take it anymore. You are too strong of an oppressor for me. As a victim, I cannot take it anymore. I am leaving you." She says, "I cannot withstand such heavy pressure anymore." Can we still see her leaving you as an act of betrayal if we look at the situation from this point of view?

— *She was stronger than me.*

— Hmm … then why did she call you a tyrant? Why didn't she say, "I am such a strong tyrant that a weak victim like you doesn't satisfy me? I will find myself a stronger victim." Why did not she say that?

— *That's an interesting turn. Perhaps, there is a tyrant hiding in me.*

— Yes, you are not accepting your inner tyrant; you see her as a tyrant. In that case, why are not you happy with her leaving you? The tyrant who tyrannized you for many years has finally decided to release you from prison. "Get out of here," the tyrant said.

You have been thrown into a prison. A guard is beating you daily. One beautiful morning the guard walks into a cell and says: "I don't want to beat you anymore." He opens the door and says: "Get lost." Who releases whom here? This is the question. Did she release you? Did you release her?

— This is quite an interesting turn of events. You have a very flexible mind. I will read your books and come to your webinars. When I was preparing for this conversation, I thought, "What did I gain by her leaving me?" I came to the conclusion that I had a subconscious desire to have sex with other women. I could not allow myself to do that while we were married. I was brought up in an old fashion family. My mom used to say, "A family man should not cheat on his wife." When my wife left me, I felt ashamed. But I also found myself free to sleep with other women.

— Your personal program was inculcated with an idea that woman is a saint, who will never betray you. Thus, if you have a relationship on a side, you betray her sainthood. It is equivalent to desecrating an icon in church. One part of you, the subconscious part, desires to be with other women, but another, conscious and very active part of you says, "I must be faithful to my wife. Marriage is sacred. I cannot be with other women."

It is as if you were to come to church and to have sex there. Afterward, you will blame yourself for that. You will be miserable. You will contemplate eternal damnation. The defense system inbuilt into your personal structure is very strong. You wanted to be with other women. The only way for you to be with them was to see your "saintly" wife in a negative light. So, you have created a situation in which she betrayed

184

you. Now, you can say: "Aha! If you are such a bitch, I can go and sleep with other bitches." Am I right?

— *Yes.*

— So, did you extract a profit out of her leaving you or not? Did your shadow part extract a profit out of it? Did this shadow part of yours participate in a creation of this "tyrant" situation?

— *Yes, it probably did.*

— Of course, it did. Your shadow part has created this situation. I am not saying your wife did not participate in it. She had a part that was interested in this outcome, too. Both parts of two of you—hers and yours—received what they wanted. Can you still say she betrayed you?

— *I forgave her already. But why can't I create a new family?*

— Wait a minute. Wait a minute. What did you forgive her for? We have just concluded that she was not guilty. Two businessmen get together. They have negotiated a business contract and signed it. They celebrate. They are drinking champagne. Suddenly, one of them says, "I forgive you for signing this contract." The other replies, "I forgive you, too." Is this funny or what?

— *It is funny.*

— But that's exactly what happened here. What is there to forgive? You have signed the contract. You did exactly what you had to do. The only thing that remains in you is the condemnation of the part that continues to consider her and other women saints. However, you have started to have sex with these "saints" now. How can you have sex with a saint? You should pray to a saint, not have sex with her. The image of an ideal family you have been inculcated with presupposes life with a saint. You can have sex with a woman, but you cannot create a family with her, because family, the way you

185

see it, requires a woman-saint. That's what was inculcated into your personal program.

— *"I am a remarkable woman," she used to say.*

— Great. You can tell her: "That's exactly who I was looking for. I had a role for you in my show. I needed a partner like you." Then she flipped, allowing you to express your other side, which wanted to have sex with other, less remarkable women.

You have two parts in you. One part wants to have a family. It sees women as saints. Another, opposite part, says: "These women are not saints. They are bitches."

Here is how the dilemma appears. Where do I find a saint now, when I don't believe women are saints anymore? Do you follow me? If your goal is to create a family, you need to reevaluate this situation and accept it. The real question is why? What is your aim? The aim is written in your personal program and it upsets you. Why would you create a family and who will you create it with? Are you ready to accept these two aspects of a woman—a mother and a whore—and to start searching for a wife with this new understanding?

It looks like you need to reevaluate your attitude toward a woman. You need to see two parts of a woman: a mother and a whore. Then, you can decide whether you are ready to get married to such a dual woman or not. You must understand that we are dual creatures. Every man and every woman is dual.

— *Thank you.*

— Thank you. Next, please.

— *I cannot formulate my question. I have started to feel the energy of the money lately. Money is not just a piece of paper. Money is energy. When I started to investigate where I spent my energy, expressed in the form of money, I saw that my personality is strongly fixated on one part. I tried to redistribute this energy. I took some money allocated to my son and paid for the webinar with it. I have also spent some money having fun. What is the relationship between money and emotional center?*

— What is the relationship between money and *your* emotional center? Does money excite you? How do you react to money emotionally?

— *Money excites me. I feel guilty for spending money on things I don't find important. I love to play a doctor and to take care of the people around me. I spent ninety percent of my money on that.*

— So, you doctor people around you.

— *Yes.*

— You doctor them, and you pay them money for this. Do I read you right?

— *Well, what I mean is … I feel sad when my kids or one of my relatives get sick. I plan and arrange for doctors to visit them. I buy medicines for them.*

— I got it, you take care of people. You do not doctor them yourself. You doctor them using real doctors. Do you like doing that?

— *Yes. I like it a lot. I like it to the point of being nauseated by it.*

— What exactly do you feel when you do that?

— *I feel I am saving the world.*

— You spend your money to support your self-identification with a savior of the world. You are the savior of the world.

— *Yes, I am.*

— You like it so much, you are willing to spend all your money to maintain your self-identification with this role, and for other people to see you as such.

— *I have two kids: a boy and a girl. I have conducted an experiment last week. I took some of the money I planned to spend on my sick daughter's medicine and spent it on my son. I took him to a circus. My daughter got better.*

— She said: "Why do I have to spend my time lying in bed sick, while he gets to go to a circus?" And she got better.

— *Her symptoms resolved completely. Usually, when she gets sick, she is sick for weeks. This time her cold only lasted two days.*

— She enjoys being sick, right?

— *She does. Moreover, she accepts my treatments with gratitude. She loves it.*

— Aha, enemas at night. She says: "Mom, check my blood pressure! Check my temperature! I don't feel well. I am going to have a heart attack! Please, give me an enema!"

— *Yes.*

— Let's explore this situation in detail. First, for you to be the savior of these people, they need to be sick. Who are you going to save if they are healthy? You are not rescuing them from earthquakes and fires, right? You are not rescuing them from financial disasters. You need them to be sick. Then you can play the role of a savior.

— *Yes. My personality experiences kaif, when people around me get sick.*

— One day, you will open your own hospital.

— *I can open a small clinic now. My mother in law came over last night. What do you know? She broke her leg this morning.*

— Wow! Your mother in law comes to spend a weekend with you, and you immediately make a patient out of her. Come to me sick and injured! Is that your motto?

— *Yes.*

— So, you are interested in people being sick. Then, you can play the role of a savior, the role which makes you happy. What do you need to do to play this game? First, you must have a sick kid. That's the first prerequisite that must be met for you to be happy.

— *Yes. When kids grow up and leave the house, I will start to doctor my husband.*

— There are many sick people in Russia. Just stop by a train station. You will find many patients there.

— *I don't need to go to a train station. My office is full of sick people.*

— They are a pleasure to your eyes. You remind me of a car dealer who inspects a lot of new cars, "Wow! So many nice cars!" You go to a train station, "Wow! So many sick people! Great!"

— *It's funny. I work at a train station. I come to work every morning thinking: "Why do I come here?" Now I understand.*

— Why? You need to see all these sick, maimed people. Russia is full of sick people and their number is growing. God will not leave you without work. One morning you will wake up and say: "Listen up, kids! I am finished with you. I have to organize an orphanage for sick noble girls." Sick noble girls will gather around you. You will give them enemas."

— *They will resist, but I will do what needs to be done. That will be great.*

— They will have to resist. They will scream: "We are not sick! We are not sick!" But, you will prevail. Screaming, "No! You are sick!" you will give them enemas.

— *Hmm ... where is the catch here?*

— Do you remember the main axiom of our School? **The external world reflects your inner world.** The situation you have brought up shows us that there are a doctor and a sick patient in your world. This sick patient is also you. It *appears* to you that you are a doctor and only a doctor, but in reality, you are a sick patient at the same time.

— *This is interesting. I played the opposite role before kids were born. I was sick and everyone in the family was doctoring me.*

— This is how it should be. You are investigating duality "doctor—patient" from different sides. Perhaps you have reached a point of seeing this show holistically inside yourself. Perhaps you need to accumulate more of this experience in a role of a doctor now. Sooner or later, you will get to fully understand why you have been working so hard on the field of illnesses and doctoring. Have you approached this stage yet?

— *I want to believe I did.*

— Who is it in you that wants to believe that?

— *My personality wants to believe that.*

— Wait a minute. Your personality contains both: a doctor and a patient. So, which one of them wants to believe that? Is it a sick patient who wants to believe that he doesn't have to be sick anymore or a doctor who wants to believe that he is ready to close his office?

— *It seems to me that both the doctor and the patient are so tired of this game that they are ready for something else.*

— "The Hospital" is your favorite game.

— Yes. That was my favorite childhood game.

— "How many patients are in the waiting room, nurse?" the doctor asks. "We have four more, doc. We have a broken leg, two chest pains, and chronic constipation." "I've had enough," the doctor says, "I am tired. I can't take it anymore."

— *Patients are also getting tired of being sick.*

— Perhaps, it is time to change the billboard on your house from "The Hospital" to something else? What other names can you think of?

— "The circus."

— Great! You have announced that from now on the billboard on your house will read, "The circus." What will be happening there? We have sick people moaning and groaning

190

there now. Doctors are bored and tired of patients. They are drinking beer and flirting with nurses.

— *There will be actors and audience there. Everyone will have fun. The new house will be full of joy and laughter.*

— You will build a Comedy Club. Okay. But what will your patients and doctors do? They will continue to play the "The Hospital" game. Do you understand? This is not just a change of personnel when the old actors are taken away and new actors are brought in. Those are your actors. Are your patients and doctors ready to participate in the rehearsals of your circus?

— *I think they are ready. They are tired of playing the "sick" role. They want to be happy. They want to express their positive emotions too.*

— One of your patients starts to laugh after an enema. Some water was added to his system and now he can laugh and cry. It is laughter through tears. He laughs and cries, laughs and cries. Sick people get together and discuss their symptoms. They are happy. They smile at each other. One says: "They have cut off my leg, ha-ha-ha." Another says: "My finger was crushed. They bandaged it, ha-ha-ha." What exactly will your actors do? This is not clear to me yet. Your actors are still there. They have been given different roles. Is your troop ready to act in a different show? Are you ready to change the name of your show to a new name? Currently, you are still running the old "Hospital" show. Are you ready for this change? What about your actors? Are they ready to play the new roles? How will they play these new roles? What are these roles? This is something you need to investigate.

— *Thank you.*

— Thank you.

— *I have been stressed out before this webinar. I am new here. I am not even a first grader. I am still a preschooler. A few days after my first*

191

webinar I heard a song on the radio, "Get up and sing." I have been trying to analyze everything before. This song pushed me in a different direction. I am not sure how to say what I want to say. After the last few webinars I have developed a dependency—I am waiting for the next webinar impatiently.

— Is it dependency or interest? This is a very important distinction.

— *Interest. I even defined it for myself: I came to Pint full of interest. I did not have questions. What I had was an interest.*

— Wow. What are you doing? As soon as you like someone and get interested in him, you declare you are developing a dependency and you say: "Go away! Get lost! I am not going to depend on you."

— *I participated in one of your seminars. When I came, I told you I was looking to experience an emotional state. A day after the seminar, my oldest son, who is usually very calm, started to yell at me. I told him: "Stop screaming! You can't talk to me like that!" I could not understand what was going on. I was sitting there looking at him trying to figure out what he wanted to say. On my way to work the next morning, I understood that everything I was saying to him I was saying to myself. I told him, "You cannot talk like that!" I suddenly understood that it was me who could not talk like that. I told him to study psychology. I was saying it to myself. I came to work. My colleague was talking about her cat being spoiled. I told her: "A cat just reflects the owner. It's you who are spoiled." Evening comes, and I understand that it is me who is spoiled. Everything I was saying, I was saying it to myself. That lasted the entire week. As soon as I would say something to someone, I would realize I said it to myself.*

— Did you stop talking?

— *No, I did not. When the topic of this webinar was announced, I reviewed my life looking for situations of betrayal. When was I betrayed? Who did I betray? I have experienced betrayal in my life. I have experienced a divorce. But to tell you the truth, I did not experience pain.*

I have nursed my husband through a terrible accident. He was paralyzed for two years. I never thought he would betray me after that. We have been married for thirteen years. I was his "queen." Suddenly, I was dethroned.

A thought came to me yesterday. Roman said he associates Pint with a father figure. I associate Pint with a male figure. Six months have passed since that seminar. During that time, I did not read any of your books. I did not attend your webinars or seminars. An inner struggle was going on in me. Suddenly, I received an email from Pint. He was offering me his friendship. Wow! I understood that it was my own inner man. He was offering friendship to my woman, my inner woman.

— *Suddenly, I became aware that every man in my life taught me to be a woman. I was spoiled by the attention of men. I was spoiled by my parents' attention. I was spoiled by the attention of the people around me. People are talking about pain, but my situation is different.*

— Why would all of them try to discover a woman in you if you are already a woman?

— *I don't know.*

— So, are you a woman or not?

— I am a woman.

— I need to know who I am talking to. Why do you consider yourself to be a woman?

— *I am a woman because I have a woman's body. However, my father has been installing a man's program in me since the day I was born. I was only interested in math as a child. I had no interest in girly toys.*

— Let's not talk math now. Can you flirt with me?

— *Yes, I can.*

— Do it.

— *I flirt non-stop. That is how I betray my man. I attract every man around me.*

— How do you attract men?

— I don't know how I attract them, but as soon as they are attracted to me, I push them away. I ignite them, but as soon as they are aflame, I cool them off.

— How do you ignite them?

— *They start to experience sexual desire around me. Something crazy happened at work yesterday. A man came over from another department, and one of the interns liked him. When she shared that she was attracted to him with the older colleagues, they told her not to introduce him to me. They told her I would take him away.*

— Where would you take him?

— *I don't know. This is not something I do consciously. Something happened to me when I was young, and that's what I subconsciously do now.*

— Okay. You are a woman. Where would you take him? What would you do to him? C'mon! I want your inner woman to wake up! People are talking already. They say: "Do not introduce him to Tatiana. She would take him away." My question is where you would take him?" He is strolling around the office. Suddenly you show up. Where would you take him?

— *Well, I may take him to my place.*

— Okay. So, two of you go to your place. What happens there?

— *I have two other men there. I have my two sons there.*

— Wow! Two other men?!

— *They spoil me too.*

— So, these sons of yours, they say: "Wow! Who is this? Another man. Come over. Help us spoil our mom." The new guy has a bewildered smile on his face, "Why did you bring me here?"

— *I cannot express my feelings. I suppress my feelings all the time.*

194

— Do you have any feelings? Do you have any feelings to express? Please, express some of your feelings to me. What do you feel toward me?

— *I admire you.*

— What exactly do you admire?

— *Hmmm?*

— Here you go. Your intellectual center starts to work now: "What? Why? Where?" You have lost it. You are in your mind now. You don't feel anything.

— *After the last seminar, I felt grateful to you.*

— That's a noble feeling.

— *And I wanted to express my gratitude. Next day I received a message from Roman: "Thank you for your participation in the webinar." I wrote him a thank you note, but the only thing he received was a letter "n." I can't even express my gratitude.*

— That's who Pint must work with. He will go nuts. There are twenty women around him, but neither one of them can say a good thing about him.

— *I constantly suppress my desires. I suppress my feelings, too.*

— You suppress them to such a degree, they disappear completely. That's horrible.

— *I have a weight problem. I understand that this is a psychological problem. I started to gain weight when I started to suppress my feelings.*

— You are getting overweight. You will have to spend all your money to buy new clothes. Would not it be easier to express your feelings to Pint? Do it!

— *Pint ... I ... I ... I ... I don't know ... I am going to cry now.*

— Pint can't take it anymore. Are you done crying? It is Pint's turn to cry now.

— *I am grateful to you. I want to hug you.*

— You can't hug me yet. We still have things to do. You need to express your gratitude on the emotional level. You need to say something warm to Pint.

— *I need Pint to kick my butt.*

— Is that what you are going to use Pint for, to kick your butt? I don't want to kick anybody's butt. I ask you to say something nice to me. But no, you say: "Pint will play an oppressor." What are you doing to Pint? Why do you want to make an oppressor out of him?

— *Pint gives everyone a push. He helps us to formulate our questions.*

— Pint has been begging for a warm word since yesterday. Did he get it? No. That's how Pint lives. He keeps talking about consciousness and awareness, but no one says a warm word to him. His life is hard.

— *I want to scream: "Help!"*

— Help me, Tatiana, help me! Tatiana screams: "Help me! Help me!" Pint screams: "Help me, Tatiana! Help me!" A blind man is screaming to a deaf man, "Show me God." And a deaf man screams back: "Let me hear God." That is the conversation they have. So, that is what we are going to have until Tatiana says something nice to Pint, who is in dire need to hear something nice. This is our main task now.

— *Do I have to figure out what to say to Pint?*

— You must **feel** something toward Pint.

— *I had this experience once… Let's call it "A wish for unrequited love."*

— Do I want to be loved, or do I want to love someone?

— *I wanted to experience unrequited love. And it happened to me exactly as I wanted it to happen. This love expressed itself toward a man.*

— Really?

196

— *When I felt it, I was shocked. Why him? Why this man? He was a very interesting and handsome man. He was younger than me.*

— A younger man. How beautiful.

— *He was tall, young, and handsome, but that did not prevent me from suppressing my feelings.*

— "You are too young and too handsome," she told him, "I need somebody older and uglier than you."

— *Stop that! I thought: "Why him? He would never love me." We worked together, and when I looked at him, he felt me staring at him. I have never said a word to him, but he felt it. I think he felt it on a different level, on the emotional or some other level. I cannot say.*

— We can call this painting, "An older woman cognizing love of a younger man."

— *I kept asking myself: "What do I feel? What do I feel?"*

— This is horrible. You should have told him: "Listen, young and handsome. Do you like me? I am a boring, intellectual, aging woman." He might have said something back to you. This is so boring, I am going to cry now.

— *Please, don't cry.*

— Something life-affirming … anyone … please.

— *This was a feeling. I can't express it in words. It was a breath of fresh air.*

— Such a serious talk about love?!

— *I was trying to understand myself. Do you understand?*

— I understand, but to talk about love so seriously?

— *Perhaps, it was not love.*

— We are discussing feelings, but our listeners are dying of boredom. They ask: "What do they discuss? Do they discuss love? No. They analyze love." Do you want to analyze love, or do you want to love? You are analyzing love of the young men. You will kill them with your analysis. They will go nuts. I can stomach that. I am a seasoned, old man. But what will happen to a young, romantic man fate brought to you? You will make him impotent if you continue to psychoanalyze this whole thing.

— *But that's what I do. I am a psychoanalyst.*

— This is horrible. You are cutting young trees to the roots. If you continue to do that, we will lose all our perspective, young men. We will be left with analysts sharing stories: "I have met a woman. I thought I loved her." And they will analyze it for two hours.

— *I am not using this energy. It is wasted on me.*

— I'll tell you what you need to do, Tania. Fall in love with an old, ugly, fat man. You need to feel this love. Write him a letter: "I want to have sex with you in an abandoned building by the cemetery." Run there. While waiting for him there, you will experience some amazing states. You will tell him about these states when he finally gets there with his walker. Then, two of you will have wild, passionate sex. Two of you will wake up the entire neighborhood. Dead will rise from their graves screaming: "What's going on here?" That's what Holistic Psychologist Pint recommends you do. I want to thank you for your analysis of love. I hope you *start to feel* something soon.

— *Thank you.*

— Thank you.

— *I would like to return to the topic of betrayal. I have been in a relationship with a woman for three years. Lately, it has taken an unusual turn.*

— We are going to the movies now. We used to sleep together, but now we just go to the movies.

— *Yes, something like that. I would like to discuss the excitement my personality experiences while it is looking for and discovers the facts of cheating, lies, and betrayal.*

— Is this excitement sexual in nature?

—   This excitement is three centered. All
three of my centers get excited.

— A private detective, ah?

— *I have expected our conversation to proceed in a more serious tone.*

— You want to make me sad too, eh? I am tired of your
sadness. C'mon, bring some fun to our webinar.

— *It is about kaif. I have experienced betrayal before. My
personality has suffered from betrayal many times. But, on the other hand
…*

— Great. Describe the pleasures of betrayal to us.

— *I have tried to experience this kaif. I have broken into her email
box. I observed myself reading her emails. I was trying to experience this
kaif, but I could not. There was still some kaif there, but …*

— Why so much sadness in your voice? Tell your story
differently: "I broke into her email box! As I read her email, I
visualized her having sex with another man! I got a hard-on! I
felt a strong desire to join them!" Bring some excitement into
your story. Your story is pathetic. I don't believe you. If you
really feel excitement, all of us should feel it. God damn you,
psychoanalysts. A patient is on a couch, and you slowly fall
asleep asking him one question per hour. "What happened
then?" you ask, and you fall asleep. C'mon, if you experience
this excitement, then bring it to us.

— *I am sorry Alexander Alexandrovich, there was so much static
coming from Sergei's microphone, I had to put him on mute.*

— Sergei got overexcited! That what happens to a man
when after suppressing his excitement for a long time he allows
himself to express it.

Okay. Next, please.

— *Why do I have to experience betrayals so frequently? What does
it show me? On one hand, I have a tremendous fear of being betrayed. Is
there a subconscious desire to be betrayed behind this fear?*

— Yes, behind your fear of being betrayed is your desire to be betrayed. As your desire of being betrayed is very strong, you constantly create situations of betrayal around you. Try to see what is behind this desire? What is it that you really want to experience? What state are you after?

— *Perhaps that is how my personality asserts itself as being good. Looks like I am a saint. There is pride there.*

— Are not you tired of playing a saint yet?

— *I am tired of it.*

— Are you really tired of it? Perhaps, you still want to play this game.

— *No, I am done with this game. First time in my life, I was able to finish this game without breaking up with a woman. It took me three years.*

— Three years? Wow! That was a long orgasm. My compliments to you, stud.

— *It was a great experience. My self-investigator saw many interesting things.*

— You can shoot a porno movie. Two people are having sex. They come. They get up. They get dressed and discuss the feelings they had during sex.

— *While you were laughing, talking to a student before me, I observed I was wearing a mask of seriousness on my face. I got stuck wearing it.*

— Everyone is stuck here. Do you understand? It is a scourge. It is a scourge of people who are on the search.

— *I felt great. I really enjoyed your sense of humor.*

— **You need to learn to laugh over what you are crying over. That's a skill. As any skill, it must be learned. It will provide you with fun and laughter for the rest of your life.**

— *Is that true?*

— Gosh, there is so much sadness in your voice.

— *I just realized how far away I am from that point.*

— Move on fast to the fun side. Throw some fun into your self-investigation. Otherwise, you will go nuts. With a thousand books on your shelves and this serious face of yours, you will go crazy. Have some fun, laugh about all this esoteric stuff. Take a book, read it, and laugh.

— *Thank you for your help.*

— With God's help. God is crying already: "Stop this tragedy. I can't take it anymore." God is tired of this tragedy. Let's have some fun. Investigate, but enough of these sullen faces. I am conveying God's words to you.

— *I thought self-investigation was a serious business.*

— Yes, you must get red in the face, sweat, and strain. Only then it can be called an investigation. Fifty years later, you will tell your grandchildren, "My face got red. I was sweating all over. That is how I got my first present of awareness."

— *I have a tough time swallowing all of this. Is there another self-importance here?*

— Laugh over your self-importance for God's sake! You are constantly throwing it at me: "I am so important. My self-importance is here. My self-importance is there." Another one comes: "I am more important than you."

— *Thank you.*

— Thank you. You have puffed, and you have strained, but you were so serious, you did not fart. I had to puncture and release your tension to harmonize our webinar. I hope I harmonized this mess somehow.

Let's call it a good night. Please, share your experience regarding paying for this webinar and what you got out of it on our forum. Please share and discuss what's going on with you and in you, so each one of you knows what's going on with him and with the group.

I wish everyone good night and dreams of awareness.

CHAPTER 5

HOW TO STOP THE FIGHT OF YOUR PERSONAL OPPOSITIONS AND TO BECOME WHOLE IN THE DUALITIES "CONDEMNATION—GUILT" AND "PITY—EMPATHY"

•❖•❖•❖•❖•❖•❖•❖•❖•❖•❖•❖•❖•❖•❖•❖•

— I would like to say something about our webinars. Every webinar has its own theme. Every theme deals with becoming whole in one or another duality. Previously, you could have freely asked me any question you wanted to ask. Many of you have asked questions that were not related to the themes of the webinars. I have a feeling, you don't read our website and don't get prepared to discuss the subject specified. **Our work requires you to apply effort.** I want to remind you that awareness will be bestowed upon you according to the effort you apply. Your personality doesn't want to hear that. Personality wants everything, and it wants it now. That's not how it is going to happen here. Therefore, I will present material in a different format today. We will explore the specified subject step by step. I will ask you questions and you will answer them. Let's start.

How often do you become aware of the fact that you condemn other people or yourself? How often do you become aware of the fact that you are experiencing the feeling of guilt? The states of condemnation and guilt are indicators pointing to the fact that our personality is dual, i.e. that its opposite sides are in conflict. You feel and experience the consequences of this conflict as states of condemnation and guilt. But as chronic patients get used to their pain, people get used to their states, including the states of condemnation and guilt. Being in the state of chronic conflict of opposite personal parts, people are not even aware of the war that rages inside them. I frequently use terms *to be conscious of* and *to be aware of.* These terms carry a different meaning. **In my terminology, *to be conscious* of something is *to notice* it. For example, you can become conscious of a thought that appeared in your head, "I don't like this man," or "I want an ice-cream," or "I feel cold."** *To become aware* of something is *to see two opposite sides of something*—**conscious and subconscious**—**simultaneously. To be conscious of something and to be aware of something are different things. I have used the word "conscious" earlier. However, quite frequently we are not conscious of the states of condemnation and guilt, even though we experience them.**

Let me use an analogy here. There are many programs in a computer, but we only bring the programs we currently work with to the desktop. It doesn't mean that all other programs in our computer disappear. You see your conscious part. The subconscious part is hidden from you. Usually, we are not conscious of our inner conflict, because it is chronic. **For us to feel and to notice the states of condemnation and guilt, we need to have a visible external conflict.** When someone screams at and condemns you, you start to feel inner conflict—you either condemn your opponent or you experience guilt. This will be the first part of our meeting. Please, answer my questions: "Have you observed yourself experiencing the state of condemnation? Have you condemned someone last week? In which situations did you experience these states? Who did you condemn? Have you observed yourself experiencing the state of guilt? In connection with what did it arise?"

— I experienced a feeling of guilt as soon as you said that some of us have asked the questions that were not related to the themes of the webinars. I am guilty of asking these questions, too. On the other hand, I immediately condemned you for limiting me; I can ask whatever I want. I have just experienced both states.

A few weeks ago I met a friend who expressed the idea that we should not condemn anyone. I retorted that by his nature a man is unable not to experience condemnation. As soon as I said that, I realized that I condemned him.

— That's true. A man, the way he is now, is unable not to condemn other people. Why does this happen?

— According to the knowledge you pass on to us, there are two opposite parts in us: one part condemns, another part experiences guilt. They flip back and forth all the time.

— That's right. When we enter this reality, we receive a personal program—a program of conflict and fight. Birth of a child in this reality is the birth of a new fighter. Our personality is this fighter. Every side of duality wants to prove to the opposite side that it is more important, that it is a winner, that the other side is wrong.

— I agree with that. The side that experiences guilt retreats, gets stronger and hits back. At this point, these two sides flip. The side that felt guilty starts to condemn now.

— I have been experiencing the states of condemnation and guilt since birth. These feelings are chronic, and the frequency that this seesaw is flipping with is getting faster and faster. Finally, I started to investigate the reasons for my condemnation. When I observe my condemnation, tension diminishes.

I can also tell you that I love the state of condemnation. I recently took my friend's son for a walk. He asked me to go to a shooting range, but I came up with an excuse not to go there. I recalled my own childhood. My mom had always forbidden us from going to the range. My mom was always in a state of condemnation.

— What did you condemn the kid for?

— This is about duality "to give—to take." I condemned the request itself. At some point, when I was a kid, I forbade myself to ask people for anything, to cry, and to be afraid.

— Okay. So, you have condemned the kid for asking you to do something. As soon as you encounter an external request, the mechanism of condemnation is triggered in you. I will remind you that this is happening inside you.

— I can share many other examples of condemnation with you. I am a painter. A few months ago, I have accepted an order from a man. He asked me to create a certain product for his firm with an aim of manufacturing and selling this product. I did what he asked me to do, and I emailed him the final pictures. Days are passing by, but I don't hear from him. He doesn't answer my emails. He doesn't answer my phone calls. I started to condemn him for not paying attention to me. This comes straight from my childhood, "I am good. I did everything well and fast. Why do they ignore me?" The financial part of this situation is also important. I still can't sort this situation out.

— It is very important to start to become aware of the states of guilt and condemnation, as they are behind every conflict and war in this world. Every personal program is built on these states. I want to emphasize that to investigate your personal programs, we need to use real examples. When a mechanic takes a carburetor apart, every small part of it is important and must be accounted for. We are dealing with something similar here. We need to see how your personal program works.

— *I agree with you. When I started to see the basic mechanism my personality works on, I felt a relief. But I feel it is just a small thread out of the ball of yarn which has formed at the beginning of my current incarnation. I am unraveling it slowly. Thank you.*

— Thank you. Next, please.

— *I have just experienced a strong feeling of condemnation followed by a feeling of guilt. As soon as this webinar started, my kid woke up. I silently condemned him for that. I am sitting here waiting for my turn to speak. He sits in front of me crying. I feel guilty. Eugene speaks in a very slow, monotonous tone of voice. I condemn him, too.*

— You should condemn Pint for not interrupting Eugene, too. Then, you should condemn Pint's parents for giving birth to Pint, who doesn't interrupt Eugene, who speaks in a slow, monotonous voice. The reasons to condemn are many. **If you know your ancestral lines, you can track these reasons down.** What did you condemn your son for?

— *I feel anxiety now. You can probably hear it my voice. I condemn myself for manifesting emotions. I block them. Dad condemned all emotional manifestations at home. He didn't allow mom to laugh or cry. When I was young, he would lock me in a dark room for laughing or crying. So, according to my program, people turn away from me when I manifest emotions. Whenever I laugh or cry, I am always afraid people will get angry with me and leave. I am very nervous now. My voice trembles. I condemn myself for that.*

— Every personal program is a program of conflict and fight. The key figures of this conflict are a man and a woman. A child is born of a man and a woman, and it carries two ancestral lines: maternal and paternal—conflict occurs between these two lines. Romeo and Juliet fell in love with each other, but their families were at war with each other. They did not remember the reason for this feud, but they wanted to destroy each other. That's what each one of us is dealing with. We live in a hypnotic state. One human being gets an order to destroy another human being. He completes the mission. This mission is hidden, silent, and not easily visible. Many of us don't want to see it. If you start to talk about this at a party, people will get upset. But this is the game that is played on this playground. In your case, your father—mind wants to suppress your mother—feelings. This is war until death. Different strategies are being used. These strategies are invisible. They are camouflaged. People could be gentle and tender. They may talk about love and God. Those are the strategies they use waging their war. This is not easy to see. There are open battles, during which one takes a knife or a gun and assaults his opponent. But most battles are silent and invisible—a nindzya is silently sneaking on his opponent at dawn.

— I also condemn people for wasting my time. If someone wants to chat with me online or talk on skype, I feel a surge of condemnation: "Don't you have better things to do? Why do you want to waste my time?" When my son opens his mouth in the middle of my conversation with someone and starts to talk gibberish, I immediately feel guilty. He is taking my friend's time. He shouldn't be doing that. I have not brought him up properly. I position myself as a serious, professional woman.

— Here you go. You manifest two sides at once: masculine and feminine. Your inner man condemns every manifestation of emotions. He offers clarity and rationality at the expense of emotional manifestations. He suppresses all of them.

Let's move to the second part of our conversation.

I will start with a question: **"Do you understand that condemnation gives birth to guilt, while guilt gives birth to condemnation?"** Guilt and condemnation are connected as yin and yang. They can be seen as Gemini sign; two human beings sit with their backs touching each other, looking in the opposite directions. We usually condemn someone, who, in our opinion, is wrong. We defend our point of view, and we condemn our opponent for his truth, which is opposite to our truth. Actually, we condemn ourselves, because other people only reflect the projections of our personal parts to us. After we condemned someone, we experience guilt, because, in reality, we condemn ourselves. We are not aware of this. We condemn our opposite part, which we project onto another human being. When we feel guilty, we want to get rid of this inner state, as it is heavier than condemnation. When you condemn, you feel you are right. As a righteous public prosecutor, you lean on the law. You lean on the truth the way you understand it. The feeling of guilt, however, is connected to you experiencing your own mistake. You feel that you are in the wrong, and you want to get rid of this heavy feeling. Frequently, we condemn someone we feel guilty around even more. This leads to a vicious cycle of defense and offense, which we cannot exit unless we are aware of this mechanism. That's what we do here. Our work is to become aware of this mechanism. I will ask you to share

how you experience this vicious cycle of condemnation and guilt in your life. How are these two states interconnected in you?

— In my case, condemnation and guilt are glued together. I am ashamed to discuss anything I consider to be personal with other people. I feel guilty when I do that, and I simultaneously condemn myself. This happens automatically. When I decide to do some kind of work, I condemn myself if I don't do it or do it slowly. I also feel guilty for that.

— Here you go. **This is a drug addiction.** It is precisely this interaction between condemnation and guilt, crime and punishment that gives birth to the state of narcotic excitation, which later manifests itself in conflicts and dramas. This is the inner mechanism of personality survival. Personality doesn't want to change itself. It fights for its survival; it wants to preserve itself the way it is. This is the reason we experience such difficulty in becoming aware of the mechanisms of its actions.

— I am ashamed to talk about the states I experience. I understand I need to speak up and talk about my every experience. I understand it is very important to do that. You are right, this is the vicious cycle we cannot exit. If I don't vocalize these states, I experience kaif: condemnation and guilt are here right away.

— Your profit is a continuation of this drug addiction. If you understand that, everything starts to make sense. Otherwise, it is not clear why people do what they don't want to do. They want to stop doing something, but they continue to do it. Why? They continue to do it because their personalities extract profit from these activities.

— Yes, it is in this state of swinging back and forth between condemnation and guilt, accompanied by suffering where kaif lies.

— This kaif is produced by the cycles of guilt and condemnation. You are talking about shame. You are

210

discussing the very intimate experience. You feel like you are undressing in public. Conversations we have here are looked down upon and condemned by the society. All of us have been taught not to talk about these states. "How can I talk to people about such intimate things? Who will they take me for?" we ask ourselves. We are afraid people will condemn us for our sincerity, for revealing our deepest feelings. And they will condemn us. Everyone condemns everyone here, and all of us support this system. That's how society's morals operate. People constantly watch each other.

— *I behave as a spy. I start to talk to a man, and I watch his reactions—will he condemn me or not? Based on his reactions, I decide whether I want to talk to him or not.*

— People are asleep. A sleeping man fights without even knowing it. In the end, he will use everything you said against you. It will happen sooner or later. That's why everyone here is afraid and keeps his silence because everything you say will be used against you. After having a glass of wine, you can share something personal, something that was hurting you for a long time, but you will condemn yourself for it in the morning. You will hate this man or woman for knowing something intimate about you. Two human being got together. Then, they parted. What a big deal? But what do we see? Pain. Suffering. Hysterical outbursts. Why? Because they shared something intimate with each other. While together, you got to know each other. People who are close to us get to know our weak spots and they hit us there. Sooner or later, our partner will hit our weak spot and we will hit him back. That's the way our relationships are set up.

— *In my case, condemnation occurs in the inner pair: mother—child. My inner child condemns my inner mother for not wanting to give birth to him; the mother feels guilty. When I was fifteen, I told my girlfriend I would never give birth to a child. I told her I would adopt one. When I met my husband, he expressed a strong desire to have a child, and I gave birth to our son. When I was young, I felt that my parents didn't want to give birth to me. The feelings of condemnation and guilt I experience are connected to that.*

— Let's investigate this situation a bit closer. If your parents did not want to give birth to you, they would not have given birth to you. Let's start with that premise.

So, they wanted to give birth to you. Why?

— *My husband wanted to have a child. I never did. I feel guilty about that. Condemnation follows.*

— Do you feel guilty for not wanting to give birth to a child or for not seeing yourself as a whole? I am broadening the notion of guilt and condemnation now. We are dealing with mundane, daily situations, but in reality, we experience guilt and condemnation because we are not Whole. We don't remember who we are. We don't remember why we came here. We don't remember where we are going. Those are the real reasons behind guilt and condemnation we experience every day. These states manifest themselves in difficult situations we experience every day. We need to sort these situations out. Unless we do that, we will not become whole. We will not recall who we are. We will not understand why we are here. We are here to get to know how divided we are and to become Whole. Let's take a look at your situation. You say you did not want to give birth to this child. Why did you do that then?

— *In my case, the role of mother was buried deep in the subconsciousness. Deep down, subconsciously I wanted to feel what it is to give birth to a child.*

— You assert that it was your subconscious desire to feel what it means to walk around for nine months with a swollen belly, to scream in pain delivering a child, and then feed and foster him for the rest of your life.

— *I can't think of anything else.*

— Presently, you are exploring the positive moments of childbirth.

— *When I was fifteen, I thought I would never want to experience the pain of childbirth. I thought I would never want to have a child. I thought I would never want to take care of a child.*

— Then, why did you give birth? We investigate everything from the standpoint of war of the sexes. What role does your child play in your conflict with your husband? Why did this kid show up? What kind of bets do you place on him? Why did you decide to go through all these problems: delivery, sleepless nights, a need to take care of your kid?

— *Perhaps I am using my kid as a tool to manipulate my husband? We got a divorce a few years ago. As soon as we did that, we started to split this kid in two. Each one of us wants the kid to live with him.*

— Of course. You want to hurt each other as hard as you can. Why separate peacefully? That's no fun. You want to traumatize each other as hard as you can. You need to divide everything, including kids.

— *Yes, this war continues. When the kid goes to my ex-husband, his grades drop. When he is with me, his grades pick up, because I keep an eye on him. Hmm, looks like I am using his grades to fight my ex-husband, too.*

— Now, take a look at your child. What is happening to him? You don't care much about him, because you spent all your energy to fight your husband. A soldier is not interested in his gun if it is shooting all right.

— ***I feel guilty because as every other child my kid wants to live with both of his parents. But we are divorced, and this is impossible.***

— A child wants to live with his parents, but parents don't want to live together; they want to destroy each other. That's what they download into a child. That's how the personal program gets created, with its conflict of the opposites, the conflict between a man and a woman. We can clearly see that here.

— *After reading many smartbooks, which taught me not to condemn people, I got into a trap. On the level of the mind, I don't condemn anyone. However, I cannot resolve this conflict; it is hiding deep inside me, and it is very strong. It is so strong, I don't want to see myself in the mirror.*

— When you forbid yourself to condemn other people, you start to condemn yourself. In essence, it is the same thing, but a sleeping man separates it in two. Many spiritual leaders insist you must love other people, including your enemies. You have to respect and understand everyone. But no one takes into consideration the fact that we are programs, created to experience conflict and war. Unless you investigate and transform your program into a program of different quality, all you can do is redirect this conflict inside yourself. Instead of condemning and hurting other people, you will condemn and traumatize yourself.

— *That's what I do. My condemnation manifests itself quite exquisitely—in a form of irony. I am stuck in the grips of condemnation to such a degree, I am hurting all over. I want to see every nuance of my condemnation. I need to free myself from it.*

— So, you feel guilty when you condemn other people. As you are unable not to condemn, the feeling of condemnation metamorphoses into sarcasm and irony.

— *Yes, when my sarcastic remark hurt someone, I feel satisfaction.*

— Your story confirms my thesis that a human being is a dual, paradoxical creature. We need to accept both sides of

214

ourselves. Do not run away from negative emotions—manifest and investigate them. That's the only way to see them. That's the only way to liberation.

Every ideology here is based on *have to*, i.e. on duty. But you cannot become Whole out of duty. You cannot free yourself from condemnation and guilt out of duty. You cannot understand yourself out of duty. Duty is a key position here, but where did it bring us?

— *That's what I do. Instead of hurting other people, I condemn and hurt myself.*

— I will offer you a simple working-class solution. Express your condemnation in a simple, direct way. Find someone and condemn him or her.

— *I don't like my boss. He is a nasty son of a bitch. He only thinks of himself. I work in a medical field. He only thinks about money. He doesn't give a damn about patients. He doesn't give a damn about his colleagues.*

— Okay. You can express yourself here, in our group. Can you say that anywhere else?

— *No. I have tried to bring the subject at work, but I was threatened with being fired.*

— That's the climate we live in. Why do we see such forms of distorted condemnation as irony and sarcasm? It happens because we are afraid to express ourselves freely. We can lose our job. We can even be killed. That's how illusory society morals are maintained. That blocks every opportunity we have to become aware of ourselves. How can we combine things we discuss here with what is happening in your life?

— *I found the solution in irony, but I am starting to understand how dangerous it is now.*

— **The irony will not get you anywhere. The irony is an acceptable method of expressing condemnation in this**

215

world. But does it help you to see yourself? No, it hides things even more.

— *How do I get out of this trap?*

— I do not offer any premade solutions here. I cannot solve this situation for you. We are on the path. You have to walk your path. My webinars and seminars invite you to the path I follow. I am constantly on a move. I will not advise you to quit your job. I will not advise you on what to say to your boss. That will not solve anything. **The external action that is not based on understanding that everything that surrounds you is a result of your inner world will entangle you even more. You need to sort this situation inside yourself. This is our Process.** This is our path. There will be many steps on our way.

We have started with a question, "How does condemnation give birth to guilt?" You have described your condemnation. Tell us about the guilt you experience.

— *I feel guilty around my mother. She is not happy with me. She constantly tells me that I occupy myself with rubbish. She says that the fight for justice and fairness is nonsense.*

— And what does she offer? What is not "rubbish" to her?

— *She says I need to adapt.*

— That's exactly what you do. Instead of openly condemning people and fighting for your rights, you occupy yourself with irony and sarcasm. Is not this adaptation?

— *That doesn't make me feel better.*

— You will not feel better until you become aware of your program.

— Recently, I started to see the traits I condemn my boss for in myself. Sometimes, I treat people as harshly as he does.

— Great! This is a very important moment. **You start to see the part you project onto other people and condemn them for in yourself.** This is what the process of becoming aware of yourself, of your shadow sides, and adding them to yourself is all about. What happens when you see your inner oppressor? Does your attitude to the external oppressor, to your boss, change?

— *Yes, I feel better.*

— Do you feel better because you became aware of the part your boss expresses as of your own part?

— *How can I condemn him, if I have something similar in me?*

— People are occupied with only one thing here: they either condemn or feel guilty. **I invite you to investigate. Continue to condemn as you did before. Continue to feel guilty as you did before. But investigate these states.** Then, your energy will not be wasted on condemnation and guilt alone. It will be used to investigate these phenomena and the inner mechanisms that give birth to these states. This is the answer to your question, "What can I do?" To start to understand the knowledge I share with you, you have to transform many things. You may think there are faster and simpler ways to do that. That's an illusion.

— *I have started to see how the states of condemnation and guilt are interconnected. I see how they transform one into another. I am in constant conflict with my dad. Sometimes, when he screams at me, I do not say anything back—I accumulate condemnation. But as soon as I spill my emotions, I feel guilty. This is an interesting mechanism of defense: in order not to feel guilty, I suppress my emotions. My boss is a woman. She is very emotional. I constantly condemn her for being so emotional.*

— You have touched upon a very interesting topic. The pleasure the oppressor experiences is a pleasure of condemnation. The pleasure that the victim experiences is a

217

pleasure of guiltiness. When you condemn someone, you collect points in the role of the oppressor. Your victim doesn't accumulate any points at this time. Your victim is waiting patiently to get to the stage; it accumulates energy. The condemning part—the oppressor, uses its energy to condemn. Your victim saves up the energy necessary for a punch back. It is not easy to see what's going on here as the victim can jump out and punch someone else, someone who is not involved in the situation; you cannot punch your boss, but you can punch your kid, your wife, your husband, or your dog.

— *I can see how condemnation and guilt are interconnected, but I cannot understand that they are one whole. Perhaps this is the first step.*

— Yes, this is the first step. We will investigate everything very thoroughly and in minute details. The investigation is a slow, step by step process. We are sawing a seed that will bring many fruits. The process of investigation will lead you to experience increased clarity in your holistic perception of yourself.

Our next question, **"For what reasons do you actively condemn yourself and other people? What do you feel guilty about?"**

The main reason behind condemnation is our inability to accept the qualities we consider to be bad in ourselves. **Not accepting and not seeing these so-called negative qualities in ourselves, we project these qualities onto other people and condemn them for having these qualities.** Later, we feel guilty for that. One of our parts acts as an oppressor, the opposite part acts as a victim. The oppressor experiences the state of condemnation. The victim experiences guilt. This happens inside us. Which of these states we are conscious of depends on which part we experience consciously and which subconsciously. That's the way this

218

fight between a victim and an oppressor occurs. Each one of them carries his own weapons. You need to know and see your weapons. You need to see how one part of you uses these weapons waging its war against your other, opposite part. Let's investigate this by using examples from your daily life.

— *Recently, I have noticed that I condemn men for desiring me sexually. I probably feel guilty for my own desire, and I project my condemnation onto men around me.*

— Let me comment on that. We have talked about sexuality at length yesterday. There are two types of sexuality here: masculine and feminine. A man wants a woman. The way nature has it, for an animal of male sex to possess an animal of the female sex, it must fight other male animals, who also want to possess the female animal. The winner will have sex. A male animal is driven by strong desire. A female animal reacts to the desire of a male animal. She feels she is being desired; that creates excitement, i.e. electrical excitation in her.

— *She might also resist.*

— She only resists in order to escalate this excitement. You say you condemn this behavior in men. But what you condemn, you want. You condemn your own part that wants it.

— *I did not see that. I did not see that I also wanted it. I always looked for a reason to refuse to have sex with men. Only the most persistent one is allowed to have sex with me.*

— That's exactly what happens in the animal kingdom. You create a certain situation. Men start to fight. The strongest one wins. You get excited about it.

— *Yes, but multiple social and inner prohibitions get in a way. Open desire gets obscured by moral norms.*

— If you were to get in bed with a man before the wedding day fifty years ago, many people would have condemned you.

Things changed nowadays. But, nevertheless, a man still manifests activity, while a woman manifests alleged passivity, even rejection. A woman constantly stops a man. A man gets excited from his own activity, while a woman gets excited from her own passivity.

— *I didn't see that. So, the more obstacles a man overcomes, the stronger his charge is going to get.*

— He shows you the strength of his desire. When the strength of his desire reaches the level you find acceptable, you agree to his advances and have sex with him.

— *I condemn myself for dating this guy … I cannot figure out whether I like him or not. I condemn myself for giving him hope. I condemn him because he is not what I need. This is so complicated. This is so entangled.*

— My job is to untangle whatever is entangled. As I mentioned already, we are living in the world of *appearances*. It *appears* to you that you attract men to live happily thereafter. It *appears* to you that you want to attract a good partner. In reality, you attract a man to condemn him. You attract a man and you start to condemn him. Then, you start to feel guilty for allegedly giving him hope. "He is not what I need. Why do I give him hope if I am not planning to be with him?" That's what one of your parts asserts. But you continue to encourage him. Thus, it is not because you offer him hope that you feel guilty. No. You feel guilty because you condemn him, i.e. yourself. Condemnation. That's your kaif. But while you condemn, you also feel guilty.

— *Exactly. I do not accept many of my qualities. That's why I attract such partners. One I don't like for his physical appearance. Another I cannot stand because he is not very smart. The third one drinks too much.*

— In reality, it just *appears* to you that you are looking for a man to love. In reality, you meet your own shadow parts, parts you condemn. Your main game is self-condemnation. Let's get deeper. What do you condemn these men for?

— *One is fat. I cannot accept his physical appearance. Another is plain and stupid. The third one drinks so much, I cannot take him anywhere.*

— You collect men to condemn. You condemn all these qualities in yourself. You will either continue to attract lines of men to condemn, or you will become aware of this situation. In that case, the lines of men searching to be condemned by you will wither and disappear.

— *I also attract people in whose presence I feel like an idiot. So, I condemn those, and in the presence of others, I feel not worthy.*

— Yes, that's how it works. First, you condemn someone for being fat. Then, someone condemns you for not having a perfect body. Everyone experiences this. The question is why do we do that?

— *Are we doing it to accept ourselves?*

— We do that to receive the experience of both sides of duality, to see the situation from the point of view of two opposite sides. People acquire this experience, but they do not understand why they are given it. You are given this two-sided experience so you can start to see yourself holistically, i.e. from two sides. When you condemn a fat man, you don't know what he experiences. To understand that, you must get into a similar situation, where some gym junky will condemn you for having skinny legs.

— *Yes, when one experiences these situations from both sides, one feels a certain calmness. One doesn't condemn a fat guy so strongly anymore and doesn't feel so humiliated next to a gym junky.*

221

— Exactly. That happens because the level of excitation in this duality drops. When do you experience the strongest excitation in a duality? You experience it when you are on one side—you either idealize the opposite side or hold it in contempt. When you move to experience the opposite side, excitation diminishes. Try to see how much this double experience offers you.

— *This happens when I become aware of the experience of both sides. They start to connect. Otherwise, I sink to one side.*

— Uhum. It is precisely the states of victim and oppressor and accompanying them states of stress or excitation, that people call life here. This is not life. This is survival. But those are the strongest experiences people strive toward. People want to experience these states. You are upset some gym junky gave you a dirty look. You are upset someone called you stupid. It causes a storm of emotions in you. It *appears* to you that you long for other states. No, that is exactly what you need. You need this experience. Without it, you are bored.

— *Yes, these interactions allow us to experience strong emotions.*

— To humiliate someone and to be humiliated by someone—that's the basic game the matrix of survival offers. When you humiliate someone, you rise above him or her. When someone humiliates you, you rise on a different side of a polarity. You equally want to experience both states. (See Wikipedia, *Stockholm syndrome* and *The Night Porter* by Liliana Cavani, 1974. Translator note)

— *I am not aware of that. This is painful.*

— This painful experience is kaif at the same time. But you are right, you are not aware of it. When you start to become aware of it, you will not be able to play this game anymore. I am explaining the entire structure, rules, and mechanisms of the game of duality. When you start to see it in detail, these games will not interest you anymore. Your ego-personality will lose this game; it resists that loss strongly. It wants to play this game eternally.

— *That's exactly what I have experienced. At first, I experienced stress, excitation, and fear. Then, we got to the peak of it. When we openly acknowledged everything we went through, excitation disappeared. I felt: "Okay. We stand open in front of each other. What is next?" It seems to me that without this excitation, there is nothing to do here. Perhaps that's where the switch to another fuel, the fuel that is different from fear, lies?*

— That's a big question. Your game with this partner has ended. This is a fact. It has ended because you have said something that cannot be said here. How does a process of seduction occur? A man gets puffed up. He advances. A woman gets red in the face. She covers her eyes. People call it to flirt. It is kaif. Suddenly, they look at each other and start to laugh; both know the game. Can they flirt afterward? No. Look at people faces. They are serious. They have suffering written all over them. What if they were to see their game and to laugh at it? They will not be able to play it anymore. You can only play this game if you firmly observe the rules of this game, i.e. if you only see one half of it. People would not play this game of survival if they were to clearly see it. It would be absurd. Our Supreme aspects observe our games and laughs. At one point I asked them, "Why are you laughing all the time?" "We are not making fun of you. We are just having a good time," they said. Well, we are not having such a good time here. That's why we play this game so hard. What do I want to say? The fact that you decoded the game doesn't mean you have switched to a new fuel. You just saw something you were not supposed to see.

— *Okay. So, the situation got discharged. What do I do next? Do I have to decode every single duality?*

— Let me illustrate this situation by using the example of a couple having sex. A man orgasmed and fell asleep. Those smart Chinese have invented the "Dao of love." They can have sex three days in a row without climaxing. A Russian guy has a beer, gets on top of his woman, and ten minutes later he is done. He is done. He doesn't have any more energy. You have experienced something of a similar nature. It doesn't mean you have switched to a new fuel. You have exhausted your energy, and you are not interested in this game anymore. Later, our guy will simply drink beer at night or switch to vodka. He will not even remember he wanted to have sex. Everything started with sex but ended with vodka. That happens all the time. People continue to play the game of survival because they cannot imagine any other game. Refusal to play this game is perceived as death. That's why people experience such a strong resistance to see this game.

— *Presently, I observe. I have started to see the kaif I receive from negative experiences. That's where I am now.*

— Transfer to the new game occurs in a few steps. First, everybody plays, but no one sees anything. And they should not see anything. The cycle of guilt and condemnation repeats itself thousands of times. To get out of it, you need to experience kaif of the game. You need to see that what you consider to be horrible, is kaif for you. This is step two. You will start to see that you experience kaif when you feel guilty. You experience kaif when you condemn. You experience kaif in the role of the oppressor and you experience kaif in the role of a victim. You experience kaif when you get scared. When you start to experience and observe this fear, condemnation, and guilt as kaif, you are ready for the next step. That is the road toward the exit. It consists of many steps.

224

When you start to feel this kaif, you start to allow yourself to do things you prohibited yourself from doing before. That will provide you with an opportunity to see what you do. The "sleeping" man plays the game of survival blindly. He doesn't see the game he is playing. When you start to feel pleasure experiencing opposite sides of duality, you start to see the game, and slowly but surely you lose interest in it. That's when you will start to search for another game, for a game of different quality. This is the Quantum leap I am talking about. Those who will find themselves ready to jump to the next level of the game will jump. Those who will not be ready will find themselves playing the same game of survival on another planet. They will continue to play this game until they are bored with it.

— *Do we still find the old game attractive? Is that why we cannot talk about anything else?*

— I'll let you ponder over this question on your own. Let's move to the next topic, **"How does your victim attract an oppressor to receive punishment for the guilt it experiences?"** No oppressor can exist without a victim, and no victim can exist without an oppressor. This is very important to understand. We frequently hear on TV, "Innocent victims have suffered …" Then, we hear of the oppressors who hurt those "innocent" victims. In reality, no one suffers here without a reason. A victim always attracts an oppressor to experience the state of victimhood. **I repeat, a victim always attracts an oppressor.** It's not just an oppressor who is looking for a victim. No! A victim is in search of an oppressor, too. That's how every victim oppresses its oppressor. There is an oppressor in every victim, and there is a victim in every oppressor.

A victim feels guilty. The state of guilt is a heavy, difficult state to carry. A victim wants to be punished, as punishment will remove this guilt, either totally or partially—it searches for an oppressor, who will punish it. **A victim searches for an oppressor.** I will ask you to share with me the ways your inner victim attracts these external oppressors. Why does it do that? What kind of guilt does it carry? Why is it searching for punishment?

— The topic of condemnation and guilt is very important to me. I will try to connect it to victim and oppressor. I always blamed men for not taking care of their kids. They play with a child for two hours and they are good fathers. The fact that mothers spend days and nights with their kids doesn't concern people. Today, I experienced a severe feeling of guilt. One of my sons is sick, but instead of being with him, I am here, at the webinar. My mother was so upset and angry, she picked up my child and took him to her place. She thinks I have gone nuts. According to her, I should be sitting next to my child's bed. But instead, I am listening to Pint.

I don't know what to do. I cannot drop the webinar and run to my child, who got even sicker after yesterday's webinar. As soon as I started to see my "Hospital" game, my kid got sick. "What's going on? Where is this mother of mine?"

— Patients get upset. Where did this damn doctor go? The doctor got sick of patients and went outside to have a cigarette. The whole hell broke loose.

— Yes, the doctor needs to come back. Let's make the doctor feel guilty.

— Who is who here? Who is an oppressor? Who is a victim? At first glance, your kid is a victim. He is sick.

— Yes, he is a victim. Mom doesn't care. She left him to take care of her business.

226

— It *appears* to us that the kid is the victim here. But turns out, the victim doesn't want the oppressor to leave. As soon as the oppressor moves to the door, the victim starts to scream.

— *As soon as I stop giving him pills and let my attention go somewhere else, the situation escalates. We have been admitted to a hospital three times already.*

— How does a victim attracts and keeps an oppressor next to it? You have your answer. The doctor prescribed medicine. A patient lays there quietly drinking his medicine. That's one thing. We are dealing with exacerbation of symptoms here. Who creates this exacerbation? It's the kid who creates this exacerbation. He doesn't understand that, but that is what he does because he needs to keep the doctor next to him. Is the victim innocent?

— *That's his way of manipulating me. He doesn't want me to go to the webinars.*

— He doesn't want you to go anywhere. All he wants you to do is to wipe his nose. He wants you to keep him warm and comfortable. That's how your kid sees your role. Later, he will get angry with another patient, his sister, if you spend more time with her. Then, these kids or patients of yours will fight each other trying to determine who is sicker. That will induce severe suffering in you, the doctor. This is the war you will see at home. Kids are torturing mom. Finally, they will join forces, and as soon as you decide to go to work, both will get sick.

— *That's exactly what is going on in my house. It is not funny. It is a tragedy.*

— As long as the state of fear you are in continues to escalate, this tragedy will continue to get worse. But as soon as you start to laugh, your patients will get bewildered. The doctor comes in laughing, "Have you died, yet?" With sad, solemn faces, they will show you their zits. The doctor was panicking,

227

now she is laughing: "Keep scratching your zits." Kids are puzzled: "What's going on? You used to forbid that?" "Scratch your zits until they bleed," you say, "You will feel better." This is the way to transfer from a doctor to a comedian. This will not be easy for a doctor, but she will have to become a comedian. Patients don't understand. They expect medicine, but she comes in laughing. That's the only way to put your sick kids on their feet. A patient is sick because it is profitable for him to be sick. He doesn't want to refuse this profit. In your kid's case, his profit is your attention. When the kid is healthy, smiling, and gets straight A's in school, nobody notices him.

— *Yes. When he fails at school or sick, he gets my full attention. I cannot part with this horrible scenario. It continues. If I keep doing that, it means I like it. Yesterday, I tried to imagine another game. I could not. The "Hospital" is my only game.*

— Nothing else is needed, just two more bottles of medicine. Soon, you are going to give birth to another child. You will be a doctor and a mother at the same time. Our hospital has one more unoccupied bed. Let's get it filled. I will get you another patient in nine months. The "Hospital" game continues.

— *Thank you.*

— Thank you.

— *Lately, I have been feeling guilty about missing the webinars. Sometimes, I am late to the webinar. Sometimes, I have to leave earlier. This happens all the time. I pay for every webinar, but I still feel guilty. Will you forgive my sins?*

— I will. You will have to get on your knees and pray to Pint's picture before bedtime. Why do you feel guilty?

— *I feel guilty because I can miss something important and not become aware of something. That's where the feeling of guilt is coming from.*

228

— A man comes to a store, pays for a bag of groceries, and walks out without taking it. One part of you wants something, and it pays for it. Then, another part comes to the scene. It doesn't want it. It says, "Let's go" and it leaves. Let's figure out what exactly this part doesn't want. It is this part that makes you miss, come late, or leave a webinar early.

— *Perhaps this part is afraid. Something may happen here, because of which my entire life will change.*

— God forbid the work of transformation will lead to transformation. That's what every "seeker" experiences. The seeker seeks. He sweats. But when he finally gets to the point of transformation, he runs back.

This is a common scenario. People walk around searching for transformation. When I ask them, "What do you want?" they cannot say anything. Everything is foggy.

— *As soon as we see the light, we run away from it.*

— The same story with cockroaches. You turn the light on, and they run away looking for the darkest spot. They are afraid of the light. Everyone screams, "Let's go to the light. Let's go to God. Let's go to the next dimension!" But, as soon as the light shines from above, you run for cover.

— *I want to thank you for your attention, patience, and love. I don't understand a lot. I am frequently in the dark. I will do as much as I can. Thank you again.*

— Thank you. I serve. This is how I serve. I am aware of my assignment. My assignment is to serve. I serve Wholeness. I serve my Supreme Aspect. I serve those who send me. This is not an easy work, but I am getting stronger. I have experienced different feelings in the process. I used to get irritated when people didn't understand me. I have passed this stage. I arrived at servitude. This is the state that allows me to do what I do best. You will come to it, too. You will walk your own path, but you will come to this stage. When you serve, your doubts disappear.

Our next topic will answer the question, **"What inner scenario of the oppressor—victim game was transmitted to you by your parents?"** We have discussed the oppressor—victim game quite at length already. Every dual game that is played in this reality is the oppressor—victim game. One side plays a victim role, another act as an oppressor. The states of condemnation and guilt appear because both the oppressor and the victim are fighting inside you. The scripts of these games were inculcated into your personal programs by your parents. If you want to become aware of the mechanisms of these conflicts, you will have to become aware of your personal program. You will see that every duality we explore has been inculcated in your personal program. Let's look at the reasons you were condemned for by your parents. What were you pitied for? Which one of your parents did you see as the oppressor? Which one did you see as a victim? What strategies did your parents use fighting each other? How do you use these strategies now?

— *Both of my parents were oppressors. Mom tried to get pity out of dad and us, kids by playing a victim. She never succeeded. She felt self-pity because no one pitied her. Dad oppressed her by not manifesting oppression. A joke comes to mind. "Hurt me! Hurt me!" masochist begs. "I will not hurt you!" sadist replies.*

— This is a perverted form of oppression: a victim is waiting to be hurt, but an oppressor just stands there smiling, refusing to punish it.

— *My father, as on oppressor, forbade every manifestation of feelings at home. Being in a victim, I wanted to cry, but I was not allowed to do that. My own oppressor is even harder on my victim. As soon as a victim opens her mouth, he is on top of her.*

230

— A victim has his or her own medals, "A victim of the fight with my husband," "A victim of the fight with my son." You have many medals. Your victim, as any other victim, has her own medals and her own pride.

— *A victim wants to show her medals, but the oppressor doesn't allow that.*

— A victim will put another medal on its chest for that.

— *I do have this desire to manifest myself as a victim, but I don't allow myself to do that.*

— I can't say you don't. Every victim enjoys pity. It allows it to experience self-pity.

— *I don't feel that. I don't accept this feeling. I don't pity other people and I don't pity myself. When someone pities me, I experience aggression.*

— Why don't you pity Pint?

— *What can I pity him for?*

— What can you pity Pint for?

— *Hmm ... I can pity him. He has to deal with all of us ... all our ... problems.*

— Pint could have been having dinner with a beautiful woman now. Instead, he must deal with your problems.

— *I feel condemnation now. At first, I felt pity, but now I feel condemnation. Why do you have to play a victim?*

— What else can you pity Pint for?

— *He has suffered for many years to open up all these dualities.*

— He was born a small, quiet boy. And look what fate gave him. He suffered. Oh, he suffered. He had to enter tragedies, and he had to exit them. Let's pity this small boy, whose childhood was shattered to multiple dual fragments. Can't you pity him as a woman?

— *As a woman, eh? That's a good question. Where is this woman? Why do you bother me with your little boy? Look at me! Look at my wounds. You should pity me!*

— Wait a minute! Wait a minute! Don't forget we are pitying Pint. Let's finish pitying him. Then, we will pity you. Pity is a feeling. A feeling is a woman. I am asking your woman: "Please, take pity on me!"

— *She is crying: "What did you do to Pint? Ah, what did you do for Pint?"*

— Finally. Here you go. Now, people who will listen to this webinar will cry too. Please, continue. You should bring it up a notch. Bring it up so Pint can cry over himself too. Can you do that?

— *It will take some time.*

— It will take years. Pint will die. Then, you will cry.

— *Yes, if you die, I will cry.*

— After Pint's death, you will come to his grave and cry.

— *I do feel pity now. If I were to lose you, I would feel pity. I would really cry.*

— Of course. Pint is not eternal. It seems to you these webinars will go on forever. Why shall we hurry? This is not the case. Who knows what fate has in mind for Pint? Who knows when he will be called back?

— *I am crying now. I am pitying myself for not making it on time.*

— So, use this opportunity to pity yourself while Pint is still here. Start to pity yourself for not listening to Pint. Pint knew a lot, but you didn't listen to him.

— *I do pity myself now. I had an opportunity to learn from him, but he is gone. The only thing I can do is to wallow in self-pity. Nothing will help me now.*

— You will wake up in the middle of the night, look at his books and cry. Pint will look at you from above and say: "Enough already, let me go!"

— *Is that why I should pity you? You didn't love us.*

— You will feel guilty for saying that later.

— *Why?*

— Because he did love you.

— *We didn't understand that this was love.*

— When did you cry last time?

— *I was watching a documentary a few weeks ago. A scientist was talking about Earth being destroyed. I shed a tear or two.*

— Hmm, look at the level of a cataclysm you need to start crying. Look around you. People cry for different reasons. Someone called Anna stupid a few days ago. She cried for two weeks. The level of your sensitivity is very low. Your emotional body is very hard.

— *My request for this webinar is to find out why I need my inner woman. What is her function? Who needs these feelings? What do people need feelings for?*

— One can have sex with a woman.

— *What will I get out of it?*

— What do you mean? You can still have sex, can't you?

— *I need a real man. I can't find a real man here.*

— One day, Terminator will come and he will take you to bed.

— *My program will not allow that. I dream of him, but he never comes.*

— You need to wait. What do you need a woman for? You need a woman to feel. People need a woman not to forget that this world is not only about rational aims; there are feelings here, too. You need a woman to feel! Women disappear from this planet. Women are turning into men. They turn into strong men. They become so strong, men are getting afraid of them. So, where is this feeling woman of yours?

— *What is the benefit of feelings? I don't understand that. This is so irrational. Feelings just get in my way.*

— You can only connect to God through the emotional center. If the emotional center is hard and closed, as it is in your case, there will be no connection. That's what you need a woman for. Let's get back to Pint. Why did he open the matrix of survival? He did that because his emotional center was open. His pain was so severe, it allowed him to open the structure of the matrix. Otherwise, he would have died. That's the reason you need the emotional center. That's why you need your inner woman. That's why you need to feel.

— *My man understands that to be tough he needs to cooperate with a woman.*

— Your so-called tough man can only determine his toughness by using the help of the opposite side—his woman. By rejecting your woman, you are cutting a branch you are sitting on. In that case, you are not a man, either. You will need to use another word to define yourself. Perhaps you can use the word, "Terminator." We don't know who Terminator is. Is Terminator a man or a woman? You do not pay attention to duality when you move from one side to another. Thus, you don't understand who you are. We always need a comparison. The tougher the man, the more feminine his woman is. Otherwise, this man is neither fish nor meat. He is not even a man.

— *My inner man is uncomfortable now.*

— You need to get rid of your identification with a Terminator. A man can only be conscious of himself as a man in comparison to a woman. This is how the system of identifications is built here. A smart man can only get to know that he is smart if he has someone stupid on the background. Beauty—ugliness. Hot—cold. Soft—hard. Without these comparisons, we would not be able to use these notions. We would not even know them. If we have them, we know them through experience, i.e. experience of comparison. That's why we need to experience these dualities on both sides. Only by living through and becoming aware of our experience on both sides of a duality, we can become aware of this duality. Unless we have this experience, all our conversations are useless. You must always lean on your experience here. What people call change is just a move to another side of duality. That is what change is. A man was healthy—now he is sick. A man was successful—oops, he just failed. He is not successful anymore.

— *Ahh, I understand now why betrayal is change. (*Very delicate subject. In the Russian language, the root of the word betrayal and change is the same. We lose something in translation).*

— People betray but they don't change. That's what happens. What is a betrayal? Betrayal is change. To change is to move to the opposite side of a duality. If you have betrayed, you will be betrayed too. This is not a punishment for your sins. This is a way to learn both sides of the duality. That's the reason we are here. We are here to investigate dualities. But we turn them into sin; we call one side ugly and horrible.

— *Thank you.*

— Thank you. Next, please.

— *Yesterday, you shed some light on my husband tragic death. I came home, and I started to think. I should have felt guilty, but I didn't. I have only experienced grudge toward my Supreme Aspect: "Why me?" I don't know what to do with this now. I have never allowed myself to feel guilty. I can critique anyone, but I have never allowed anyone to make me feel guilty. I have been working as a manager for eighteen years. I have always tried to collect the information and to come up with judgment. When I condemn someone, I say: "I would have never done that!" However, I have done what I condemned others for doing quite a few times. I always connected it with karma.*

— What's karma for you? Is karma a retribution for sins?

235

— No. If you did something wrong, it will come back to you—you will experience what you did to another human being. That's how I understand karma. A man should think about the consequences of his actions before he acts. You should think before you do something to another human being. You should ask yourself, "Am I ready to experience what my actions caused him to experience?"

— Think about it coming your way ten times and don't do it. My approach is totally different. You can't avoid doing what you do. You can think a hundred times whether you want to do it or not, but you can't avoid doing it.

— I started to do it differently lately. I used to search for love, for something good. Do you know how my condemnation returned to me? When my husband died, I felt guilty for a long time. Prior to that, no one could make me feel guilty.

— He had to die so you could start to feel.

— I could feel myself be feeling other people pain since I was a kid.

— Pity and empathy are two different things.

— I understand. I could empathize with people when I was a kid. Then, I closed myself up, because it was very painful. I experienced terrible pain seeing what was going on around me. A man would share his experience with me, and I would feel his pain. This was unbearable. I had to close my emotional center.

— But that's the only way for you to become aware of yourself and to move to wholeness. **Work on our emotional center is the most important part of our work. You must have a very sensitive emotional center. You want to turn it off not to feel pain. But in that case, you would turn off the indicators of your disbalance. Your physical center will have to absorb this disbalance. You will get sick. You will get into an accident.**

— Yes. My emotional center was closed.

— Why was it closed? That's what I ask you. It did not close on its own. You have closed it! Why did you close it?

— I could handle physical pain—pills helped, but I could not take the pain of the emotional center. It was so heavy, I could not take it.

— How did Pint open the dual matrix of survival?

— You have started with the emotional center. I have started with the mind.

— Yes, you have started not where you have lost. You don't know what you are searching for. You forgot what you are searching for. And what did Pint do? He did not do anything. It wasn't his choice. Pint's program was created in such a way, that he could not lower the level of pain he was in. He had to experience a tremendous amount of pain. That pain forced him to search for the exit. Do you listen to what he says? Pint describes to you what he had experienced. It was very important for him to experience this pain. When we speak of wholeness, we speak of accepting our shadow sides. How can you see your shadow sides, if you turned the indicator off? **Pain and suffering serve as the indicators of a disbalance in one or another duality.** When these indicators are turned off, it *appears* to you that you are okay.

— It is easier for me to accept the negative sides that do not cause pain. I can accept duality beauty—ugliness, for example.

— Those lessons are easy. You don't give a fifth grader the assignment you give to a first grader; he will solve it in no time. You are in the fifth grade, and you need to solve the assignments that are assigned to your class. To solve these assignments, you need indicators. What hurts you the most? That's where the strongest disbalance lies. That's where the shadow side that you don't see lies. It has been activated. Your emotional center must be very sensitive for you to have the indicators to do this work of accepting your shadow sides. Our emotional center must be open. It must be very sensitive to do this work.

— *I have been experiencing an incessant inner dialogue for two weeks. Two dualities are talking in my head. Is it a ploy to distract me from more important things?*

— That's one of the strongest temptations. It *appears* to you your mind can solve everything here. I keep telling you that you can only obtain Wholeness when all three of your centers—mental, emotional, and physical—are in balance. We start with a mental center. The emotional center follows. As a result, our physical center changes. You have gotten to the third story of your house and you say you know the entire house. You have not been to other floors, yet.

— *You have said that a man can only cognize himself next to a woman. How can I solve this equation inside myself?*

— **You will not be able to solve anything inside yourself, because you will not be able to see anything inside. The external world is given to you so you can see yourself in its mirror. Your question can be solved outside, in the physical world. You need to use real situations and real people.**

— *I guess I need to move from theory to practice. To become aware of myself, I need to be around people.*

— There are plenty of people around you as it is.

— *I have separated myself. During yesterday's webinar, I talk to you as if we were equal—man to man. Afterward, I felt my inner woman. She woke up. I started to feel.*

— What did she say?

— *I could easily accomplish what I wanted to accomplish before. Now, I want to put my hands down.*

— To put one's hands down is not to stop to accomplish things. To put one's hands down is to stop the fight.

238

— I don't want to accomplish things through conflict anymore, as I used to. Now, when I hit a wall trying to accomplish something, I stop, and I think what is wrong with my structure.

— How do you do that?

— I try to use my emotional center. I try to feel what's going on. I observe. I have tried to get rid of the negative emotions before, now I am interested in them. I ask myself, "Why did that happen? What is it that I don't like? Why don't I like it?"

— Do you need the knowledge of duality to do that?

— I do. I need it not to become upset and resentful.

— Many people offer knowledge here. Why did you come to Pint?

— I have checked a number of schools before coming here. Neither one of them offered what I need. You are the only one who offers your own experience. I have a strong feeling you have experienced everything you say you did. I have not felt it anywhere else.

— We study duality here. You discuss understanding through feelings and sensations. This is the understanding of an insect, which, not having a developed brain, only experiences different sensations. It cannot comprehend them. It can only experience reality through reflex programs downloaded into it. A human being has an opportunity to become aware of what he experiences. I offer my vision, i.e. a certain conception, which describes the dual make-up of this world to you. Perceiving what I discuss with your mind, you start to understand what you experience. I want to emphasize that everything in this world is dual. You are not talking about that.

— I did everything using logic before. I used to calculate my every step. One day, I realized that I don't want my relationship with a man to be based on fear.

— We are sorting out very important things here. I constantly remind you that this training playground is dual. The dual nature of this reality is the most important discovery I have made. I am talking about dualities personality of every human being consists of. I am showing something to you again. What is it?

— *Are you implying I don't see duality?*

— Exactly. You will not be able to see anything here, including your fear and what is behind it, unless you use the key of duality. Many people talk about fear nowadays. I don't just talk about it, I explain to you the mechanisms of its appearance. I keep telling you that **a human being is a factory that manufactures fear**. If we are discussing a factory, describe how this factory works. In that case, you will be able to explain why things you experience, things you insist you don't want to experience, continue to occur.

I teach you the laws polar sides of the personality of human being operate upon.

— *I want to learn everything I can about these laws.*

— Okay. Let's move on. Why does the feeling of pity appear? What does it point you to? We have discussed the feeling of guilt at length. Now, we have come to pity. **When you pity other people, you pity yourself.** We frequently feel pity for the people around us. In reality, we pity ourselves. The feeling of pity arises because something *appears* not to be right to us, something *appears* not to be fair to us. It *appears* to you that life is unfair to you or to somebody else. Is that really the case? In reality, our notions of fairness are distorted and illusory. Life shows us things the way they are. Do we want to see things the way they are, or do we want to pity ourselves and other people because life doesn't treat us fair? What is opposite to the feeling of pity? What kind of feeling appears when you see things the way they are? What do you feel when you start to see that every event that happens to you and people around you represent an assignment you and they are passing through? What do you feel when you start to see everything that happens to you as an assignment that helps you to evolve your consciousness? Our main assignment here is to evolve and expand our consciousness. This is what process of wholeness or gathering ourselves in one whole is about. Coming here from the other worlds, we got fragmented. We are facing the opposite process now. We must gather all our fragments in one whole.

Opposite to pity is empathy. Empathy appears when you start to see things you considered to be bad from a point of view assignment that needs to be solved here. When you start to see things from this point of view, you start to see that even horrible diseases, brutal killings, and rapes are lessons you and other people are passing through. At this moment you develop compassion and empathy. You know what this human being experiences. Seeing a sick man after being sick yourself, you don't pity him, you understand the state he is in. This understanding comes as a result of you seeing that he goes through an assignment to get to the next level of consciousness. Pity doesn't offer this vision, empathy does. Let us now explore the reasons you experience pity by using examples from your daily life.

— *My parents wanted a girl. My older sister had drawn in a river, and they wanted a girl. When my mom was seven months pregnant with me, she fell. I was born with a broken finger. The first thing I felt coming out of Mom was the feeling of pity. When she was told she delivered a boy, she said, "Push him back where he came from." I remember that. The algorithm I experience since is, "I am not the one they expected." I perceive pity as love. It has been manifested multiple times in my life. Later, my*

241

personality started to use pity as a tool. When I complete an order at work, I make my customer wait for a long time before I release the product. I keep him in a state of impatience. I discuss the difficulties I had experienced in getting the job done. Eventually, when he is totally lost, I push the price up. When he agrees with the markup, I release the product to him and push for immediate payment. I create all this commotion so he will not understand what had happened. This program was inculcated in me during childhood, and it manifests itself in one way or another in different situations.

One more thing. Mom prohibited me from manifesting masculine qualities. She would only express her love to me on that condition. I had to suppress all my masculine qualities. I had to be a girl at home. I could only be a boy outside. At home, I am not a man. I started to use this too.

— You twist a situation in such a way that you appear to be a victim. That allows you to experience self-pity. That's how your program was conditioned; it continues to play in your life. Let's change this situation so instead of self-pity you can experience compassion toward yourself. Look at the circumstances of your appearance in this world as an assignment you are here to solve. Can you tell us why these conditions were given to you at birth? Why were you provided with such a unique family?

— *I thought about it. I was a warrior in many of my past lives.*

— Let's not bring past lives into this. Let's use your current life. We can get all the information we need from your current life. Why were you given these conditions at birth?

— *I was given these conditions so I can start to feel empathy. I was given these conditions so I can stop the victim—oppressor seesaw.*

— Great. Have you acquired enough experience of suffering? If you did, you can transform the state of self-pity you wallow in by starting to understand the assignment you came here to solve.

— *I experience self-pity less frequently now. When I feel it, I start to investigate. I try to figure out where it is coming from. My intellectual center is not well developed. I am a man of feelings. I can feel a three months old baby. I know what he wants right away.*

— Where is your disharmony? Which center is it in: emotional or intellectual?

— *I think it is my inner Mom. She was fast to condemn people. She has inculcated this quality into me.*

— Which center is most important for you: emotional or intellectual?

— *I am primarily in my mental center. I suppress my desires. I suppress pain.*

— After being in the emotional center for a long time, you moved to the mental center and started to suppress your emotions. You need to regulate this. You are experiencing a conflict between your emotional and mental centers, between a boy and a girl, between a man and a woman. You must see every mechanism of this conflict. This experience has been fully accumulated—you can become aware of this duality.

— *Thank you very much, Alexander Alexandrovich.*

— Let's finish for today. Tomorrow we will discuss school work. I want you to understand that you do this work not for our School but for yourself. The first line or leg of this work is to participate in the webinars and to investigate your programs. The second line or leg of this work is your participation in School life. You will not be able to jump using only one leg, you will need to use both legs. I will also recommend you use our forum to become aware of yourself. This forum is our School playground. It is free of condemnation and guilt. You can write whatever you want there. This is very important. You can see for yourself how difficult it is for you to verbalize your thoughts. By writing, expressing your states in thoughts, you will move in a very important direction. You will start to formulate something that you don't clearly understand yet. Publish your thoughts and feelings on our forum. You may be afraid to do that. This is not what people commonly do. But it is very important to publish things you consider to be very intimate. That will allow you to see and observe yourself from a side. As you may know, observation is the most important part of our work. I can talk about Pint in the third person. I can say different things about Pint. Why? Because I can see him from a side. This is a very important activity on the road of becoming aware of ourselves. Use our forum to do that.

I want to thank all of you for this webinar.

CHAPTER 6

HOW TO STOP THE FIGHT OF YOUR PERSONAL OPPOSITIONS AND TO BECOME WHOLE IN DUALITIES "TO ORDER—TO OBEY," "TO FORBID—TO ALLOW," "TO PRAISE—TO REPRIMAND" AND "TO PUNISH—TO FOSTER"

•◆•◆• •◆•◆• •◆•◆• •◆•◆• •◆•◆• •◆•◆• •◆•◆• •◆•◆• •◆•◆• •◆•◆• •◆•◆• •◆•◆• •◆•◆•

— We are going to explore dualities "to order—to obey," "to forbid—to allow," "to praise—to reprimand," "to punish—to foster" today. Behind all these dualities is management. We live in the world where management is a global notion. When we start to look at the world through the prism of this global factor, some very interesting questions arise. One of these questions is, "Who rules this world?" Things we see in our daily life are the results of management conducted by entities we don't even see. Many of them are not even here. They are not of this world. But at the same time, this world is part of a huge Cosmic Organization. What was the aim of the creation of our world? Who rules it? We are not going to address all these questions today. We are going to address the questions that are much closer to home. We are dealing with the results of management, which manifest themselves in our world in the form of presidents who rule over the countries we live in and CEOs who manage corporations we work for. These results manifest themselves in the form of our parents, who inculcate programs of management, i.e. our personal programs into us, and in people who are close to us: our wives, husbands, children, etc. Management is everywhere.

Perhaps, you think otherwise? Perhaps, you think you are not being managed by anyone. Perhaps you don't want to be managed. Is that possible? Can someone who lives here not be managed? Can you exist here and not interact with everything that exists? No. This is impossible.

So, let's explore these dualities, which actions we experience on our personalities. Most people don't like to be in a subservient position. They don't like to be ordered around. People get irritated. They complain nobody is interested in their opinion. They complain they are ordered to do things they don't want to do. That's the way relationships in the army are built. You can say you are not in the army. You can say you don't have to obey the way soldiers obey. But as we can see, you go to work, and you obey your boss the same way soldiers obey their drill sergeant. You also have bosses in your family. This topic is broader than it appears to be, and it touches every sphere of our life. I invite you to explore this topic from the standpoint of your personal program, which contains mechanisms that determine the ways you react to management, i.e. to orders, condemnation, punishment, etc. These mechanisms or mechanical reactions are recorded in our programs. They were inculcated by our parents in the process of our upbringing, i.e. in the process of formation of our personality. These mechanisms have been operating and continue to operate in our life.

People see the subject we are about to discuss differently. To sort out the specific ways you react to orders, prohibitions, praise, and punishment, we need to know the specifics of your personal program in detail, as every mechanical reaction you exhibit—intellectual, emotional, and physical—comes from your program. So, let's start our investigation with the first question I posted on our site last week in preparation for this webinar, **"What do you prefer: to order or to obey?"**

— *I prefer to obey. It's very difficult for me to order people around.*

— Why do you find it difficult to order people around?

— *My mom brought me up to be a nice, obedient girl. I used to listen to her carefully. I used to do everything she ordered me to do. I used to comply with her every instruction. It is not easy for me to come up with my own instructions now. I do what my boss tells me to do.*

— So, your mom made a good subordinate out of you. Let's sort this out. Who do you subordinate to, how, and when? You don't subordinate to everyone, right? Moreover, you experience certain reactions to orders given to you. What kind of a subordinate are you?

— *I bring very little trouble to my boss. I bring very little trouble at home. I try not to express my thoughts and feelings. When I am ordered to do something, I do it as fast and as good as I can. However, my irritation accumulates, and at a certain point I get fed up and I blow up. I quit my job or separate from a man I was living with forever.*

— As the opposite side of obeying orders is giving orders, you will not be able to only obey orders all the time.

— *Yes, up to a certain moment ...*

— Where is this line below which you will not go? When do you say, "Enough is enough!"

247

— I listened to my mom until I was twenty. I used to ask her what to do and how to do things all the time. But one day, I said, "This is it! I want to live on my own!" She objected. She said, "No! You cannot do that." I left.

— So, you left one boss. And who did you go to?

— I wound up with another boss—my husband.

— Did he look exactly like the first one?

— Yes, he did.

— They must look alike. So, the situation that played out between you and mom started to play itself out between you and your husband. Am I right?

— Yes.

— The conflicts you have experienced at home with your mom, you started to experience now with your husband, right?

— Yes, I experience the same conflicts living with him now. He objects to me coming to the seminars. He says: "Stay home!" He doesn't explain anything. "Stay home!" That's it. I say, "No! I am leaving!" and I leave. For me to do something, I need someone to forbid me to do that. This resistance energizes me, and I do something. So, for me to do something, I need someone to push me. Otherwise, I will fall asleep on a couch.

— We are seeing one of the most common mechanisms that allow people to accomplish things in this reality. You have described it very well. You said: "In order for me to do something, I need someone to resist me." Experiencing this resistance, you start to receive energy you need to be active. You cannot do anything without this energy. You need resistance. You will reinforce this tendency, but resistance will also escalate. That's how you reach a level of energy necessary for you to do what you plan to do.

— That's exactly how it is. I don't know what I would do without these people.

— It looks like we need these type of relationships. We create them, and we maintain them. When people start to oppress and order us what to do without considering our desires, we scream: "What do they do to me?! I will not allow them to do that!" You say that, start to resist, and eventually, come up doing something as if despite them.

— *Yes, in the process we get the energy necessary to do that.*

— Yes, we receive the energy we need, and as we can see now, we need these people.

— *Yes, we need them badly.*

— We need them, because otherwise, without them we will not be able to do anything. Imagine you are on your own. No one told you what to do for a year. What would happen? What would you do? Would you even do anything?

— *Hmm ... I will not even get up from a chair. I get my energy from people who are close to me, from my interactions with colleagues and family members. These interactions provide me with the energy to move forward, to hate, to love, to feel happy.*

— Yes. This is very interesting. People say: "They never praise me. They scream and yell at me. They reprimand me. They forbid me to do things I want to do. If they only praised me more." But, in reality, most people need this negative stimulation.

— *Yes. This is also attention, but it carries the opposite charge. Mom punished me severely when I was a kid. I was punished on every level: mental, emotional, and physical. I was imprinted hard. Mom used punishment to create these imprints, not praise. She used a different type of attention, or we can say it was a different type of love and care.*

— Let's get back to something I am not tired of repeating. Our parents create our personal program by inculcating us with the mechanisms of survival they know. What does it mean? Well, as a minimum, we must do something. Otherwise, we will not survive. How do our parents inculcate us with these mechanisms of survival? They can use a carrot—praise, or a stick—punishment. As we can see, a stick is used more frequently. If you were to look at donkeys and horses, you would see that they are frequently screamed at and beaten with a stick: "Go! Go!" You will see this rough type of training used more frequently than praise and gentle petting. Quite frequently, human beings need to be beaten, too. That's the only way to make some people do something. Most people react to praise with euphoric laziness. People say they want to be dealt with nicely. They say they want to be praised. But what will happen if they are dealt with this way, especially if in order to function the program they are inculcated with requires a harsh stimulus, such as a rough word, a slap, or a reprimand?

What are we dealing with here? People who receive these programs, start to attract actors with corresponding programs. Why did not you leave your mom and find someone who would treat you differently?

— *Beats me. Why can't I find someone and order him around?*

— Exactly. Why can't you? I'll tell you why. Half of your program—to obey orders—is inculcated on the conscious level, the second half—to give orders—is inculcated on the subconscious level. You have the same drill sergeant in your mom has.

— *You are right. And I manifest this drill sergeant too. I have kids. I must order them around.*

— What does this *have to* mean? In this world, everyone *has to* do something. Your mom gave birth to you because she *had to*. Then, she *had to* spend twenty years to bring you up. Now, you *have to* bring up your kids the same way she did and you will. You will apply the same stick your mom applied, and you will inculcate them with the same program you received.

250

— *Hmmm. I have not punished my son once while he was growing up. He was allowed to do everything he wanted. I have made a horrible tyrant out of him.*

— You have brought up your own tyrant.

— *Yes. He will have me cry for the rest of my life. When I read your books, I decided to make some corrections. I punish him the same way mom used to punish me.*

— Attention everyone! Take a look at what is happening here. We have been inculcated with a program. Our every action is limited by this program. We order people what to do and we obey people according to this program. Every program carries certain unique subprograms, but no one can step outside the borders of this program—your family life will repeat the life of your parents. Your supervisors and colleagues at work will deal with you the same way your parents dealt with you. We are dealing with a very strict program. Your every move has been written in it.

A question arises, "What does it mean? Will I have to experience all of this? Is there anything else here?" I will say that for a sleeping man, this is the only option. If a man wants to get married and to find out what kind of life he is going to have with his wife, he just needs to look at his parents' life. He will experience the same conflicts in his own family. Does this vision make you happy?

— *Hmmm ... Why not? Why should not it make me happy?*

— Your parents used to scream at you: "You don't understand us! What are you doing?!" Now you can tell them: "I understand you now!"

— *Yes, I understand them now. I understand what they went through when I was a teenager. I experience now what they had experienced then. I am a parent now, and I will have to face the same script bringing up my kids.*

251

— One day they will say: "You don't understand us." Then, just before you die, they will say: "I understand what you went through, now. I am sorry I did what I did." What a melodramatic life.

— *Yes. But all of us like this game. Otherwise, we would not play it.*

— Great. Some of the students are happy to play their program along.

— *She says: "I have such a great program, I am going to play it to the end."*

— A professional killer happily discusses how he killed his first, second, and third victim, thinking: "Why should I change anything? I have a great program." People around him nod their heads: "You do have a great program."

— *I used to be very upset with my program. I feel Okay now. That's where I am.*

— What do you need Pint for then? Do you need him to show you all of this for you to say: "This is great!" Is that how you see my role?

— *No. This is not how I see your role. What can I say? I can see the roles I play. I can see some of the dualities I am stuck in. I am trying to move from one side of duality to another to experience a full spectrum of it and to become aware of it.*

— Good. You are about to start on a hard road. You must start giving orders. You must pull out a whip and start to reprimand people around you.

— *Yes. I will have to walk this side of this duality. I will not be able to avoid it.*

— Does it make you happy?

— *And why not?*

— She feels happy again. Okay. Order or reprimand me for doing something!

— *Order? Reprimand?*

— Yes, you said you are ready to move to the opposite side, to the side that gives orders. Let's start with me. Order me to do something!

— *What do you mean? What do you want me to do?*

— A general stands in front of his platoon scratching his head. The entire unit is on attention. He is thinking, "What should I order them to do?"

— *I got it. Don't go to Egypt, Alexander Alexandrovich! There is nothing to do there!*

— Good. Do continue. "Go to Egypt, but don't eat breakfast there!"

— *Yes. Don't eat dinner there either.*

— Go to Egypt, but don't talk to anyone there!

— *Don't swim there either! There are sharks there.*

— Not bad, not bad. But I want to hear steel in your voice. I want your voice to make me jump. What kind of a general are you? "Dear soldiers. Would you mind digging a trench here? I hope you will not find it too tiresome." Is that how you give orders?

— *I am not good at it.*

— Where is your commanding tone of voice?

— *Who are you talking to?!!!*

— Exactly. "Don't you know who you are talking to, private?! You are talking to a three-star general!"

— *Okay. Let me be.*

— What kind of a general are you? You have started on the road called "To give orders!" but you have not even made a step forward. You march in the same spot.

— *It is not easy for me to do that.*

— Shut up, idiot! Silence!

— *I am silent…*

— Good!

— You will not silence me! I will say what I want!

— Hmmm … What do we have now? We have resistance. Look, you are good at manifesting resistance, but you can't give orders.

— You are right. My husband never does what I order him to do. He just looks at me funny, "Why are you screaming at me?"

— Why doesn't he obey you?

— I am not sure.

— What do you need for people to obey you?

— I don't know. Perhaps it is a certain tone of voice … a tone of voice that doesn't tolerate any objections.

— That's what people feel right away. A human being may talk nicely and smile, but at the same time, you feel he is not going to tolerate disobedience. Right?

— Yes.

— So, it is not about the form that the order comes in. It is about the essence of a man who gives the orders.

— Yes.

— Then, your task is to feel this side in you that gives the orders.

— Alexander! Get up and close the door!

— Here you go. Now, this is an order. Look, sometimes it is enough to give someone a look. You don't need to say anything. When two wolves meet to address territorial issues, they rarely fight. It is frequently enough for one of them to give another a look, and the opponent is running away, tail between his legs. What's behind this?

— There is an inner power behind it: "This is my territory!"

— Yes, that's how a man who is accustomed to giving orders *sees* the situation. You can't play it. It is impossible. If you try to play it, people will laugh at you. You either feel it or you don't. What does a human being who can really give orders feel?

— *He feels he is the boss. He will not tolerate any resistance.*

— And where does he get this notion that he is the boss from? Why don't other people feel that way?

— *I don't know. Hmm ... where does he get it from?*

— This is the question we will leave you with.

— *Okay. Thank you.*

— Thank you. Who is next?

— *That was a very interesting dialogue. I am not sure what I prefer: to order or to obey? I cannot answer this question. Lately, I prefer to give orders. But I don't like to be responsible for critical decisions. I can be bossy at home. I scream at my kids, but they don't pay much attention to me.*

— You remind me of a TV set. It works all the time. No one is watching it.

— *Yes. When I try to say something in a harsh, commanding tone of voice, my husband and my sons pretend they don't hear me. It looks like I am talking to myself. I command them to do something, but they just sit there. I try to make them feel guilty, thinking they will do something for me, but that doesn't work either. This is very strange. When someone is rough with me, I immediately do what they order me to do.*

— Okay. So, when someone gives you an order, you do what you are ordered to do, and you do it fast. Let's look at people who give you orders, those you obey. What are their main characteristics?

— *There were two such people in my childhood. My grandmother. She would just glance at me, and full of fear, I would do anything she wanted. She had never hurt me, but I was always afraid of her.*

— Were you afraid of mental, emotional, or physical punishment?

— I was afraid of physical punishment. I was brought up on a farm. We had animals. I have seen how people train animals. She could have pulled me by the hair. She could have spanked me. She used to ask: "Do you want me to spank you?!" and I would run and do everything she asked me to do. I was scared …

— So, you felt grandma could hurt you?

— Yes.

— That was your basic fear?

— I saw her spank other kids. Dad used to tell me how she punished him when he was a kid. I was terribly afraid of her.

— Here you go! Attention everyone! Here is the formula: "Beat your own people, so strangers will be afraid of you!"

— But I was not a stranger?!

— When mafia tough guys need to collect money from a "law-abiding citizen," they don't hurt him right away. They bring him to a place where they torture someone. It might be their own guy who stole something from their boss or somebody else they torture for something. They ask the guy they brought to the scene, who is standing there shaking with fear: "What do you think? Would you like to experience that?" He usually says: "I'll give you anything you want!"

— Ah! I remember now. Grandma used to beat her animals. I saw her do that. Oh my God! That's how she trained us. Once, when her hens had young cheeks, she brought her cat over and gave it a beating in front of them. The cat runs away and had not shown its face home for days. I thought: "Wow! If I were to do something bad, I would get a similar beating."

— Great! It's a funny reality we live in. That's how our programs get inculcated. The key moment here is fear of punishment.

— I am also afraid of aggression. When someone raises his voice at me, I feel scared. I feel I might be beaten. Even though I have never beaten, I do everything I can to avoid being physically hurt.

— You don't need to be beaten. You are well inculcated with fear to do everything they ask you to do.

— Yes.

— They don't need to kill you. They just need you to obey them.

— Yes. There is one more interesting thing here. When I got older, I stood my grounds firm. No one was able to control me. I have been threatened with physical beating many times, but I never obeyed.

— So, you are a revolutionary.

— Yes, that's who I was in adolescence. It was a matter of honor, "I will not obey! You can cut me to pieces, but I will not do what you want."

— Yes. Earth was, and it still is a planet of slaves. People were used, and they continue to be used as slaves. Essences that manage them continue to receive what they want to receive from them. This is not coincidental. Why do parents use such harsh methods to bring up their children? Why do governments use such violent methods to control their citizens? Why is the world run the way it is run? Where is this violence coming from? Everything comes from above, as they say, from the boss. I am sharing this information with you to broaden the level of your consciousness. Moreover, people do not want to obey anymore. They start to talk about their rights. What do you want to say about your rights, Dina?

— Eventually, I realized that this revolutionary attitude threatens my physical body, and I entered another period. I learned diplomacy. I learned how to avoid conflict. When I got married, I expected my husband to demand things from me, but he never did. I was free to do what I wanted to do. I was shocked. I expected him to forbid me to do certain things. I

thought I would be able to suffer a little bit on this account, but he never prohibited me from doing anything I wanted to do.

— Oh my God! This is horrible.

— *This is strange, but I like it. The only thing that bothers me—I don't work. I am home all day. I do what I want most of the day, but when my husband goes to work, I have to get up and feed him. I have to prepare his lunch. The fact that I need to comply with this stupid regimen irritates the hell out of me.*

— What would you do if you didn't have this "stupid regimen"?

— *I would do something interesting. I thought I would not be able to live without regimen but turned out I can live and do something out of interest. For example, I may suddenly experience a strong desire to cook something special for my husband.*

— Do you ever experience a strong desire to drop some sulfuric acid into his coffee?

— *What for?*

— Nothing, forget it, just my sick fantasies.

— *No. Sometimes I contemplate on how to make him feel more important so he would bring more money home and provide us with a better quality of survival.*

— Find a woman. Bring her home and tell him: "I found another woman for you. From now on, both of us are going to obey you." The level of his self-importance will double.

— *You are too much, Alexander Alexandrovich!*

— I am going crazy from these webinars.

— *We are discussing different methods of management. How do I manage my man? I make him feel very important. I tell him I admire his skills. I don't need another woman. Who knows what kind of policies she will introduce.*

— A woman shared her story with me once. "That's my fate," she said, "My last husband was good for nothing when I

258

found him. I dressed him up. I fed him. I elevated the level of his self-esteem. He became very important. One day he looked at me and he said: "You are stupid. You don't understand anything. I can't live with you anymore." And he left me for a woman who was smarter than me.

— *This is interesting. My husband also tells me that I am stupid, but he usually says it in a playful way.*

— That's great, Dina. It looks to me, we have lost the topic of our discussion. Do you remember what we started with?

— *Yes, we have started with a question of what I like the most: to order or to obey? I like to order more. But, in the case of serious decisions, I like to obey. When someone needs to take responsibility for a decision family's livelihood depends upon, such as to move to another country or not, I obey.*

— You are talking about a decision someone's life depends upon. "Go and take a bath!" Is that such a decision?

— *No.*

— Imagine someone went to take a bath and drowned.

— *That's funny.*

— Not really. People do drown in bathtubs.

— *Not in my case. Theoretically, it is possible, but I will make sure that everything is okay.*

— Life of a human being depends on every step he makes. You can serve fish to your husband and have him choke on a bone.

— *That's impossible. I carefully check his plate for bones every time I serve him dinner. What else can happen?*

— He can chock on a piece of meat.

— *I'll cut his stake for him from now on.*

— Imagine, you call him from your bedroom. He runs toward you, falls, and breaks his leg.

— *Well, you are right, anything can happen. I try to be as careful as I can. I try to warn him of every obstacle. I warn him when I see a puddle of water on his way.*

— Do you have signs all over your house, "Don't drown in the toilet"? "Don't cut yourself with a fork!" We got to a topic that deals with the subject of ordering and interest. All these difficult states you experience when you order people to do something you need to be done and obeying people who give you orders usually come out of duty.

— *Out of duty? Hmmm. When I obey, I obey out of duty. That's right. When I order, I order out of pleasure.*

— Wait a minute. Don't you think there is duty behind all these things? When you are in the army, you deal with a soldier's or officer's duty. The idea of duty, which is based on bylaws is the key here. A similar book of bylaws—written and unwritten—exists in a family. You deal with a similar book of bylaws at work. These books of bylaws are everywhere. Finally, there is a constitution of a country you live in; everyone must obey it. Suddenly, you say, "I don't want to obey Constitution!" What will happen?

— *This is not a duty. This is fear.*

— Wait a minute! How does fear appear?

— *This is the fear of punishment.*

— Okay. Why should you be punished? If you are being punished, that means you have done something wrong. In that case, there is also something that is right. Am I correct?

— Yes.

— Rules and bylaws stipulate what is right and what is wrong. Constitution and army bylaws are documents that determine what is right and what is wrong. If you don't obey them, you will be punished.

— *Yes.*

— So, do you have a duty to perform what is considered to be right here or not? We are talking duty. Our entire life here is regimented, but we don't see it. We don't perceive it that way.

— *Yes. This is interesting. I have never perceived this as my duty.*

— You had a great life. Suddenly, Pint shows up and starts to talk about duty. Now you know about it.

— *Hmmm, you are right. This is a duty. Why should I cook for my husband? It is my duty.*

— Of course.

— *I didn't think about it before.*

— Do you have to be a woman?

— *Yes. I was born in a woman's body and I should behave as a woman.*

— Exactly. You were born in a woman's body and your duty is to be a woman. If you were born in a cat's body, you would not give a damn about the constitution.

— *Is this my illusion that if I am in a woman's body it is my duty to behave as a woman? I take it as my choice. I can behave like a man, but I don't want to.*

— You are not even aware of the fact that while in the woman's body you obey certain rules, rules that were accepted here to regulate the behavior of a human being who is considered to be a woman. You are not even aware of this fact. What if your husband were to start to behave like a woman? How would you like that?

— *What do you mean?*

— What if he were to put a skirt on and to wiggle his ass in front of you seductively?

— *Oh my God! I will not feel comfortable with that. I don't know what to think.*

— So, there is a big difference between duty and interest.

— *Okay. I agree with the duty part. When I got married, I felt this duty as an oppression. I tried to resist it.*

— You should join the army. No, that would be too hard. I suggest you do something easier. Go to a supermarket and break one of the consumer's laws. Break the law that prohibits to peeing in a supermarket. Squat down in the middle of a supermarket and pee. A guard will materialize and say: "What are you doing?"

— *I am afraid to do something that will bring up a guard. I get scared when my kids pull cereal boxes from the shelves.*

— Exactly. The concept of duty is everywhere. There are rules here and you should obey these rules. If you are not aware of them, it is your problem.

— *I used to perceive the word "duty" as something very serious—a duty to protect Motherland, etc.*

— No, in your case, it is a duty in front of a supermarket, a duty in front of a street. You have a duty not to spit at the citizens of Panama. You have a duty not to step on their toes. You have not done it before, and it seems to you there is no duty, but there is plenty of duty you must comply with here. Okay. I think you had enough material to contemplate on.

— *I think I do. Thank you.*

— Thank you.

— *Let me answer the second question: "Which situations connected to obedience cause you to experience the strongest objection?" I cannot obey stupid orders. When my boss orders me to do something, he has not thought through ...*

— Why do you think he didn't think his order through? Perhaps, he thought about it for a long time. Perhaps, you don't understand what he was thinking about.

— *Let me use an example. A young man was sent to my office last week. Some office work had to be done and he was sent to do it. I immediately felt he was not experienced enough to do this work. I was asked to show him around and to make sure he gets the work done in time. I was very polite to him. I took two days out of my busy schedule and I explained everything to him in minute details.*

— Wait a minute. How does this situation relate to the question you wanted to answer?

— *Finally, I got angry and I screamed at him, "Just do it already!" I left the office. In two hours everything was done. Now, he is a key figure in this operation. I just had to "kick his butt" at a certain time, and the work was done.*

— Wait a minute. You "kicked his butt," but the question was, "What happens when your butt gets kicked?" What happens when you need to obey? I order you to answer my question!

— *In order for me to get him moving, I had to bring myself to this state, to the state where I clearly saw that I didn't have another choice but to kick him.*

— Is that what you want me to do now. Do you want me to bring you to that state?

— *This is my mechanism. That's the only way you can make me obey you. I will nod my head and pretend to agree with you, but I will continue to do my own stuff. That's what I am doing right now.*

— Yes, that's what you are doing. That's what you do. You torture me. I am getting tired. You have gathered here to torture me. You don't want Pint to live to see the Quantum Leap.

Take a look at what your parents gave you. That's your inheritance. I can't even use profanities when I talk to you. Everything here is built on fear, but I can't use fear to do this work. I have to do it differently.

A priest can scare you with the devil, "If you don't pray, the devil will take you." Parents can scare you with the police,

"If you don't go to school, police will come and take you." That's the way they bring you up. And that works.

I use awareness. Does it work?

— *We are really trying. I'll be honest with you...*

— We are having a webinar. I conduct this webinar. I have a set of questions that we need to address. And I came here expecting you to answer these questions. You do not answer them. So, how can I manage this PROCESS? *(*Quantum physicists have recently come up with the definition of Consciousness. Consciousness is a PROCESS in the structure of the universe. Sir Roger Penrose, The Emperor's New Mind. Translator's note) How can I make you interested in these questions? I ask you a question. You answer me. But your answer has nothing to do with my question. What should I do? Should I sit here until cows go home listening to your gibberish? What kind of principles is our relationship built upon? I can tell you that you have a duty in front of the fourth dimension. If you do not do what you supposed to do, you will not get there. But I will not tell you that. So, what is going to happen next? Everyone here works using the concept of duty, rules, and laws that can't be broken. When you break the rules, you get punished. I can't punish you. So, what shall I do?

— *We have to develop interest and start to ask you questions.*

— Great. We have touched upon the topic of interest earlier. What's the difference between duty and interest?

— *When I am interested in the order I receive, everything goes nice and smooth. I experience no conflict or condemnation. Time flies without me noticing it. Sometimes my wife calls me from the bedroom, "Come to bed. It's four in the morning."*

— Okay. Are you interested in what we do here?

— *Yes, I am very interested in what we do here.*

264

— You are interested in what we do because you are not bound by duty here. Am I correct? The concept of duty is present everywhere, but it is absent here. What we do here, in our group is based on interest. The difference between duty and interest is enormous. But a human being is not even aware of the fact that he has a duty. That's what we just sorted out with Dina. A human being does not even understand what duty is. How can he understand the difference between duty and interest?

— *A system that is based on duty is a dead system. It kills creativity.*

— However, this system prevails in our reality. Everything here is based on duty. Take a look at your life. Everything you do, whether at home or at work, you do out of duty.

— *A man who creates is free of duty. He is free. But this reality doesn't need free people. They are difficult to manage.*

— Have you ever seen these so-called free people here? Perhaps the whole idea of freedom is a myth?

— *When a small screw stops to work properly, it gets removed.*

— Exactly. So, what kind of a machine are we dealing with? What kind of a reality are we living in? What kind of parts does this reality need? It needs parts that perform certain functions, parts such as a wheel, a hub, a sleeve, and a crankshaft. Suddenly, a wheel says: "I don't want to be a wheel anymore. I want to be a sleeve." Boom! Your automobile has changed; you cannot drive it anymore. What kind of freedom is this? This is anarchy. What is the difference between order and anarchy? And remind you, things that are related to management are connected to order. Different people have a different understanding of order, but everyone tries to bring order into his life the way he sees it. But what is an order for one man is disorder for another man. Everyone tries to establish order the way he sees fit. Take a family unit. A man

265

and a woman get married. A week later each one of them tries to establish his own order. A child has been born; he needs to know what order is and who to obey.

— *We are dealing with a hierarchical system. It has been operating here for centuries and it will continue to operate.*

— Okay. But how do we live in this hierarchical system?

— *We mechanically obey certain orders. This world is a reflection of our mind. Our mind is a mechanical structure, and this world is equally mechanical.*

— Yes. You bring up good theoretical thoughts to our table, but I am interested in your factual experience. Look, we are dealing with a certain order of survival. I have spent a lifetime investigating it, and I clearly see how this mechanism works. It works great. Someone manages this mechanism and it continues to operate according to the plan.

But what are we talking about here, in School? We are talking about something entirely different than survival. But how aware are you of the mechanism you happen to be in? You are a small part of the global mechanism of survival. That's what we do here. We have to sort out every minute mechanism of survival. Then, we face another question. What will we have outside of this mechanism? Spiritual people like to talk about enlightenment and getting out of here. I would like to ask them a question: "Where are you planning to go to?" A man has spent his entire life in jail. Suddenly, his jail door opens and he is free to go anywhere he wants. He doesn't know what to do. He will create the same jail for himself. He will jump from one jail to another because he doesn't know anything better.

— *The system of notions his machine is attuned with corresponds to the terrain he occupies. We are dealing with a mirror principle. In order*

266

to go higher, we need to convert our machine, i.e. our mind to a different algorithm.

— Yes! But how can you even ask a question of going anywhere if you don't even understand the algorithm you happen to operate on at the present time? This is the main theme of the Quantum Leap. Why do people get so stressed out talking about Quantum Leap? What stresses them out so much? They are stressing out thinking about what is going to happen to them over there, i.e. how will they survive there? They are not stressing out about what will happen and what will it lead to. No! They are stressing out about their bodies, their way of life, their prison that is starting to become endangered as they think in connection with Quantum Leap.

— *That's understandable. We don't have any other notions and we cannot get them anywhere else. Our machine is attuned to this reality. We can't even imagine …*

— You can't even imagine what is about to come. Pint talks about it, but no one listens. Perhaps Pint should leave. This is an interesting paradox. We are discussing a topic that can get you out of the survival mode. But how do you see it? It turns out, most of you don't even see that everything you do, you do out of duty.

— *Perhaps I didn't make myself clear. We are discussing a very difficult new topic. We are searching for something new. We are ready to change our perception and to see things in a new light.*

— Yes, your readiness to change your perception is of paramount importance here. If you want to move from point "A" to point "B," to begin with, you have to understand that presently you happen to be at point "A." To move out of it, you need to understand where you presently are. Otherwise, you will not do anything at all. You also need to have an idea, or at least be able to imagine, what point "B" where you want to get to looks like. In my terminology, point "A" represents survival. Point "B" represents life. So, what is the difference between survival and life?

— *We can define survival as a harsh system of conditioning that was forced upon us.*

— It's a system of duties. "You have to survive! You have to survive!" That's the main program parents inculcate into a child.

— Yes. "You have to live. You have to survive!" That's what my parents kept telling me when I was a kid.

— Pay attention here. In my terminology "To live" and "To survive" are two totally different things. What is the difference between these two terms? Survival presupposes duty. You must comply with this duty. But what is opposite to duty?

— *I think it is creativity.*

— Yes. But creativity is just a notion. What kind of a state does a human being experience while he creates?

— *Is it freedom?*

— Hmm ... this is not easy to understand. That's the peculiarity of language we use. I am asking you to talk about something that is not easy to talk about—about your states. What kind of a state does a man experiences while he creates?

— *Is it happiness?*

— No. In that case, happiness would be opposite to duty, but some people are happy when they perform their duties.

— *I don't understand ...*

— I understand that you don't understand. This is not an easy topic. You cannot discern it.

— *I don't know ... it is some kind of general state of excitation ... you are right I can't discern it yet ... but I feel it intuitively.*

— Okay, name the prevailing states you experience during the webinars.

— *I fluctuate between pain, stupidity, and brief flashes of interest.*

— Here you go. Primitive men used to rub two wooden sticks together to strike a fire. By rubbing our pain and suffering, we strike out interest. Interest. It is interest that is opposite to duty. This is the key! Does anyone obligate you to come to Pint's seminars? Do you attend them out of duty?

— *No, I come here out of interest. I am not obligated to come here. The interest I experience coming here is similar to the interest I experienced as a child, when these survival mechanisms were not installed in me, yet.*

— So, the key moment here is interest. I would ask all of you to discern between how you understand duty and interest. Every question we have discussed today dealt with duty. The way things are here, you will be punished for not doing something you are supposed to do. What do people ask you to do? They ask you to do what you are supposed to do. What do people praise and reprimand you for? They praise you for doing what you are supposed to be doing and they reprimand you for not doing what you are supposed to be doing. They would not be able to either praise or reprimand you if you were not inculcated with the idea of duty, i.e. what you are supposed to be doing since childhood. The idea of duty penetrates everything here. You will discover it in formal government laws and in informal family laws. You don't see these laws framed on your family room wall, but everyone knows them. Moreover, everyone tries to reinforce them. Everything here is connected to duty. Every woman knows what her husband should do and how he should behave. Every man knows what his wife should do and how she should behave. Every parent knows what his or her children should do and how they should behave. The idea of duty has been inculcated into every personal program.

Let's move on to our next question, "Which situations, linked to obedience, call you to experience strong protest?"

— *Recently, I have decided, "I will only do things out of interest." Next day I was fired from my job. At the time, I felt disappointment— my survival was at risk. But then I realized that this part of me, let's call it "the part that manifests interest," was very pushy. I have not worked on this part before. Previously, when I insisted on doing something my way, I thought I did it out of interest. Suddenly, I discovered that this was not the case. The ongoing conflict between me and my mother continued. I was financially in debt as well. Finally, I saw that I was resisting and fighting my mother. She was sending me a message, "You have to survive!" I screamed back: "No! I want to live. I am not interested in survival. I want to live!" That was an illusion. I was not interested in living. To bring my attention to this fact, I was dealt with harshly. My boss fired me. My mother used to curtail my every interest when I was a kid. My ex-husband did that too. They did what they did to me until I saw that I was not in the interest you speak of.*

— You have touched upon a very important moment. Let's take a look at the interplay of these dualities. You say "duty." I go further and say that opposite to the side called duty is interest. But when you start to investigate yourself, you will see that in your program opposite to "duty" stands "negation of duty."

Your mom says: "You should do that! It's your duty to do that!" "I will not do that! That's not my duty!" you retort. She tells you: "You should…" You say: "No, I should not." There is no interest here. To get to the level of interest is to get to the Supreme Aspect. It is not easy. I know that based on my own experience. You will always be dealing with a dual nature of your personal structure, i.e. you will try to oppose whatever is being imposed on you. Whenever someone will try to impose a rule on you, you will scream: "No! I will not do that!" Whenever someone will try to impose a feeling on you, you will scream: "No! I will not feel that!" Whenever someone will try to impose a thought on you, you will scream: "No! I will not think that way!" That's the way your personality is built—it has been built on negation. Every personality is built on negation.

There are good boys and girls and there are bad boys and girls. Good boys and girls follow the instructions they are given. Bad boys and girls reject what they are told. Those are two sides of one duality. Those who accept what they are told will finally reach a point of getting fed up with following the instructions they were given and start to reject them. Those who reject what they are told eventually will start to accept it. When will they do that? That's irrelevant. I want you to see that the only thing you can do here is to swing between two sides: you either accept or reject what you are told.

— *Yes.*

— Where does this message—whether to accept things or to reject things—comes from? It comes from the outside. That's how the personality of a human being is formed. When a child is born, he doesn't know anything. Parents start to inculcate a child with the notions they are familiar with. Later, this child starts to relate to everything he was inculcated with in two ways: he either accepts or rejects it. He gets on one side of duality while being submerged in a conflict between two of its opposite sides. Irrespective of the side he finds himself on, all he can do is fight. That's the way this wonderful mechanism of survival is built.

— *I noticed that I resist. I got so taken by this resistance, I only have slogans instead of interests. I have lost connection with my Supreme aspect.*

271

I thought I was swimming in the interest as a child, but that was not the case. This conflict took all my energy.

— Exactly. And when a slogan about your interest appears, you scream: "Don't push me around with your demands. I have my own interest." Pay attention that you continue to fight under the slogan, "This is my interest!" But what's hiding behind this slogan is your refusal to do what another human being demands you to do.

— *Yes. And that's how personality carries me away.*

— Exactly. You have to remember that personality is conflict. Personality is attracted by conflicts and fights in all their manifestations. The matrix of survival was constructed amazingly well—everyone here will be offered what to fight for. That's what holds us in the axiom of survival. Conflict, struggle, and fight. That's what personality likes the best. Slogans and reasons behind conflicts can change. It's funny, but some people say: "No! Not me. I am not fighting. I am for peace and love. I am for awareness," and they fight for it. Conflict is everywhere. People get carried away with it. A man says, "I am not interested in this conflict, and I am not interested in that conflict. But, wait a minute, I am interested in that conflict," and he pulls out his sword. This is not easy to see. I have experienced it on my own skin. It took me five years to start to discern and to experience real interest. TO E-X-P-E-R-I-E-N-C-E. Not just to say these words, but to feel where this interest is coming from. I can tell you about my interest now. **My interest is the interest of a self-investigator.** It is not dual. It cannot be dual, because an investigator investigates duality. An investigator is interested in both sides of the duality. An investigator is interested in everything. He investigates the mechanisms of his personal program. The interest of an investigator is outside the frame of the matrix of survival, i.e.

272

matrix of conflict. That's why it is not dual. You will never be able to lean on one side of duality—you will be thrown from one side to another as a pendulum.

Let's move along. You see the questions on the screen. You can choose any one of them.

— *I will take: "What is the worst punishment for you and why?" The worst punishment for me is silent treatment. I started to talk when I was three years old. A few days later, I was bitten by a dog, and I started to stutter. I didn't talk much for the next five years, and my parents didn't talk much to me either. Now, I feel horrible when after having a fight, my husband gives me a silent treatment. I would do anything to avoid that.*

— People react differently to silent treatment. Some say: "He is not talking to me. Great!" But in your case, in response to the painful stimulus you have experienced as a child, you see silent treatment as a horrible punishment.

Let's take a closer look at this situation. Why do you find it to be so bad? He is not talking to you. He doesn't scream at you. He doesn't beat you. He doesn't ask anything of you. Why are you so afraid of it?

— *When someone screams at me or wants something from me, I exist.*

— What exactly are you afraid of? Are you afraid of not having to do anything? Are you afraid no one will tell you: "Go and do that"?

— *I am a machine. When someone tells me what to do, I know what to do. I get up and I do it.*

— Okay. What will happen if no one orders you around? You are sitting quietly in your room. Is that very difficult for you?

— *Yes.*

— Let me clarify it. Are you afraid of not having to do anything or are you afraid you are not going to exist? When

273

your husband orders you to do something, you come to a conclusion that you exist, "I was told what to do. I have done it. Therefore, I exist." But when you are not told what to do when you are ignored, you feel pain, "I don't exist. No one notices me."

— *This is it. You got it. Sometimes, a thought pops into my head, "I am such a good person. How come no one talks to me?"*

— Whether you are good or not is another question. Right now, we are trying to figure out whether you exist or not. It looks like when no one tells you what to do, you take it as a sign that you don't exist.

— *Yes.*

— Why don't you contemplate on this for a while? This is the **key feature** of your personal structure.

— *Thank you.*

— Thank you.

— *I will try to answer the question, "Which punishment scares you the most?" I am terribly afraid of being condemned by a big group of people. That's how Mom used to punish me, and I experience it now, in my adult life, too—punishment by condemnation. I do something wrong and I get condemned in the presence of many people. I feel horribly guilty. With all these people around me, the state of guilt I experience quadruples.*

— Let's take a look at this. Where is your profit here? A big crowd of people has gathered to be told that you are a bad girl. They look at you, and you know that they look at you because you are bad. Now all of them know that Lilly is bad. They also know that you exist.

— *Yes. She is bad, but she is here.*

— Exactly. What happens to the movie stars? They get famous. When their fame starts to fade away, they start to do crazy things to draw attention to themselves. If no one says a good thing about them, they do something bad, and bingo—everyone is talking about them again. That's what they do.

Every personality wants to keep people attention drawn to it. Whether this attention carries a positive sign or a negative sign—nobody cares. So, what's your profit in this situation?

— *My profit is the attention I get, and I get it from a big crowd of people.*

— Look, we are dealing with a very interesting situation here. I ask a man: "What do you want?" "I want attention," he replies. I say: "Let me hit you and give you a black eye. Do you want this type of attention?" "No. I don't want this type of attention," he replies. But, in reality, that's exactly what he wants. His personal program has been inculcated with a subprogram which receives attention, i.e. energy when he gets into negative, adversarial situations. Many people are inculcated with similar programs.

What is attention? It is an acknowledgment of your existence. Imagine no one praises you. No one reprimands you. You walk down a street—people don't even notice you.

— *This is interesting.*

— Yes. Let's review this interesting situation. A man says: "People reprimand me. They force me to do things. They insult me sometimes. I don't like it, but they keep doing that." You sit down and you talk to him for a while. Turns out, he creates these situations himself. The question arises, "Why does he do it?" When you ask him that question, he replies, "I don't want to do that. I don't need that." But as it turns out, he needs these situations. We have just figured out why he needs these situations—this is the only way he can feel he exists. Descartes said, "I think. Thus, I exist." Here, we can say, "I get punished. Thus, I exist." Do you understand? "Someone called me stupid—I exist. Someone called me a slut—I exist." People frequently identify with the negative side of their personality and start to maintain a negative image of themselves. What kind of image is it? That's another question. People who carry this negative self-image create negative situations in their lives and experience negative states. But when you ask them why they do what they do, they tell you they don't want to do that. In reality, however, these situations provide them with a profit—other people acknowledge their existence.

— *Thank you. I am not ready to discuss this further at present time.*

— Okay. Next.

— *According to my program, when I am ordered to do something, I obey. However, I resist. I protest. I reject these orders. My days are spent in a state of constant, chronic resistance. Irrespective of what I am told— I resist. When someone says I am good, I insist I am bad. When someone says I am bad, I insist I am good. This happens all the time, even during the seminars. I get stressed out of my mind, then I create a very strong resistance. That's the only way for me to get to the seminar.*

— You are resistance itself.

— *Yes, I am. I resist everything. A man shows up. I don't even know him. He starts to talk to me. I immediately say something that goes against what he says.*

— Great! Why do you need this resistance?

— *That's how my personality was formed. As a kid, I had to resist my parents. I had to resist my brother. When I resist, I exist.*

— So, your personality gets to know itself when it resists.

— *Yes.*

— The more it resists, the more it exists.

— *Exactly.*

— Okay. So, how is life?

— *Not so good. I have started to see this game lately. I see how I create it. But I don't know how to stop it. I am in it up to my gills.*

276

— You have spent your entire life playing this game. Tell us about its pleasures.

— *Pleasures? I have my own opinion on every single topic. Someone says something—I blurt my opinion right away.*

— So, you are a woman who has her own opinion, right?

— *No, I am a contrarian woman. My job is to oppose the opinions of other people.*

— Okay. And what does it give you? Why do you do that?

— *When I do that, I feel like an individual. I feel I am different. I have an opinion on every topic. I like it. I like having my own opinion.*

— So, you form your opinion instantly, and you reject the opinions of the people around you.

— *Yes, that's what I do. Also, it is hard for me to order someone to do something because that will be an expression of my own opinion.*

— It turns out you don't have your own opinion.

— *Yes. That's why it is difficult for me to order someone to do something.*

— You need someone to order you to do something. Then, you can say: "Get lost, idiot! We should not be doing this."

— *Yes.*

— Then you can prove that there was something wrong with the order you were given; a totally opposite thing needed to be done.

— *At the same time, someone who knows about this mechanism can easily manipulate me.*

— I will tell you more: "It's impossible *not* to manipulate you." You are a great object for manipulation. You can advertise in a newspaper, "A girl for manipulation. Manipulators be aware—Alina is waiting for you!"

— *Ugum ...*

277

— What do you mean, "Ugum"? You need to object Pint now. Tell Pint to get lost.

— *It is not easy to tell you to get lost.*

— Why? Why is it so difficult for you?

— *Well, I cannot do it this way. I have to do it differently. I have to do it a sly way.*

— Let's shoot a movie, "Outplay Pint." Tough personalities will challenge Pint.

— *No one can outplay you.*

— Why? Why is it so difficult to outplay Pint?

— *You are equally strong playing both sides of the duality. You can flip from one side to another very fast. I would not be able to beat you. I need a "sleeping man," who I can easily tip out of balance and drug into my game.*

— Exactly. I am like a roly-poly. You push me—I roll and I bounce back right away.

— *Yes. I do exactly the same thing. I convince a man that something is right. When he is finally convinced, I turn a hundred eighty degrees and I start to convince him that the opposite thing is right.*

— That's an interesting game. Let's call it, "Outplay a roly-poly."

— *That's what attracted me to you. You are not about conflict. You don't compete with us. I try to assert my power, but you use this technique as an instrument, as a carpenter uses a screwdriver.*

— Yes, but take a look at what happens next. I offer a challenge to the personalities who want to outplay me. I think this is one of the strongest interest that drugs many of you here. "What kind of a roly-poly is he? Let me outplay him!" Pint says, "Okay. Come! Ask your questions!" So, you are interested in competition, right?

— *Yes.*

— You don't just resist, you want to outplay Pint.

— Yes, I want to flip my opponent. I want to destroy his opinion completely.

— Great. We are dealing with an arm wrestling contest. One arm showed up; the second arm brings it down immediately. In our case, these two arms are two opposite opinions. Actually, everyone here specializes in this game. Every personality around you wants to win this competition.

— Yes. I am waiting for my turn. I take a bite at you here and there during your seminars. I am scanning you for weak spots non-stop.

— Where is Pint's Achilles heel?

— Yes. I sit there quietly and I keep an eye on my opponent. I feel him. I get to know his weak spots. You are a very interesting and unusual game.

— Invite your friends to our webinars. Let them try to tip Pint over. So, you want to outplay Pint. This is your main interest. Do you have other sparing partners aside from Pint?

— I do.

— Who are they? How do you find partners to play this game?

— Presently, this game has been transferred inside. Two of my parts are fighting: good part and bad part. My bad part tries to outfox my good part.

— Ugum … So, your bad part needs to knock your good part down.

— It's scary, but it provides me with a lot of adrenalin.

— That's what every personality wants. Pint talks about a world of partnership, a world free of conflict. You listen to him. Why? Do you listen to him to knock him down?

— It seems to be the case.

— Great! Okay. Next. Who else wants to arm-wrestle Pint?

— *I want to explore the question,* **"For what reasons and how were you rewarded during childhood?"** *My personality did not take your conversation with students you spoke to before me well. It took it as a sign of rejection—I was not rewarded. I usually come to the webinar laughing and you laugh with me. You encourage and reward me with your laughter. But suddenly, today, you said, "You don't understand anything—go away. I will talk to somebody else." What's that?! No, I will prove myself to Pint! He will reward me! I am going to prove to you ...*

— Okay. Prove it to me now.

— *No, I can't prove anything to you.*

— You have to participate. This is important to you. It's not victory, but participation that is important to you.

— *No. One of the reasons I choose you as a teacher was your total rejection of flattery. You don't buy it. I will not be able to flip to that side, the side I usually manifest. But, I found a way out of it, too. After the webinar, I will describe our conversation online, expecting other students to admire me.*

— Moreover, Pint will read your post, too. He will read your post and he will say, "Wow! She is great!"

— *If not on Pint, flattery works pretty well on many students. Some of them will praise me, "Great post, Dina!"*

— Great. So, what's your question?

— *When I was praised as a kid, I would always try to do more, expecting to be praised more. Now, when people don't notice my work, I try to do it better. If that doesn't work, I do something else. I find what they like and do it the way they like it, "Look, I did it!" They smile and say, "Dina is such a good girl!"*

— Dina, you are an ideal woman.

— *Wow! You are killing me. My husband started to praise me lately, too. I got mad at him. I think he praises me so I would work harder*

280

and harder for him. I think he figured me out and tries to control me this way.

— So, do you like to be praised or not?

— *If it is not a manipulation, I like it. I don't know why, but I frequently see praise as manipulation. I often get irritated by it.*

— What if I am a very good manipulator? What if I am so good, you can't see my manipulations? Perhaps I am waiting to be flattered. I am waiting to be flattered, but I pretend not to care for flattery.

— *I don't believe you! That's not what Pint is about.*

— Who knows Pint better: you or me?

— *Well, Okay. I will flatter Pint in my post, and he will single me out among other students. Thank you for a tip. He will cry reading my post tomorrow.*

— Here you go. Make Pint cry.

— *That might be a good way to bring you down as a teacher, as an authority.*

— By using praise and flattery?

— *Yes.*

— How about cursing me?

— *Naah. That will not work. I will praise and flatter you to death.*

— What else do we have here except praise and punishment?

— *I am not interested in anyone bringing Pint down. I want him to be able to withstand any blow, and I want to learn from him. I will learn his skills and I will use them. People say, "He can neither be bent nor broken." That's a compliment.*

When I am harshly oppressed by duty and can't stand it anymore, something shifts in my head, and I say, "I am not doing it because I am obligated to do it. No. I am interested in doing it!"

— Are you just saying it or you really feel that way?

— I feel this inner switch. I really feel how interest arises. I feel a desire to do it.

— How can you discern between a dual desire and a non-dual interest?

— I have learned today that duty and interest are two sides of one duality. How can I discern between them? When one moves toward interest, one moves away from duty.

— Wait a minute. We have just figured out that opposite to "duty" is "rejection of duty." Alina manifests this "rejection of duty" strongly. I have to use words that are commonly used here. All these words have their own dual opposites. What I call **interest** is not dual. Let me use a different word: **intention. Intention** carries the same energy as interest. Let's say **the intention is a mental construct;** **interest is the emotional component of intention.**

— Let's talk about the intention for a minute. Let's say my intention is to come to every seminar. This is priority number one for me. But it is also my duty, right? I vocalized an intention, but it is perceived by me as my primary duty now.

— This is a great point. Everything that comes out of Supreme Aspect is not dual, but as soon as it gets to the level of personality it immediately becomes dual. You will say: "Wow. What a great seminar! Pint is great, too!" But in a few days, you will suddenly cool down toward Pint and his seminars. That will happen. When you start to observe, you will notice this happens everywhere. Things you like will sooner or later bore you. Things you strived for, will sooner or later repel you. That's the paradox of this reality.

— That's true. I have felt that many times. I decided to attend every webinar irrespective of how I feel. When I feel resistance, I investigate what is behind it.

— Okay. But can you allow yourself not to attend one or two webinars?

— *Yes, I can.*

— Conduct your investigation when you do that. You need to investigate both sides. Otherwise, you will think, "My Supreme Aspect told me to go to every webinar, but I cannot come to every one of them. I am worthless. I can't even do that. I am not ready for this work. The hell with it." Don't strive to be an ideal student. Ideals are created so people can condemn themselves and other people for not being ideal. "The ideal of communism." "The ideal of Christianity." They have made an ideal out of Jesus. No one can follow Jesus's footsteps, but every man can accuse his neighbor of living in sin. Let's not create another ideal out of awareness. Next thing you know, your personality is fighting other people—they are not aware enough.

— *Thank you.*

— Okay. Do you want to discuss something else?

— *No, I think we are done. Perhaps you want to ask me a question.*

— What's the weather like in Panama today?

— *Why don't you stick to the topic of the webinar?*

— Here you go. You put Pint right in his place. Pint has decided to speak about something that interests him, and you immediately reprimand him, "What are you talking about?!" Pint says, "I like hamburgers." "I don't care what you like. Let's talk about duty and guilt," she replies.

— *I feel stupid now. It looks like I am going to go home without you praising me.*

— Okay. Next.

— *I will take the question: "What do you prefer: to order or to obey?" My personality thinks it can order and obey equally well, but most of the time it orders people around. I was thrown out of a military school*

283

for disobedience. I am a freelancer. To think about it, I don't like to obey anyone.

— And what exactly don't you like the most when you are ordered to do something?

— I get nuts when something is wrong with the order.

— What exactly are you talking about? Be specific.

— I don't like stupid orders.

— Have anyone given you a stupid order last week?

— Hmmm. I can't recall anyone doing that at work. No one orders me around the house, but my son doesn't do anything I order him to do. He takes every order of mine as a personal offense. The only way for me to get him to do something is to ask him nicely.

— What kind of orders do you give him? Be specific.

— I may ask him to do his homework, "Will you please go to your room and study?" If I order him to do that, he would just sit there, brooding, but if I ask him nicely, he would finish his homework in ten minutes. I don't order him around anymore; it is useless.

— Okay. What is the difference between ordering someone to do something and asking them to do it nicely?

— What happens when I ask someone to do something? There is probably a hidden order there. I know how to influence people softly. I do it with tact. I know how not to get people upset. I know who to say what and which tone of voice to use with every colleague at work. I feel the situation and I act based on my feeling.

— Okay. So, if we were to see it as a method of manipulation, what is the difference between manipulation in the form of an order and manipulation in the form of asking someone to do something?

— When you ask someone to do something, you understand you can be refused; you take it into consideration. When you order someone to do something, you expect it to be done no matter what.

284

— Yes. There is a great difference here. When do we order people to do something and when do we ask people to do something for us? Let's investigate real-life situations. When can't you ask your colleague to do something you need to have done? When do you have to order it to be done?

— *I can't recall a specific situation now.*

— Let's think of our daily life. I use the order form when I am afraid that a human being I am dealing with is not going to do what he supposed to do. That scares me. That's why I put my request in a form of a command. If I ask a man to do something for me, I can accept him doing what I ask him to do or not doing it; I can accept both. I am not overly stressed about it.

— *When you ask someone to do something and it is not done, you have to do it yourself.*

— Okay. Let's look at our relationships with people who are close to us: friends and family members. Which aspects of these relationships are stressed to the point where we need to use the order form, where you know that if he or she doesn't do what you ask them to do, you would get mad? You may kill for it. Every personality has these zones.

— *I don't know. Usually, I try to see these situations as mirrors. I try to figure out what these mirrors reflect me. Frequently, I don't understand what a situation mirrors me right away. Sometimes, it takes me a long time to see that I am dealing with my own part—the situation simply reflects one of my parts to me. One of my coworkers was screaming at me daily for three months. He would not allow me to open my mouth. As soon as I would try to say something, he would scream at me. Finally, I saw he reflected my inner tyrant to me. I behave this way, too. As soon as I saw it, he stopped screaming at me.*

— Okay. Why did he behave the way he behaved? Why did he scream at you? Why did he refuse to hear what you had to say?

— *I behave this way too sometimes. I have a part in me that considers itself to be smarter than anyone. It thinks it can shut everyone up.*

— What are we dealing with here? Do you think this situation recurs because this part is very smart and knows everything or because this part is terribly afraid that its orders will not be carried through?

Imagine a scenario. It's a war situation. The officer in command sees his soldiers running away from the enemy. What should he do? Should he scream at them: "Stop! Get back! I will shoot you!" Should he shoot a couple of them? Or, should he speak softly to them: "Listen to me, my friends! Don't run away. Please, come back."

— *One should always behave according to the situation one is in.*

— Exactly. I am asking you to discuss the situations where you cannot be nice. If this officer's soldiers desert, he will be court marshaled and shot.

— *I do encounter similar situations at work. When I see drunkards around my construction site, I order my workers to throw them out. They are in danger to themselves and to others.*

— For example, one of your workers starts to do something opposite to what he is supposed to be doing. He is supposed to be building a house, but you see him demolishing a house. You come to him and you say: "Don't do that!" He continues to break it. You are his boss. You oversee the project. The wall should be finished today. Instead, he is breaking it. I am exaggerating this situation so we can understand what's going on. Similar situations occur in other spheres of our life. That's when we start to scream. We get red in the face. We start to order people what to do. Why? We do that because we are afraid that something we are afraid of will happen. That's when we start to order people what to do. **Why do people scream, yell, and order other people around? They don't do that because they are smart. They do it because they are scared.** They think something they are very afraid of is about to happen, and they get scared. That's the reason they scream, argue, and use profanities. People don't scream without a reason.

— *You are right. A man fell out of the window at one of my construction sites a few months ago. He broke his back. It was a break of basic safety precautions. He was not supposed to be there. When I see safety rules broken, I start to scream at my workers. I order them what to do and God helps them if they don't do it fast.*

— Exactly. I'll tell you more. Who cares if some drunk falls out of a window and breaks his back? It's his business. But if it is my construction site and if I am responsible for safety there, I will try to prevent this situation from happening the best way I can.

— *I am afraid of him dying, too.*

— Truth be told, I am afraid for my own survival. It's me who will be held accountable. If I am not the one responsible for the site's safety, let him do whatever he wants. What do I care? If I am responsible for it, he will not get close to my site; I can be punished for him being there. If this idiot wants to break his head, it is his business. The fact that I will be reprimanded is what stresses me out. That's when I become aggressive. The most important part of our discussion is fear. We are afraid of something, and we manifest our fear by ordering people around us to do things that we think will prevent these accidents.

— *In these situations, one cannot think straight. One starts to scream. It is as if we were screaming for help.*

287

— Exactly. Now, look at people who scream all the time and throw orders left and right. Now, you can feel what they feel. Do they scream because they feel important and know a lot? No. They scream because they are scared shitless.

— *The guy who screamed at me, said: "I spent my life on construction sites. I am responsible for three deaths already." At the time, we had drunk bums wandering around our property. Perhaps that's why he screamed.*

— Yes, that's why he screamed. Let me reiterate. Why would any man raise his voice and waste his energy? He would only do that if he is scared. At the base of every order is fear. FEAR! And it is one's own fear, not somebody else's fear. When a human being screams at another human being, it means he is scared. He is scared for his safety. He is not afraid for anyone else. He is afraid for his own safety and only his own safety.

— *I have never seen it that way.*

— I know. This point of view is very important and virtually unknown here. It is important because it allows you to see where a human being who screams at you and insists you do something is coming from. He screams because he is afraid. Behind every conflict and war on this planet is fear.

— *Hmmm. So, the only way to get out of these situations is to see that behind every one of them is fear. As soon as you see this, you can resolve them.*

— Exactly. Now, let's look at how people use fear to their advantage. Let's say you need to create a war in a small country of your choice. All you need to do is to intensify fear in its population. If fear is present in a human being, and as we know it is always present, it can be intensified. New technologies are being developed to do that. All you need to do is to activate fear—it will manifest itself in the external world.

288

I want you to notice that your phone is ringing. This is interference. It points to the fact that topic we discuss is a complicated one; this interference relates to you. It is *your* phone that is ringing. *This is a sign.* It's time for you to start seeing signs and how they work.

— *Yes, I know. I have noticed my phone ringing in stressful situations before.*

— Observe what happens around you. These signs will point your attention to your subconscious parts. A man has been courting a woman for ten years. He is telling her about his love and offering her his heart. At this precise moment, his phone rings. His broker calls him to discuss a financial transaction. This sign clearly shows what happens to this man.

— *Is it his opposite side that calls him? Does it attract these situations to prevent him from seeing something?*

— Exactly. If we don't see ourselves holistically, if we don't understand what is happening in our consciousness and subconsciousness, we can easily be manipulated. I just showed you how easy it is to do that. Multiple organizations occupy themselves with this task and they perform it quite well. They create coup d'états or so-called "Orange revolutions" in other countries. These technologies are applied to countries and individual human beings.

— *Thank you.*

— *I will take the question: "How and for what reasons have you been punished as a child?" I don't remember ever being punished, but my older brothers used to play a weird game with me. We had a big house. They would trick me to a dark room situated in the most distant corner of the house promising me a candy and leave me there. I would cry and run around like crazy trying to find the exit. Eventually, I would get to the kitchen where they were hiding. That's how I was punished. I was left alone in a dark room.*

— Interesting. There is another interesting moment here. They seduced you into this dark room by using a candy, right?

— *Yes!*

— What is a "candy" for you now, in your adult life? How are you being seduced into similar situations now?

— *I am not sure I understand you. Candy?*

— Someone offers you a candy. You come to get it—there is darkness there.

— *I live with an illusion that I can save people. Perhaps that's my candy. I find myself incapable of doing it again and again. I can't save anyone. I feel disappointed. I am alone again. There is no candy. I am in the dark again.*

— Why did you follow them to that room when you were a kid?

— *I wanted to have something sweet.*

— Sweet. Okay. And what is sweet for you now? What is candy for you now? You are being lured by a candy, but you receive darkness and loneliness. What is this candy?

— *Candy? Oh, my God?! Perhaps I subconsciously want to kill all these people. I can't think of anything else.*

— Good. You have something to work with.

— *Thank you. I would also like to discuss, "Which situations connected to obedience cause you to experience the strongest objection or who forbids you to do things?" The main objection I have ever experienced was related to my mom's saying, "Now that you are married, you will have to spend your life with your husband. You will have to build your family life to be happy until death do you apart." At first, I agreed with her. But when I started to live with my husband ...*

— You wound up on your own.

— *Yes.*

— Here is another realization of the situation you experienced as a child. This time, the candy is called, "To live with a husband happily until death do us apart." This is a very sweet candy.

— *I tried to prove that I could do it for a long time, but after a while, I realized it was too burdensome. Finally, there was no one to prove to that I was happy. I kept doing what Mom prohibited me from doing—I kept destroying my family. I maintained the image of a happy family for a while, but then, the force of resistance kicked in. I could not bear to be in the same room with my husband anymore.*

— Have you decided to destroy what you have created?

— *Yes, I destroyed this sweet candy.*

— So, you had something sweat. Then, you started to crave for something salty?

— *Yes.*

— Take a close look here. We are dealing with a duality here. Are you aware of the fact that to leave this sweet family home of yours is your desire?

— *Yes, now I understand that I wanted it. I went all the way for it to happen.*

— Did you see that back then?

— *No, back then it was unbearable. I didn't understand anything. I was scared.*

— You need to see this. When you enter these situations with a full understanding that you want to enter them and exit these situations with a full understanding that you want to exit them, your life will change. When that happens, these opposite sides will stop fighting each other inside you. They will still be in you, but they will not be in conflict anymore.

You walked into a restroom. You did what you wanted to do. You don't sit there forever. You get out of it happy, a big smile on your face. You have done what you had to do—you can go outside and play now. Right? But for some reason, you can't do that in certain situations—you get stuck. You had a cup of tea. You don't hold the empty cup in your hand for five years, right? You put it down. You have done what you had to do. Put it down. Think about that.

— *Thank you very much.*

— *How did my parents bring me under their control? As a kid, I could never understand why I had to do things I didn't like doing. My parents used to scream at and even beat me for a long time—that didn't touch me. Then, one day, I remember it vividly, we were in the kitchen, they told me: "If you don't like living with us, go and live anywhere you want." I was shocked. They were throwing me out of the house. My parents, who insisted they love me all along, were throwing me out of my own house. That's when I realized I had to conform to their rules. I felt they didn't love me anymore. I felt they didn't need me.*

— Imagine what they felt. They have tried and tried, but you have rejected everything. You say they denied you their love, but look how you treated them.

— *I would not know what to do with a kid like that.*

— Yes, they didn't know either. They were desperate. Think about it.

— *Thank you.*

— *I would like to address the topic of obedience and subordination, too. Upbringing presupposes kids conform to the will of their parents, right?*

— Yes.

— *Quite frequently, obedience is based on total suppression of the will of a child. When we grow up, we continue to listen to every authority we encounter. Am I right?*

— Go on.

— *We talk about obedience as one side of our life. We are forced to conform and to suppress our desires according to the wishes of our parents. So, on one side we have our own desire. On the other side, we need to obey the desires of other people. That's a duality.*

— Correct.

— *That's where the conflict lies. When do I have to obey and do what another human being desires me to do and when can I manifest my own desire and insist on doing what I want to do?*

— What exactly do you mean when you speak of your own desire?

— *Let's talk about family relationships. One always deals with conflict of interest there: husband wants to watch television, but I don't want to do that. Someone must always yield. The one who obeys yields to another. We always insist on our desires to be carried through. So, our entire life consists of obeying someone or on insisting they do what we want.*

— Great. You have presented us with your philosophy. Good. What do you expect of me now?

— *I don't expect anything from you. I am just saying that we have a conflict here, and this conflict will always exist.*

— So, you don't expect anything from me. You just want to declare your worldview.

— *No. I expect you to explain to me how to stop this conflict. How can I decrease stress and irritation that appear when I need to obey someone? In certain situations, when a man or a woman I am dealing with is stronger than me, I must obey.*

— Okay. If you must obey, you will have to obey. Can you imagine you can obey differently?

— *How can I do that? Give me an example.*

— Can you imagine yourself obeying someone without being forced to obey?

— *But when I yield to someone, I suppress my own desires.*

— Let me use a subway analogy. You walk into a subway station. You get on the escalator. Then, you break down the rules of subway administration—you sit down on the steps of a moving escalator. You do not obey the rules of the subway

293

administration, which prohibit people from sitting on the steps of a moving escalator.

— *Okay.*

— Or, you stand on the steps of the escalator, and you use it the way subway administration orders people to use it, with a full understanding that this is a right way to use an escalator. Those are two different ways to obey the rules of subway administration. While in a subway, you obey the rules and regulations of subway administration. If you don't obey these rules, expect to be punished.

— *In that case, I obey out of fear of punishment.*

— I don't know why you obey.

— *That's fine. If I don't follow the rules, I can be thrown out of there or be reprimanded.*

— I don't know how you see the rules and regulation of subway administration in this particular case. So, you think you obey the rules just because these rules are specified by the rules and regulations of the subway department.

— *To a certain degree, yes. But, I also obey these rules because I think of my safety.*

— So, you do have reasons to follow these rules. Otherwise, you would have jumped down and walked down the train tracks singing, "I will not follow the stupid subway administration rules. I will do what I want. I want to walk down the tracks and I will walk down the tracks."

— *Hmmm. Any rule can oppose my desire, right?*

— Shall we talk about all the rules and how they can oppose your desires now?

— *Okay, let's take a look at one common and important rule—the rule that a wife should obey her husband. This rule is being observed in most families. It looks like women will always be burdened by this rule.*

294

— If this rule is active in your family, it means you have found a man who follows this rule. Not all people follow this rule, and those who follow it do so only to a certain degree. Then, I will ask you, "Which of your parts has found such a man? Which of your parts insist you observe this rule?"

— *Being brought up in a family that obeyed this rule, I have naturally found a man who controls me. I am subservient to him.*

— Looks like you understand everything. What's your question?

— *I experience inner tension and conflict.*

— So, you want to be happy. In that case, be happy when he asks you to obey him and be happy when you obey him.

— *No, I want to understand how I can escape this conflict, when a man orders me around and when I, as a woman, have to obey him.*

— I will say it again. You have found a man, who, as you say, is a tsar at home. Am I correct? You have found him. You come to me and you ask me, "What do I do now? What do I do with a man who insists I submit to his will?" I ask you, "Did you find him?" "Yes, I did," you reply. Then, you say, "I experience tension because of it." I say, "In that case, take it with a smile and experience it with pleasure." You have to choose between two options available to you here: you can attack your husband and establish matriarchy in your household, or you can bow submissively, "Aye aye, my husband. I will do as you say." This is your choice. Why do you ask me this question? You have found this man yourself. Now, you experience stress. But then again, "Why did you find such a man, a man with this interesting worldview?"

— *There is only one explanation here. It's my inner state. My inner state has attracted this man.*

— Yes, that's why you are dealing with this situation. What else can I say?

295

— So, until I decide to submit myself to his will, I will deal with men like him. I must feel a desire to submit to man's rule.

— First of all, the situation you experience is a result of a personal program inculcated in you. This program is your fate. If you understand that, you should ask the next question: "Why was this personal program given to me?" It was given to you so you can go through a lesson. The next question, "What kind of a lesson is it?" Your lesson is to explore, understand, and experience submission.

— I think you are right.

— Your lesson deals with submission. Until you go through it and understand it in full, it will continue. That's the reason you found this man. That's the reason you experience the stress you experience. You experience what you experience because you don't want to submit to his will because you think he appeared here out of nowhere and for no reason.

— Thank you.

— Thank you.

— I want to discuss the question, "How and for what reasons have you been punished as a child?" I was punished physically. I was punished for many reasons. When I speak to my mom about it now, she denies the fact that I was punished frequently, but that is what I remember. I was punished for not doing well in school. I was not interested. I was punished by my teachers for not doing my homework. Some of the teachers punished me physically. My elementary school teacher used to hit me with a ruler. I didn't talk to my parents about it because I knew they would not stand behind me. Dad used to whip me, but I would outsmart him by putting five pairs of pants on. I didn't feel the pain. I am not sure why, but I don't hate my parents. I have never thought of killing them or running away from them. I loved my mom, and I accepted her reprimands and beatings as something normal. This is the answer to the question "Why and how I was punished as a kid?"

I have two kids, two good boys. One is a stellar student. He has finished High school with a gold medal. I have never laid my finger on them. My mom used to scream at me when they were young, "They don't listen to you. You need to beat them." But I never did. They did what was important. I allowed them to have a lot of freedom. Perhaps, I didn't accept my parents' program of physical punishment.

When my younger boy turned nineteen, he said he was old enough to do everything he wanted. He refused to clean after himself. At the time, he was living in my house and I was paying his tuition. I told him, "If you are such a free spirit and don't want to follow the rules of this household, you can go and live on your own." I didn't know what else to do. I could not handle everything by myself. He got upset, but he started to do what he was supposed to do. I don't understand: did I accept my parents' program or not?

— You have written an essay. It's topic, "How did I spend my summer?" What is next? Do you want to sort something out or you simply reading your essay to us?

— I want to understand something. Even though I was punished physically a child, I did not pick up the program my parents tried to install in me. I don't punish my kids physically.

— What bothers you? Does the fact that you were punished physically, but do not punish your kids physically bother you?

— No. What bothers me ... the heaviest punishment for me now is that I have to do a lot of physical work. I must go to work. I must cook. I must clean. I must do all these things. I must ... I must ... I don't want to do that.

— This is your physical punishment.

— Will it continue?

— You have just told us that you have experienced physical punishment as a child. You neither punish anyone nor

297

being punished by anyone now. However, you consider your need to do any kind of physical work to be a punishment.

— *That's right. I don't know how to exit this situation. If I am to live, I must do it. It must be done. Should I do it with pleasure? I don't know. In that case, I will have to force myself. I do not experience any pleasure.*

— Where do you want to exit out of and what do you want to enter?

— *I want to exit this life I have. One of the women here said, "I am afraid to be alone." I, on the other hand, am dreaming of being alone— people don't let me.*

— Death has to be earned. Your story reminds me of the old movie. The KGB agents are torturing a man. He begs them, "Please, kill me." One of the agents replies: "Shut up! Death has to be earned!"

— *That's right. I am not afraid of being lonely. I would have spent days by myself if people were to let me. I feel shivers when people utter my name or call me.*

— What are you afraid of?

— *"Do this, do that, sit next to me, you don't spend enough time with me …"*

— So, people oppress you by forcing you to do something, right?

— *I am afraid of my family.*

— Are they so horrible?

— *No, they are not horrible.*

— Then, why do you feel so bad in their company?

— *Last night my husband was watching his stupid TV shows. He was flipping channels, "What would you like to watch, dear?" I didn't want to watch anything. I wanted to read a book. He had not read a book in his life. He can't even understand why someone would read a book.*

— So, you are surrounded by the imbeciles.

— *No, no. That's not the case.*

— What do you mean? I don't understand you.

— *We have different interests.*

— Okay. We need to use a different word to describe your family members. Right?

— *Annoying?*

— Good. Give us more. Can you use another word?

— *I don't know. I feel I am annoyed by all of them.*

— Okay. Annoying is your experience. I am asking for something else. I am asking you to define them. I am asking for a definition. Your relatives are pretty tough. Otherwise, you would not want to end this life.

— *You are right. I don't understand …*

— Okay. Let's find a proper term to define them.

— *I don't know. It looks like I have had enough. I don't want to conform to these rules that were established in my life. To tell you the truth, I have never conformed to them. I always resisted.*

— Stop beating around the bush. Use the words you want to use to call them. Speak out of the part that wants to commit suicide, not out of the part that says that everything is nice and swell.

— *This part wants to say that it is tired of this bullshit. Go to hell all of you. I don't have a word to describe them. They are the way they are. Perhaps, I don't belong to their world.*

— Okay. In that case, self-liquidate and let them live their life the way they want to.

— *I would have if it was not for the feeling of guilt: I have to bring up kids. My mom is still alive. Who would take care of her? That's what is holding me.*

— In that case, repent. Come home tonight and say, "All of you are nice, good people. I am bad. I am not worthy of living with you." And hang yourself in front of them.

— *No, they will not let me do that.*

— Use a gun. It's fast. They will not have time to react.

— *No, I have saved up some pills. I am waiting for my son to finish High school. This is my debt. I must pay it.*

— He will finish school. Then, he will get married. He will have kids. You will have to help to bring them up. Your pills will expire.

— *Hmmm ...*

— So, call them their proper names, call them according to the feelings you have toward them.

— *I don't know what to call them.*

— Get a pen and a piece of paper. Start writing.

— *Should I let them read it?*

— No, just write it down for now. We will discuss it afterward.

— *Okay. I will do that.*

— This is an assignment. Your assignment is to play a subservient role. Until you pass this lesson, your assignment will continue.

— *Thank you.*

— Thank you, everyone. Have a good week. I'll see you next Sunday.

www.ingramcontent.com/pod-product-compliance
Lightning Source LLC
Chambersburg PA
CBHW021615270326
41931CB00008B/702

* 9 7 8 1 9 4 4 7 2 2 0 8 1 *